MEDIUM ÆVUM MONOGRAPHS
NEW SERIES XIII

FROM LEGEND TO CHRONICLE

The Treatment of Epic Material in Alphonsine Historiography

D. G. PATTISON

Fellow of Magdalen College, Oxford

The Society for the Study of
Mediæval Languages and Literature
Oxford
1983

THE SOCIETY FOR THE STUDY OF
MEDIEVAL LANGUAGES AND LITERATURE

http://mediumaevum.modhist.ox.ac.uk

© 1983 D. G. Pattison

British Library Cataloguing in Publication Data

Pattison, D.G.
    From legend to chronicle: the treatment of epic
material in Alphonsine historiography.—(Medium
Ævum monographs. New series; 13)
    1. Cid.   Poem
    I. Title   II. Series
    861'.1   PQ6373

ISBN-13: 978-0-907570-03-5 (pb)
ISBN-13: 978-0-907570-78-3 (pdf e-bk)

First published 1983
This reprint first issued 2015

Typeset by Joshua Associates, Oxford

PREFACE

I began serious work on the Alphonsine chronicles in 1974, during the first of a series of visits to Spain to work on archival material there. In the course of the ensuing years I have built up a long list of debts of gratitude, the principal among which it is my pleasure now to attempt to discharge.

Among these, the chief one, as anyone will know who has worked over a period in Spanish libraries, must be to the directors and personnel of those libraries: among them I single out especially those of the Biblioteca Nacional, Madrid, the Biblioteca del Monasterio de San Lorenzo de El Escorial, the Biblioteca de la Universidad de Salamanca, and the Biblioteca Menéndez y Pelayo at Santander.

Next I must record my thanks to those institutions and individuals that have enabled me to travel to Spain and pursue my studies there. The British Academy made me grants for travel to Spain out of its Research Fund in 1977 and 1979. I have received similar help from time to time out of funds administered for the University of Oxford by the Board of the Faculty of Medieval and Modern Languages, and all this assistance is gratefully acknowledged. When in Madrid, I have been privileged to stay at the Casa de Velázquez, and offer my heartfelt thanks to successive Directors of that institution, MM. François Chevalier and Didier Ozanam for their hospitality. Nor must I forget my good friends Chris Pratt and Darrell Williams, whose willingness to put me up (and to put up with me) has eased the rigours of research in a foreign country. By no means least, I owe a great debt to my wife June, and my sons, who have had to bear the cross of a husband and father whose idea of a holiday from teaching and administrative duties has been to settle down to 'real' work on mediaeval chronicles. That they have accepted this relatively cheerfully has been a very real comfort and encouragement to me.

A number of scholars have contributed directly or indirectly to this book. Among those who have listened to papers and made pertinent comments in subsequent discussion, or who have read drafts of parts of the work, I must mention particularly Professor Colin Smith and Dr Brian Powell, as well as a number of colleagues, pupils, and research students at Oxford, not all of whom may have realised that ideas were being tried out on them. Dr Nicholas Mann, of Pembroke College, Oxford, kindly read the whole manuscript on behalf of the publishers and made a number of most helpful suggestions. A special place, however, must be reserved in this list for my friend and former colleague Professor Peter Russell. In the recent past he has performed the same functions as those just mentioned, and has been, predictably, the fairest as well as the most rigorous of critics. He may not realise, though, the full extent of his role in the genesis of the present work. No less than twenty years ago, in my final undergraduate year, I enjoyed the privilege of tutorials with Peter Russell on Alfonso *el sabio*; and although my subsequent postgraduate study led me into quite different fields, it was always clear, to me at least, that one day I would return to the subject for which he had fired me with such enthusiasm. From him I first learnt something of the difficulty of applying in a mediaeval context such anachronistic distinctions as that between 'literature' and 'history'; to him this book is respectfully and affectionately dedicated.

D. G. Pattison

CONTENTS

Preface	iii
Abbreviations	vi
Select Bibliography	vii
Introduction	1
1. Bernardo del Carpio	11
2. Fernán González	23
3. The Infantes de Lara	43
4. The Condesa Traidora and the Infante García	57
5. Mocedades del Cid	81
6. The Death of Fernando I and the Fratricidal Wars	93
7. The Cid as Hero	115
Conclusion	143
Appendix: The Chronicle Texts	151
Index	161

ABBREVIATIONS

(i) CHRONICLE TEXTS

Cr1344	Crónica de 1344
CrC	Crónica de Castilla
CVR	Crónica de Veinte Reyes
PCG	Primera Crónica General
RefTol	Refundición Toledana de la Crónica de 1344

(ii) PERIODICALS AND SERIES

AEM	Anuario de Estudios Medievales
BH	Bulletin Hispanique
BHS	Bulletin of Hispanic Studies
BRAH	Boletín de la Real Academia de la Historia
Hisp	Hispania (Madrid)
Hisp(Am)	Hispania (U.S.A.)
HR	Hispanic Review
HS	Hispania Sacra
JHP	Journal of Hispanic Philology
KRQ	Kentucky Romance Quarterly
MAe	Medium Aevum
MHRA	Modern Humanities Research Association
MLN	Modern Language Notes
MLR	Modern Language Review
N	Neophilologus
NRFH	Nueva Revista de Filología Hispánica
PhQ	Philological Quarterly
RABM	Revista de Archivos, Bibliotecas y Museos
RFE	Revista de Filología Española
RLC	Revue de Littérature Comparée
Rom	Romania
RPh	Romance Philology
RR	Romanic Review
Script	Scriptorium
SRL	Studies in Romance Languages
TRHS	Transactions of the Royal Historical Society
UCPMP	University of California Publications in Modern Philology
UNCSRL	University of North Carolina Studies in the Romance Languages and Literatures

SELECT BIBLIOGRAPHY

The following books and articles are referred to in at least two different places in the text, footnotes or textual appendix, and are cited in the abbreviated form given here. For items referred to only once, full bibliographical details will be found in the footnotes or textual appendix. For abbreviations of (i) unpublished chronicle texts and (ii) periodicals and series, see p. vi.

Armistead, 'The Enamored Doña Urraca'
: Armistead, S. G., 'The Enamored Doña Urraca in Chronicles and Balladry', *RPh*, 11 (1957-58), 26-27

Armistead, *La gesta* (abbreviated to 'Armistead' in the textual appendix)
: Armistead, S. G., '*La gesta de las Mocedades de Rodrigo*': Reflections of a Lost Epic Poem in the *'Cronica de los Reyes de Castilla'* and the *'Cronica de 1344'* (unpublished doctoral dissertation, Princeton University, 1955)

Armistead, 'The Structure of the Refundición'
: Armistead, S. G., 'The Structure of the *Refundición de las Mocedades de Rodrigo*', *RPh*, 17 (1963-64), 338-45.

Armistead, 'An Unnoticed Epic Reference'
: Armistead, S. G., 'An Unnoticed Epic Reference to Doña Elvira, Sister of Alfonso VI', *RPh*, 12 (1958-59), 143-47

Artigas, *Catálogo*
: Artigas, M., *Catálogo de los manuscritos de la Biblioteca Menéndez y Pelayo* (Santander, n.d. [1930])

Avalle-Arce, 'Clerecía y juglaría'
: Avalle-Arce, J. B., 'El *Poema de Fernán González*: Clerecía y juglaría', *PhQ*, 51 (1972), 60-73

Babbitt, *Latin Sources* (abbreviated to 'Babbitt' in the textual appendix)
: Babbitt, T., *La Crónica de Veinte Reyes: A Comparison with the Text of the Primera Crónica General and a Study of the Principal Latin Sources*, Yale Romanic Studies, 13 (New Haven, 1936)

Babbitt, 'Observations'
: Babbitt, T., 'Observations on the *Crónica de Once Reyes*', *HR*, 2 (1934), 202-16

Babbitt, 'Twelfth-Century Epic Forms'
: Babbitt, T., 'Twelfth-Century Epic Forms in Fourteenth-Century Chronicles', *RR*, 26 (1935), 128-36

Catalán, 'Crónicas generales y cantares de gesta'
: Catalán, D., 'Crónicas generales y cantares de gesta: el *Mio Cid* de Alfonso X y el del pseudo Ben-Alfaraŷ', *HR*, 31 (1963), 195-215 and 291-306

Catalán, *De Alfonso X*
: Catalán, D., *De Alfonso X al Conde de Barcelos: cuatro estudios sobre el nacimiento de la historiografía romance en Castilla y Portugal* (Madrid, 1962)

Catalán, 'Don Juan Manuel ante el modelo alfonsí'	Catalán, D., 'Don Juan Manuel ante el modelo alfonsí: el testimonio de la *Crónica abreviada*', in *Juan Manuel Studies*, edited by I. Macpherson (London, 1977), pp. 17-51
Catalán, 'Poesía y novela'	Catalán, D., 'Poesía y novela en la historiografía castellana de los siglos XIII y XIV', in *Mélanges offerts à Rita Lejeune*, 2 vols (Gembloux, 1969), I, 423-41
Catalán, 'El taller historiográfico alfonsí'	Catalán, D., 'El taller historiográfico alfonsí: métodos y problemas en el trabajo compilatorio', *Rom*, 84 (1963), 354-75
Catalán and Andrés, Cr1344	*Crónica General de España de 1344*, edited by D. Catalán and M. S. de Andrés, vol. I (Madrid, 1970)
Chalon, *L'Histoire et l'épopée*	Chalon, L., *L'Histoire et l'épopée castillane du moyen âge*, Nouvelle Bibliothèque du Moyen Âge, 5 (Paris, 1976)
Corominas, *DCELC*	Corominas, J., *Diccionario crítico etimológico de la lengua castellana*, 4 vols (Berne, 1954-57)
Cotrait, *Fernán González*	Cotrait, R., *Histoire et poésie: Le Comte Fernán González, genèse de la légende* (Grenoble, 1977)
Crónica Abreviada	Don Juan Manuel, *Crónica Abreviada*, edited by R. L. and M. B. Grismer (Minneapolis, 1958)
Crónica Najerense	*Crónica Najerense*, edited by A. Ubieto Arteta, Textos medievales, 15 (Valencia, 1966)
Cummins, 'The Chronicle Texts'	Cummins, J., 'The Chronicle Texts of the Legend of the Infantes de Lara', *BHS*, 53 (1976), 101-16
Deyermond, *Epic Poetry and the Clergy*	Deyermond, A. D., *Epic Poetry and the Clergy: Studies on the 'Mocedades de Rodrigo'* (London, 1968)
Deyermond, *The Middle Ages*	Deyermond, A. D. *The Middle Ages*, A Literary History of Spain, edited by R. O. Jones (London and New York, 1971)
Deyermond and Chaplin, 'Folk-Motifs'	Deyermond, A. D., and Margaret Chaplin, 'Folk-Motifs in the Medieval Spanish Epic', *PhQ*, 51 (1972), 36-53
Entwistle, '*La Estoria del noble varon*'	Entwistle, W. J., '*La Estoria del noble varon el Cid Ruy Diaz, sennor que fue de Valencia*', *HR*, 15 (1947), 206-11
Fraker, 'Sancho II: Epic and Chronicle'	Fraker, C. F., 'Sancho II: Epic and Chronicle', *Rom*, 95 (1974), 467-507
Franklin, 'Origins of the Legend'	Franklin, A. B., 'A Study of the Origins of the Legend of Bernardo del Carpio', *HR*, 5 (1937), 286-303
Gómez Pérez, 'Elaboración'	Gómez Pérez, J., 'Elaboración de la Primera Crónica General de España y su trans-

Gómez Pérez, 'La EE alfonsí'	misión manuscrita', *Script*, 17 (1963), 233-76 Gómez Pérez, J., 'La *Estoria de España* alfonsí de Fruela II a Fernando III', *Hisp*, 25 (1965), 485-520
Gómez Pérez, 'Fuentes y cronología'	Gómez Pérez, J., 'Fuentes y cronología de la Primera Crónica General de España', *RABM*, 67 (1959), 615-34
Grismer: see *Crónica Abreviada*	
Heinermann, *Untersuchungen*	Heinermann, M., *Untersuchungen zur Enstehungen der Sage von Bernardo del Carpio* (Halle, 1927)
H(istoria) Rod(erici)	*Historia Roderici*, in Menéndez Pidal, *España del Cid* (*q.v.*), II, 919-69
Hook, 'The Episode of the Cid's Lion'	Hook, D., 'Some Observations upon the Episode of the Cid's Lion', *MLR*, 71 (1976), 553-64
Hook, 'The Opening *Laisse* of the *PMC*'	Hook, D., 'The Opening *Laisse* of the *Poema de Mio Cid*', *RLC*, 53 (1979), 490-501
Horrent, *La Chanson de Roland*	Horrent, J., *La Chanson de Roland dans les littératures française et espagnole au moyen âge* (Paris, 1951)
Horrent, 'Santa Gadea'	Horrent, 'La jura de Santa Gadea: historia y poesía', in *Historia y poesía en torno al 'Cantar del Cid'* (Barcelona, 1973), pp. 157-93
Lathrop, *The Legend* (abbreviated to 'Lathrop' in the textual appendix)	Lathrop, T. A., *The Legend of the 'Siete Infantes de Lara'*, UNCSRL 122 (Chapel Hill, 1971)
Lindley Cintra, *Crónica*	Lindley Cintra, L. F., *Crónica Geral de Espanha de 1344*, 3 vols only published (Lisbon, 1951-61)
Lorenzo, *La traducción gallega*	Lorenzo, R., *La traducción gallega de la Crónica General y de la Crónica de Castilla*, 2 vols (Orense, 1975-77)
Menéndez Pidal, *CMC*	*Cantar de Mio Cid*, edited by R. Menéndez Pidal, 3 vols, third edition (Madrid, 1954-56)
Menéndez Pidal, 'Condesa Traidora'	Menéndez Pidal, R., 'Leyenda de la Condesa Traidora', in *Historia y epopeya* (Madrid, 1934), pp. 1-27
Menéndez Pidal, *Crónicas Generales*	Menéndez Pidal, R., *Crónicas Generales de España*, third revised edition (Madrid, 1918)
Menéndez Pidal, *España del Cid*	Menéndez Pidal, R., *La España del Cid*, 2 vols (Madrid, 1929)
Menéndez Pidal, 'Infant García'	Menéndez Pidal, R., 'El "Romanz del Infant García" y Sancho de Navarra antiemperador', in *Historia y epopeya* (Madrid, 1934), pp. 29-99

Menéndez Pidal, *La leyenda*	Menéndez Pidal, R., *La leyenda los Infantes de Lara*, revised (third) edition with additional material by D. Catalán (Madrid, 1971)
Menéndez Pidal, 'Notas para el romancero'	Menéndez Pidal, R., 'Notas para el romancero de Fernán González', in *Homenaje a Menéndez y Pelayo*, 2 vols (Madrid, 1899), I, 429-507
Menéndez Pidal, 'Relatos poéticos'	Menéndez Pidal, R., 'Relatos poéticos en las crónicas medievales', *RFE*, 10 (1923), 329-72
Menéndez Pidal, *Reliquias*	Menéndez Pidal, R., *Reliquias de la poesía épica española* (Madrid, 1951)
Menéndez Pidal, *Romancero tradicional*	Menéndez Pidal, R., *Romancero tradicional: I, Romances del Rey Rodrigo y de Bernardo del Carpio; II, Romances de los Condes de Castilla y de los Infantes de Lara* (Madrid, 1957-63)
Michael, *PMC*	*Poema de mio Cid*, edited by I. Michael, second edition (Madrid, 1980)
Najerense: see *Crónica Najerense*	
Ocampo: see Appendix, p. 152.	
Pattison, 'The *Afrenta de Corpes*'	Pattison, D. G., 'The *Afrenta de Corpes* in Fourteenth-Century Historiography', in *Mio Cid Studies*, edited by A. D. Deyermond (London, 1977), pp. 129-40
Pattison, 'The Legend of the Sons of Sancho el Mayor'	Pattison, D. G., 'The Legend of the Sons of Sancho el Mayor', *MAe*, 51 (1982), 35-54
Pattison, 'Legendary Material'	Pattison, D. G., 'Legendary Material and its Elaboration in an Idiosyncratic Alphonsine Chronicle', in *Belfast Spanish and Portuguese Papers*, edited by P. S. N. Russell-Gebbett and others (Belfast, 1979), pp. 173-81
PCG	*Primera Crónica General de España*, edited by R. Menéndez Pidal, 2 vols, second edition (Madrid, 1955)
Plumpton, *Historical Study*	Plumpton, J. E., *An Historical Study of the Legend of Garci-Fernández* (unpublished M.A. dissertation, St Andrews University, 1962)
PMC	*Poema de mio Cid*: see Michael, *PMC*
Poema (de Fernán González)	In Menéndez Pidal, *Reliquias* (q.v.), pp. 34-156
Powell, *Epic and Chronicle* (abbreviated to 'Powell' in the textual appendix)	Powell, B. J., *Epic and Chronicle: The 'Poema de mio Cid' and the 'Crónica de veinte reyes'*, MHRA Texts and Dissertations, 18 (London, 1983)
Procter, *Alfonso X*	Procter, E. S., *Alfonso X of Castile* (Oxford, 1951)

Reig, *Sancho II*	Reig, C., *El cantar de Sancho II y cerco de Zamora*, RFE Anejo 10 (Madrid, 1947)
von Richthofen, *Estudios épicos*	von Richthofen, E., *Estudios épicos medievales* (Madrid, 1954)
Ruiz Asencio, 'La rebelión de Sancho García'	Ruiz Asencio, J. M., 'La rebelión de Sancho García, heredero del Condado de Castilla', *HS*, 22 (1969), 31-67
Russell, 'San Pedro de Cardeña'	Russell, P. E., 'San Pedro de Cardeña and the Heroic History of the Cid', *MAe*, 27 (1958), 57-79
Sánchez Alonso, *Historia de la historiografía*	Sánchez Alonso, B., *Historia de la historiografía española*, 3 vols (Madrid, 1941-50)
Smalley, *Historians in the Middle Ages*	Smalley, B., *Historians in the Middle Ages* (London, 1974)
Smith, 'The Cid as Charlemagne'	Smith, C. C., 'The Cid as Charlemagne in the *Leyenda de Cardeña*', *Rom*, 97 (1976), 509-31
Smith, 'Did the Cid repay the Jews?'	Smith, C. C., 'Did the Cid repay the Jews?', *Rom*, 86 (1965), 520-38
Smith, 'The Personages of the *PMC*'	Smith, C. C., 'The Personages of the *Poema de Mio Cid* and the Date of the Poem', *MLR*, 66 (1971), 580-98
Sneyders de Vogel, 'Le *PFG* et la *Crónica General*'	Sneyders de Vogel, K., 'Le *Poema de Fernán González* et la *Crónica General*', *N*, 8 (1923), 161-80
Southern, 'Aspects of the European Tradition'	Southern, R. W., 'Aspects of the European Tradition of Historical Writing', *TRHS*, series 5, 20 (1970), 173-96, 21 (1971), 159-79, 22 (1972), 159-80
Sponsler, *Women*	Sponsler, L., *Women in the Medieval Spanish Epic and Lyric Traditions*, SRL, 13 (Lexington, 1975)
Toledano	[Rodrigo Jiménez de Rada, Archbishop of Toledo], *De Rebus Hispaniae*, in Rodericus Ximenius de Rada, *Opera*, reproduction of the edition of Madrid, 1793; Textos medievales, 22 (Valencia, 1968)
Tudense	[Lucas, Bishop of Túy], Lucae Diaconi Tudensis, *Chronicon Mundi*, in *Hispaniae Illustratae . . . opera Andreae Schotti Antwerpiensis S.J.*, IV (Frankfurt, 1608)
Zarco, *Catálogo*	Zarco Cuevas, J., *Catálogo de manuscritos de la Real Biblioteca de el Escorial*, 3 vols (Madrid, 1924-26 and El Escorial, 1929)

INTRODUCTION

Few would dispute the importance of Alfonso X, *el sabio*, as a figure in the history of Spanish historiography. Procter regarded his work as marking 'a turning-point in Spanish historical writing' (*Alfonso X*, p. 109), and Sánchez Alonso as opening 'una nueva era en la historiografía española' (*Historia de la historiografía*, I, 208). While it is not my purpose to explore in detail the reasons for such evaluations, it will be convenient to begin by looking briefly at the original features of the historiographic tradition begun by Alfonso.

Sánchez Alonso lists four such features: an ambition to use the widest possible range of sources and to blend them into a harmonious whole; the inclusion among such sources of popular poetic ones; the similar acceptance of Arabic sources; and the use of the vernacular in place of Latin (*Historia de la historiografía*, I, 206-08). Of these, it is only the last which truly forms a claim to originality; of the others, most had been foreshadowed by Latin chroniclers of the twelfth and thirteenth centuries. In particular, one might point to the use of poetic material in the twelfth-century *Crónica Najerense* and in the work of Lucas, Bishop of Tuy (el Tudense), whose *Chronicon Mundi* was finished in 1236; to the use of Arabic sources in the *Cronica Silense* of c. 1115 (see Sánchez Alonso, *Historia de la historiografía*, I, 116); to the fact that this same chronicle was one of the few early Spanish ones to be 'an attempt to write history as distinct from mere annals' (Procter, *Alfonso X*, p. 79); and, above all, to Rodrigo Ximénez de Rada, Archbishop of Toledo (el Toledano), whose *De Rebus Hispaniae* or *Historia Gothica* of 1243 could be said truly to foreshadow the distinctive features of Alphonsine historiography in every respect but the linguistic one.

One other preliminary point must be made. The works under discussion and their precursors already mentioned are basically chronicles. That is, they set out to give coherent accounts of the major events of the reigns concerned, often within an annalistic structure. It must frankly be admitted that they are seldom if ever truly original in terms of authorial viewpoint. Little in the Spanish historiography of the early Middle Ages, whether in Latin or in the vernacular, parallels the range of writing described in, for instance, Smalley's *Historians in the Middle Ages* or Southern's 'Aspects of the European Tradition'. For one thing, these chronicles were seldom if ever contemporary with their subject matter—that came later—and, as Isidore of Seville had said, the 'true historian' was limited to contemporary or near-contemporary history (Smalley, *Historians in the Middle Ages*, pp. 23-25). The best that Alfonso can offer as a justification for writing history is, in the Prologue to the *Primera Crónica General*, a translation of the Toledano's preface stating the commonplaces that the purpose of history is that knowledge should be transmitted so that it should not 'caer en oluido', and that men should profit from the example of the past (*Primera Crónica General*, pp. 3-4).

But one should not exaggerate. The Spanish chroniclers were in a tradition which went back to Isidore of Seville, to Eusebius and to Orosius: from the second of these comes the insistence on the importance of sources, including documentary ones (see Smalley, *Historians in the Middle Ages*, pp. 42-43), from the last the conception of the sweep of universal history, a sense of the importance of geography and also, perhaps, an underlying pessimism about the human condition (ibid., pp. 45-47). This should be set against the undeniable fact that the *Primera Crónica General* is, in Procter's words, 'in no sense an original work . . . its compilers' work consisted in the translation, prosification, and juxtaposition of their sources' (*Alfonso X*, pp. 103-04).

The purpose of the present work is to concentrate on one aspect of mediaeval Spanish historiography, namely its use of popular poetic—'epic'—sources. One point that must be borne in mind, of course, is that the material in question was not always historically accurate, nor should one expect it to be. The concentration by historians of literature on the chronicles as sources for otherwise lost epic texts has perhaps obscured the fact that the predilection for this material on the part of Alfonso and his successors has resulted in an unjustifiable degree of credence being given to what are often fundamentally unhistorical sources.

It must, though, be made clear that legend, literary or otherwise, played a continuing part in mediaeval historiography. Smalley reminds us of William of Malmesbury's use of Arthurian material (*Historians in the Middle Ages*, pp. 90-91), and if one turns to Spain, Alfonso's *General Estoria* made use of the French *Roman de Thèbes* and *Roman de Troie* as well as of the Spanish *Libro de Alexandre* (Procter, *Alfonso X*, p. 83). In a more parochial sphere, Alfonso's precursors, the author of the *Crónica Najerense*, the Tudense and the Toledano, have already been mentioned; the Alphonsine work differs from them in degree and in scope, for the earlier chronicles had tended to restrict their use of legendary material either to that dealing with royal personages (the *Crónica Najerense*) or to that with a regional origin (the Tudense, whose predilection is for Leonese material: Procter, *Alfonso X*, p. 80). The Toledano seems to know few such restrictions, and the compilers of the *Primera Crónica General* and its successors still fewer. It is not that the chroniclers are entirely uncritical in their use of such material: as we shall see, legendary material is cited often merely to be refuted (although, as time goes on, such an attitude becomes rarer).

The study which follows is not an historical one in any specialised sense: rather it has to do with the chroniclers' approach to the construction and detailing of a narrative which, as I have said, is in reality as much literary as historical in the parts which I shall examine most closely. With this in mind, I now turn to the chronicle texts themselves. The series of texts with which we are concerned has its ultimate origin in Alfonso X's projected *Estoria de Espanna*, begun in the second half of the thirteenth century. There is evidence that Alfonso's interest in this project antedated his accession to the throne in 1252, as by then he was already engaged on the *Estoria*. Towards the end of his reign, however, not only was his interest diverted from it by political troubles, but he also gave a change of emphasis to the work of his historiographical school, developing an interest in universal rather than Spanish history. This change was to have as its outcome the so-called *Grande e general estoria*, but it also had the effect of leaving the earlier more parochial work in a half-finished state which has puzzled and misled students of historiography over a long period. To put it shortly, it is likely that no polished and complete text of Alfonso's *History of Spain* exists. The earlier sections, dealing with the story of Roman and Visigothic Spain and of the early part of the Moorish hegemony, do appear to have been finished before the royal interest waned; but the later parts, dealing with the reconquest and the subsequent establishment and progress of the Christian kingdoms of the peninsula—in short, the periods that for reasons which will become apparent have most attracted critical attention—present a multiplicity of variant texts and confused readings which makes it difficult if not impossible to claim to reconstruct an archetype using the conventional techniques of textual criticism.

The nature and interrelationships of the texts concerned form a fascinating problem which has engaged the attention of many scholars since Ramón Menéndez Pidal first began systematically to describe and classify the manuscripts in question at the end of the last century. Pidal himself, his grandson Diego Catalán, José Gómez Pérez, the Portuguese Luis Lindley Cintra and the Americans Theodore Babbitt and Samuel Armistead are among those who have devoted themselves to the question, and it is not my purpose to describe in detail their work or to review the controversies involved. Full details will be found in the Bibliography, and a (very limited) contribution to the study of the relationship between the principal families forms an Appendix to the present work. However, it does seem appropriate to describe, with the minimum of commentary, the principal texts in question.

One should perhaps begin with the best known and most easily accessible chronicle, that usually given the title *Primera Crónica General*. That title is not itself Alphonsine and was given by Menéndez Pidal to a family of manuscripts, a critical edition of one of which he published in 1906 (second edition, with critical introduction, 1955). As the title suggests, Pidal was of the opinion that this version was a prototype of which subsequent chronicles were in some way developments, and he defended this view on many occasions, particularly against Babbitt. The so-called *Primera Crónica General* (*PCG*) is represented in its most extensive form by MS *E* (Escorial MSS Y-I-2 and X-I-4) which forms the base text for Pidal's edition, and by a large number of other more or less incomplete manuscripts. These may be divided into two basic families, one (which includes *E*) being known as the 'versión regia', the other as the 'versión vulgar'. More will be said about this question in due course.

Diego Catalán, in a series of articles and an important book published in 1962 (*De Alfonso X al Conde de Barcelos*), drew attention to the lack of physical homogeneity of MS *E*. While its first volume, comprising material down to the reign of Pelayo, has every appearance of being an Alphonsine manuscript from the royal scriptorium—and as such may deserve to be described as the 'versión regia' of the *PCG* (in other words as the officially approved final draft of Alfonso's original *Estoria de Espanna*)—the second volume is composed of a number of different parts in various hands with many erasures and interlinear corrections. It appears to be a hasty compilation made during the reign of Alfonso's son and successor Sancho IV, probably in 1289, with serious editorial defects: in short, a rough draft. For the periods covered by the second half of the chronicle—the reconquest and the subsequent history of the Christian kingdoms—we must accept, as Catalán says, that we do not have an authoritative version of Alfonso *el sabio*'s *Estoria de Espanna*.

It is for the same portion that we do, however, have a number of other versions, some of which may even be older than that represented by the *PCG* in its most widely known form: MS Escorial X-I-4 or E^2. Pride of place among those other versions should go to the *Crónica de Veinte Reyes* (*CVR*). Babbitt thought it older than the *PCG* and presented a cogent case to that effect in his book *La Crónica de Veinte Reyes* (1936); this was, however, vitiated by the fact that he considered only the published version of the *PCG*, and of that only the base text. He ignored even many of the variants noted by Pidal, and, as Catalán has pointed out, consideration of these would certainly have led him to modify his conclusions. Many of the differences between the *CVR* and the *PCG* on which Babbitt places such emphasis are no more than divergences between the main families of the *PCG*—the 'regia' and the 'vulgar'—with the latter of which the *CVR* has certain affinities. The *CVR* does, however, differ from both versions of the *PCG*, both in extent and in technique. Whereas the *PCG* begins with the history of Spain in antiquity, the *CVR* is confined to the period of the reconquest, beginning with the reign of Fruela II of León and ending, in most manuscripts, with that of Fernando III, *el santo* of León and Castile. It is thus slightly shorter than the second half, the 'tercera' and 'cuarta partes' of the four into which the *PCG* is divided. The differences of technique will become apparent later in this work.

Two other important chronicles have until recently attracted less attention than the *PCG* and the *CVR*. These are the *Crónica de (los Reyes de) Castilla* and the *Crónica de 1344*. The *Crónica de Castilla* (*CrC*) may be described as the most popular branch of the tradition, that is to say the one represented by the greatest number of manuscripts. Dating from the early fourteenth century, it comprises a large number of Castilian manuscripts, differing among themselves in many detailed aspects of arrangement, chapter division and wording, but coinciding in sources and in basic structure. The latter is that of the *PCG*, but the *CrC* is distinguished by its uncritical use of popular sources and by a very marked tendency to elaborate narrative details, dialogue and description. These features will be fully discussed below. The *CrC* proper comprises only the 'cuarta parte' of the Alphonsine *Estoria*, that is to say it begins with the accession of Fernando I of Castile to the throne of León in 1037. However, many *CrC* manuscripts were 'completed' by the addition of the whole or part of the *PCG* version of the earlier part of the chronicle. (Full details will be found in the Appendix on chronicle texts, pp. 151-59.)

The *Crónica de 1344* (*Cr1344*) is the name given to a much smaller group of manuscripts, some Castilian and some Portuguese, which appears to represent a *refundición* of the Alphonsine work done first in Portuguese. The work can be dated to 1344, and the author is reliably supposed to be Count Pedro de Barcelos; it derives from the 'versión regia' of the *PCG*, via an intermediate version in Galician-Portuguese. Subsequently the work was translated back into Castilian. At a later date (*c*. 1400), the chronicle was once again expanded (in Portuguese) and once again translated into Castilian. It covers the same chronological span as the *PCG*, though both at the beginning and at the end there are differences in sources and techniques. For the main periods here under discussion—the reigns of the kings of León and Castile up to Alfonso VI (i.e. the 'tercera' and the first sections of the 'cuarta partes')—the *Cr1344* coincides with the 'versión regia' of the *PCG* but amplifies it considerably in the light of new sources, one of which is certainly the *CrC* and which may also include *refundiciones* of epic sources.

These are the main chronicle families, but mention must be made of two other trends. One is the existence of composite versions, of which the best known and most significant is that published by Ocampo in 1541 (*Las Quatro Partes Enteras de la Crónica de España* . . .); this was called by Menéndez Pidal the *Tercera Crónica General* (the '*segunda*' being the *Cr1344*), but that term is not now in general use. Ocampo's version differs fundamentally between the 'tercera' and 'cuarta partes': the former, to which Diego Catalán has given the name *Crónica General 'Vulgata'* is an early version analogous in many ways to the 'versión vulgar' and to the *CVR*; the latter has more similarities with the *CrC*. A second type of variation consists of the development of minor interpolated versions of earlier chronicles, often existing in one or a very small number of manuscripts. Thus, a section of the *Crónica General 'Vulgata'* just described formed the basis for an idiosyncratic manuscript (Madrid, B.N. 1277) usually called the *Versión interpolada* or *Interpolación de la Tercera crónica general*; the *Cr1344* was, in the fifteenth century, used as the basis for a substantially rewritten version known as the *Refundición Toledana* or *Arreglo Toledano*. And, as a final puzzle, we have don Juan Manuel's *Crónica Abreviada*. The nephew of Alfonso X prepared an indexed summary of the chapter headings of his uncle's *Estoria de Espanna*, as he tells us in the prologue to *El conde Lucanor*; but the surviving manuscript (Madrid, B.N. 1356) does not correspond consistently in its chapter arrangement and details to any other extant version of the chronicles, rather taking features from various chronicle families and hinting at the existence of yet another now lost mixed version.

These, then, are in outline the texts on which this study is based. I have said that I do not propose to discuss in detail previous work in chronicle studies. However, it will be convenient to mention here the work of three authors of particular interest.

The first, of course, is don Ramón Menéndez Pidal. It has become something of a commonplace in Spanish mediaeval studies to acknowledge indebtedness to his pioneering work. In chronicle studies it is particularly appropriate to do so, since the scope of Pidal's groundwork can only be described as immense. First in his study of the legend of the Infantes de Lara (1896), then in his edition of the *PCG* (1906) and subsequently in important work on a range of epic legends done in the 1930s and published as *Reliquias de la poesía épica española* (1951), he identified, classified and catalogued the great majority of the known manuscripts, gave us a reading text of an important version, the *PCG*, and showed the way towards a use of this material in the reconstruction of the lost early epic poetry of Spain. Much later interpretative work—that of Babbitt on the *CVR*, that of Reig on the *Cantar de Sancho II*, that of Armistead and of Deyermond on the *Mocedades de Rodrigo*, to say nothing of other Cidian studies—could, very simply, never have been undertaken without the essential work of Menéndez Pidal. Nor, of course, could that of the other critics to be mentioned, and nor could my own. Others have continued the Pidalian tradition, the most notable being Lindley Cintra and Diego Catalán, whose work I must briefly now describe.

Pidal's grandson has inherited his mantle in chronicle studies (as in the field of the *romancero*), and has continued to develop his work. An edition of the Castilian manuscripts of the *Cr1344* has been in progress since 1970, and Catalán has written extensively on the manuscript tradition of the chronicles. Here one must single out the 1962 book *De Alfonso X* . . . already referred to, which is easily the most far-reaching and scholarly contribution to the subject yet written since Menéndez Pidal's own. It was Diego Catalán who made us properly aware of the importance of the 'versión vulgar' and the relative idiosyncrasy of a major part of the 'versión regia' of the *PCG* edited by his grandfather; he also identified and carefully described the features of many of the minor chronicle versions described above—the *Vulgata*, the *Ocampiana*, the *Versión Interpolada* —as well as setting out clearly the ascertainable facts about other major versions such as the *CrC* and *Cr1344*. My debt to Diego Catalán in this study has been a large one in two ways: first, I have found myself accepting with increasing confidence almost everything he has to say about the physical attributes of manuscripts, their dating and their palaeographic features; second, his essentially textual study contains a great deal of incidental material touching on my own concerns, and again I have come to respect his judgement with few reservations.

Lastly I must mention Louis Chalon's book *L'Histoire et l'épopée castillane du moyen âge* (1976). This book, which appeared well after I had started work on my own, covers much of the same ground, albeit from a very different perspective. Chalon's primary aim is to establish the degree of historicity present in Spanish epic legend, in the process of which he has extensive recourse to chronicle texts, including many of those also discussed here. Incidentally to his main aim, he also has a good deal to say about issues of general interest in epic and chronicle studies, notably the necessity of postulating *refundiciones* of epic poems to explain divergences in chronicle texts. However, Chalon can be criticised—as was Babbitt over forty years ago—for being insufficiently aware of the complexity of the textual difficulties surrounding the use of chronicle materials. Although he refers in his introduction and bibliography to Diego Catalán's 1962 book *De Alfonso X . . .*, he seems not to have taken sufficient note of the Spaniard's detailed conclusions: so, he consistently fails to distinguish between the 'versión regia' and 'versión vulgar' of the *PCG*; he refers to Ocampo's chronicle throughout as the *Tercera crónica general*, with scant regard to its internal complexities; and throughout his chapters dealing with the Cid he devotes separate sections to the *Crónica particular* (that is, to the version published at Burgos in 1512 by Velorado under the title *Crónica del famoso cauallero Cid Ruy Diez Campeador*), which version is now properly regarded as effectively belonging to a sub-group of the manuscripts of the *Crónica de Castilla*. These and other deficiencies do not detract from Chalon's main purpose: as he himself expresses it, it is 'une confrontation systématique de l'épopée et de la réalité historique sur laquelle elle se fonde' (p. ii), and if the subsidiary use of chronicle manuscripts is sometimes insufficiently critical and subtle, that is a relatively minor matter.

To return to the perspectives and aims of the present study, they are threefold. First, like Chalon, I have found that a study which started from a different viewpoint—in this case that of the chronicles themselves—has led to conclusions about epic poetry also. It has been necessary to sift previous theories about the historicity and the origins of the epic legends which provided the chroniclers with much of their material, and without laying any great claims to originality I hope that a coherent account may emerge of the birth and development of the major epic and other legendary material of early mediaeval Spain. Second, this work has led me towards a modest general conspectus of the nature and relationship of the various chronicle families. These complex questions crop up on many occasions in the chapters which follow, and I have tried to incorporate my conclusions into the description of manuscripts which forms an Appendix. Third, and most important, I have been concerned to show how chronicles develop and evolve. The treatment of legendary material in mediaeval historiography gives us a fascinating glimpse of how the chroniclers' craft developed, changed in emphasis and critical criteria, and led eventually to something approaching a fictional or novelesque view of the historiographic process. To trace the successive developments of the stories—be they largely factual as in the account of the fratricidal wars between the sons of Fernando I or wholly fictional as in the story of Bernardo del Carpio—is to follow a steady drift away from the respect for authoritative sources which characterises the original Alphonsine work, and towards the creation of a convincing, consistent and credible narrative which is the hallmark of the later texts. Respect for historical accuracy was largely lost on the way; but in its place we can see a new confidence and a new creativity which is by no means without relevance in the history of the development of prose fiction.

The seven chapters of this book correspond to major legends in the literature and history of early mediaeval Spain. I begin with the story of Bernardo del Carpio, go on to those of Fernán González, the Infantes de Lara and to two short accounts concerning the later Counts of Castile—the legends devoted to the 'Condesa traidora' and the 'Infante Garcia'. The remaining three chapters deal with material from the 'cuarta parte': the youthful deeds of the Cid; Fernando I's partition of his kingdoms and the subsequent fratricidal wars; and the heroic deeds of the mature Cid. These are not the only legendary subjects dealt with in the chronicles: one thinks of the account of the loss of Spain to the Moors (the legend of *el rey Rodrigo*), the Carolingian story of Mainete, that of the Moorish wife of Alfonso VI (*La mora Zaida*) and others (a concise survey of the 'epic' sources used in the chronicles is to be found in Gómez Pérez, 'Fuentes y cronología', pp. 624-27). The ones chosen, however, are both major in literary importance and complex in their development in successive chronicle versions, and it is for these reasons that the choice has been made. To have tried to take in more would have been to prolong the over-long gestation of the present work.

Chapter 1
BERNARDO DEL CARPIO

The first legend to be discussed is that of Bernardo del Carpio. This is not the earliest legendary material in the chronicles, being preceded by the important story of King Rodrigo and the loss of Spain to the Arabs, as well as by other lesser-known legends. These, however, come in parts of the chronicles relatively fixed in form at an early date, and offer less in the way of subsequent development. The story of Bernardo, on the other hand, varies from one chronicle to another in a way which suggests that a less than sure hand is at work in the manipulation of sources and the creation of an acceptable narrative.

It is clear that these sources include *cantares de gesta*. Even were it not for the explicit references in the chronicles to *cantares* and *juglares* one would suspect a popular origin for this essentially fictional story. Menéndez Pidal admitted, for all his adherence to a theory of the historicity of Spanish epic, that here is an exception: 'La leyenda de Bernardo no nace, como las demás leyendas españolas, a raíz de un suceso histórico' (*Romancero tradicional*, I. 143).[1]

There has been much debate about the nature of the epic legend (or legends) involved; here I propose to do no more than summarise the necessarily hypothetical explanations of this prehistory of the chronicle texts. First, however, it will be convenient briefly to summarise the story in its most accessible form, that found in Menéndez Pidal's edition of the *Primera Crónica General* (*PCG*).

It begins in ch. 617, corresponding to the 21st year of the reign of Alfonso II (*'el casto'*) of León, or 800 A.D. We learn how the King's sister, Jimena, secretly married the Count San Diaz de Saldanna and had a son, Bernardo. The King, outraged, imprisoned the Count and sent his sister to a convent, but brought up the young Bernardo at his court. The succeeding chapters tell how Bernardo played a key role in the defeat of

---

[1] Deyermond and Chaplin draw attention to the presence in this story of traditional motifs such as the bastard hero and the successful return of the hero ('Folk-Motifs', pp. 43-44).

Charlemagne's army at Roncesvalles (ch. 619); and how he subsequently learnt of his father's imprisonment and unsuccessfully begged the King to release him (ch. 621). There is also a reference to the possibility of Bernardo's further involvement with Charlemagne, this time helping him to defeat Marsil, the Moorish King of Saragossa and subsequently accompanying him on his return to France (ch. 623). No more is heard of Bernardo until the reign of Alfonso III '*el magno*' some twenty years later (the chronicler speculates in ch. 648 that this silence may be due to his absence from Spain with Charlemagne: *PCG*, p. 370a9-15). Bernardo then plays an important part in several campaigns against successive invasions of Moors (chs 649 and 650) and French (ch. 651). After each battle he requests the favour of his father's release, but Alfonso is as obdurate as his earlier namesake. Finally he exiles his importunate vassal (ch. 652); but after a successful campaign in which Bernardo establishes himself in his own fortress at El Carpio and harasses the royal troops over a long period (ch. 654) the King sues for peace and agrees to release the Count in return for the keys to Bernardo's stronghold. The Count, we are told, is found to have died three days previously; but the King has him bathed, dressed and mounted on horseback to meet his son. Bernardo discovers the deception too late: the castle has been surrendered and the King exiles Bernardo (ch. 655). He goes to France and, after a brief stay at the French court, settles down in Ribagorza to carve out a fief for himself and found a family. In the next chapter (ch. 656) there is a reference to his death after a return to Spain in the twenty-first year of Alfonso's reign, or 857 A.D.

This story has many unsatisfactory features which suggest some kind of composite origin. Its division between two non-consecutive reigns is unfortunate both from the point of view of chronology[2] and in that the refusal of Alfonso III to release the Count is not satisfactorily explained. It also has a degree of

[2] Even in terms of the erroneous chronology of the *PCG* there are difficulties, of which the chief is that Bernardo is said to have been born in A.D. 800 and to have played a part at Roncesvalles six years later (*PCG*, chs 617 and 619). If one takes instead the actual chronology, the difficulty is that Alfonso III reigned from 866 to 910 (and not 837-882 as in the *PCG*): Bernardo would thus be over seventy in the fourth year of that monarch's reign, when he reappears as a warrior. As for Roncesvalles, the historical battle is usually assigned to A.D. 778, i.e. before the dates given for Bernardo's birth and the accession of Alfonso II. See Defourneaux, 'La Légende de Bernardo del Carpio', *BH*, 45 (1943), 117-38 (p. 127), and Franklin, 'Origins of the Legend', pp. 289-90.

repetition: first, in that Bernardo's rôle as a military champion whose request for a well-earned favour is repeatedly denied is duplicated in the two separate reigns; and second in his absences in France, first with Charlemagne (ch. 623) then in exile (ch. 655). What is more, the references to *cantares* mentioned above introduce variants to the story which are largely inconsistent with its main points: one is the suggestion that Bernardo's mother was not donna Jimena, sister of Alfonso '*el casto*' but Timbor, sister of Charlemagne (*PCG*, p. 351a21-27). This is mentioned again in connection with his subsequent visit to the French court (ch. 655)[3] but can hardly be said to be consistent with Alfonso's outraged imprisonment of the Count San Diaz, which is in many ways the pivot of the story. Again, the account of Bernardo's alliance with Charlemagne in ch. 623 and their subsequent campaigns is mentioned only tentatively, since the chroniclers know well that the French Emperor died shortly after Roncesvalles. All the signs are that this narrative is an unsuccessful attempt to harmonise disparate sources.

In support of this it should be noted that, as Diego Catalán has pointed out, the base MS of this part of Menéndez Pidal's *PCG*, E^2 (Escorial, MS X-I-4) shows signs of a break at this point. Up to the end of folio 18 (p. 350a10 of the edition) the MS is a carefully prepared text which originally formed part of the codex E^1 (Escorial, MS Y-I-2). This original MS, which Catalán calls E^*, ends abruptly; and in E^2 it is continued in altogether more hesitant way. This may be precisely because its compilers— working after Alfonso X's death—were faced with a complex of sources giving contradictory versions of Bernardo's story.[4]

[3] On his arrival at the court, Bernardo tells the French king that 'era sobrino del rey Carlos el Grand et fijo de donna Timbor su hermana'. The King replies that 'estaua y estonces en la corte un fijo dessa donna Timbor, a quien pregunto ... si le querie recebir por hermano a Bernaldo. Et el dixo que non, ca lo non era' (*PCG*, p. 375b25-32). It is not clear whether the last phrase is part of the reported speech or an opinion of the chronicler.

[4] *De Alfonso X*, pp. 32-49. Catalán concludes: 'A mi parecer, no se trata de una simple casualidad el que precisamente en el capítulo inmediato se inicie en la *Crónica General* la historia de Bernardo del Carpio. Mientras los 'ayuntadores' alfonsíes utilizaron fuentes varias de la historiografía en latín, la labor compilatoria no presentó graves dificultades; el problema surgió al intentar conjuntar la información épica de los Cantares de Gesta con la narración 'más verídica' de los historiadores latinos (el Toledano y el Tudense, por lo general) ... En consecuencia, creo muy probable que el haberse detenido el manuscrito alfonsí E^* en el capítulo 616 sea precisamente debido a que en el capítulo siguiente se comenzaba a tratar de Bernardo y había que coordinar el relato del Tudense y el Toledano con el Cantar de Gesta' (pp. 48-49). See also Gómez Pérez, 'La *EE* alfonsí', pp. 501-02.

Before seeing how this situation was handled by the compilers of other—perhaps later—vernacular chronicles, it will be convenient briefly to consider what has been referred to above as the prehistory of the legend: in other words, the nature of the sources which caused so much difficulty. One can assume, as Catalán does, that they included on the one hand the Latin chronicles of the Tudense and the Toledano and on the other the vernacular *cantares*. The situation is complicated by the fact that the Latin historians appear in turn to have used vernacular sources. The Tudense tells a story which is in many respects similar to that which has found its way into the PCG. It includes Bernardo's Leonese origins (his mother is Jimena) and his father's imprisonment; after telling of his part in the defeat of Charlemagne at Roncesvalles it goes on to that monarch's reconciliation with Alfonso II and pilgrimage to Santiago, and his return to France accompanied by Bernardo. When the latter reappears, in the reign of Alfonso III, it is to aid that monarch and to demand his father's release in return: a release which the King promises but does not grant. Bernardo then becomes involved once again with the French, who invade under Charles III, only to be repulsed by Bernardo with the aid of Muza, Moorish King of Saragossa.[5]

The Toledano's version is less complex, in that it omits mention of the second battle against the French, and has Alfonso pardon Bernardo's father and release him; nor is Bernardo's death recorded.[6]

These different accounts have been variously explained as stemming from two basic forms of the legend, even from two separate legends. Menéndez Pidal calls one the 'Bernardo carolingio'—the story of the national hero, a counterweight to the French Roland and Charlemagne, who fought with the Moors against the French invaders; then, reconciled with Charlemagne, he goes with him to France to fight against the enemies of the Empire. The second version, the 'Bernardo alfonsí' contains more decidedly Spanish features, concentrating on Bernardo's sense of family honour and his relationship with his Spanish sovereign; he receives a Leonese mother, and the

---

[5] The relevant portion of the Tudense is reproduced in Heinermann, *Untersuchungen*, pp. 3-27.

[6] Toledano, IV. 9-11, 15-16 (pp. 82-91); also reproduced in Heinermann, *Untersuchungen*, pp. 3-27.

story of his imprisoned father is woven around his previous exploits. We lose his foreign excursions, but instead he becomes wholly caught up in the cause of Christian Spain and in his own family grievance.[7] This line of speculation is pursued further by Horrent (*La Chanson de Roland*, pp. 466-69), who regards the 'Bernardo alfonsí' not as a development of an earlier Carolingian legend but as a quite separate one, set in the reign of Alfonso III and being essentially a tale of family honour unconnected with the story of Roncesvalles.[8] Whichever of these hypotheses is correct, it is still necessary to explain the way in which they were handled, first by the Latin chroniclers and then by the Alphonsine historiographers. The Tudense appears to use both stories and to reconcile them as far as possible. This he does by dividing the material into two parts, putting Bernardo's birth (his mother being donna Jimena) and early exploits including Roncesvalles in the reign of Alfonso II; explaining his subsequent absence from the chronicle by supposing he returned to France with Charlemagne; and assigning the rest of the story of Bernardo to the reign of Alfonso III. This

[7] *Romancero tradicional*, I, 143-47. The hypotheses of Entwistle, 'The "Cantar de Gesta" of Bernardo del Carpio', *MLR*, 23 (1928), 307-22, and Franklin, 'Origins of the Legend' are not essentially different, though the former prefers to postulate a prose *estoria* in place of a second *cantar*: to this he ascribes the change from a Carolingian to a Spanish centre of gravity for the legend, and to this also the original attempt to relate legendary material to specific historical periods. Franklin prefers to stress the quasi-historical origins of the legend in various actual Bernardos active against the French in earlier centuries, to which Leonese characteristics were added in the thirteenth century. Defourneaux 'La légende de B. del C.' concentrates on the relationship between Bernardo and Charlemagne at the expense of the story of Bernardo's father, and has a different view of the probable coalescence of the elements involved. He sees the invention of Bernardo as a national hero, to take part in Roncesvalles, as the core of the legend, which was subsequently influenced first by local legends concerning a Count of Saldaña and subsequently—in the context of thirteenth-century preoccupations with the reconquest—by a desire to ally Bernardo with the forces of Christendom: hence the rapprochement with Charlemagne. See also E. von Richthofen, *Nuevos estudios épicos medievales* (Madrid, 1970), pp. 37-46; and Heinermann, *Untersuchungen*.
[8] Horrent: 'L'histoire conservée de "Bernardo" renferme deux aventures originellement différentes d'esprit et de localisation et peut-être autonomes' (*La Chanson de Roland*, p. 467); he distinguishes: (a) 'un récit de l'Espagne orientale, pyrénéenne, centré sur Roncevaux où Bernardo était un personnage mi-carolingien mi-espagnol, fils illégitime de la sœur de Charlemagne et d'un seigneur espagnol, héros de la bataille de Roncevaux et d'aventures glorieuses en France même'; and (b) 'un récit de l'Espagne léonaise, centré sur le drame familial qui oppose le roi de Léon Alphonse à son neveu Bernardo del Carpio, né des amours cachées ou illégitimes de la sœur du roi et d'un de ses vassaux. Cette histoire est absolument étrangère à Charlemagne' (ibid., pp. 468-69).

leads to the repetition noted above (see Menéndez Pidal, *Romancero tradicional*, I, 149-50).

The Toledano, on the other hand, simplifies the relationship between Bernardo and Charlemagne (who no longer makes a pilgrimage to Santiago or takes Bernardo off to France with him),[9] suppresses the second battle against the French and drops the final climax of the death of Bernardo's father.

By and large the compilers of the *PCG*, as will be seen, followed the Tudense. They take from that source the division of material between the reigns of Alfonso II and Alfonso III, and they also follow the Latin chronicler in such details as the identity of Bernardo's mother. From the Toledano they take that author's scepticism over Charlemagne's pilgrimage to Santiago and other deeds in Spain (*PCG*, pp. 355b27-357a21).[10] The *PCG*, however, as has already been mentioned, does draw attention to the existence of divergent details of poetic origin, such as the French ancestry of Bernardo. It also refers to a possible relationship between the latter and Bueso, the leader of the French invasion of ch. 651, once again ascribing this to 'algunos en sus cantares' (p. 371a25-27), and a similar scepticism attaches to the whole postscript of Bernardo's later career in France and the Pyrenees (ch. 655). In short, the authors of the *PCG* prefer what they call 'los libros autenticos, esto es ... los libros otorgados' (p. 376a24-25) and 'lo que fallamos por los latines en los libros antigos' (p. 376a32-33); but they are not sufficiently confident to discard completely the contradictory statements of the *juglares*.

The other chronicle versions which tell this story fall into four groups. Let us look first at the 'version vulgar' of the *PCG*, best represented in this section by MSS *Y*, *G*, *T*, and *Z* (see below, p. 152, for further details). Diego Catalán has pointed out that the 'versión vulgar' or, as he prefers to call it, the 'versión alfonsí' is regularly more concise and closer to its sources than the more discursive *E* ('version regia') which he dubs the 'Amplificación de 1289' (*De Alfonso X*, pp. 124-71,

---

[9] Horrent sees this as part of the Toledano's tendency to exalt the rôle of the King. '(Le Toledano) atténue fortement l'odieux de l'attitude royale envers Bernardo, en racontant que le père de ce dernier a été relâché et a obtenu le pardon du roi' (*La Chanson de Roland*, p. 478).

[10] Horrent explains this as due to the Toledano's natural hostility to the metropolitan pretensions of the Galician city; this equally explains the Tudense's enthusiasm for the same episode (ibid., p. 477).

especially 125-32). The difference is essentially a stylistic one and has little if any effect on the narrative. Examples may be seen in Catalán's study from various parts of the chronicle, including one from this section (p. 132): in ch. 651, MS Z tells of Bueso's arrival as follows:

> El rrey fue estonçes a el con grand poder e ouo con el su batalla en Orçejo, que es en tierra de Castilla, e murieron y muchos de cada parte. E algunos dizen en sus cantares que este Bueso era primo corrmano de Bernaldo (fol. 220r; cf. MS T, fol. 129v),

while MS E expands at several points:

> El rey don Alffonso, luego que estas nueuas sopo, llego su hueste et grand poder et fue contra el, et fallaronse, et ouo el rey don Alffonsso su batalla en Ordeion, que es en tierra de Castiella cercal castiello que dizen Amaya. Et dizen algunos en sus cantares, segund cuenta la estoria, que este frances Bueso que so primo era de Bernaldo (fol. 33v).

The numerous variants recorded in Menéndez Pidal's edition bear witness to similar differences of an essentially linguistic nature.

More interesting are other MSS also loosely classified as belonging to the 'version regia', namely B, U, X, and V. At this point in the chronicle (from the beginning of the Bernardo story until the end of the reign of Ordonno II, ch. 677) these MSS form a family apart which Catalán has called the 'Crónica Fragmentaria' (*De Alfonso X*, pp. 176-77). The differences between this group and the E version outlined above are not merely stylistic but of interest in the light they throw on compilatory technique. So, for instance, they insert at p. 351a8 the detail that the Count San Diaz was in prison for forty-seven years (which ties in with the chronology of the *PCG*); when denying (as E does) the alternative story that Bernardo's mother was Timbor they rightly point out that if this were só the whole story of Alfonso's wrath would be pointless;[11] and they remind us at the appropriate point of the reason for the King's intransigence in refusing to release the Count, namely his oath.[12] Thus, while the story is recognisably the same, there is more

---

[11] 'Mas sy esto fuese verdat el rey don Alfonso non auie por que gelo demandar nin auia razon por que resçibiese a Bernaldo por su sobrino' (MSS B and U, PCG, p. 351a27 variant); cf. also MSS V, fol. 137r and X, fol. 537r.

[12] '. . . çiertamente dierale su padre sinon porque auia jurado que en toda su vida del Sant Diaz nunca de aquella presion salliese mas que en ella moriese' (MSS B and U, PCG, p. 355a23 variant; cf. MSS V, fol. 141r-v and X, fol. 544r-v.

cross-referencing and more critical examination of sources: one could say that more of the scaffolding of historiographical method is visible in the 'Crónica Fragmentaria'.

All the versions so far mentioned are recognisably forms of the same narrative, perhaps preserved at differing stages of its elaboration.[13] The same cannot be said of the next group of texts, the so-called *Crónica General 'Vulgata'* or *Tercera Crónica General*, a version of which was published by Ocampo in 1541. Apart from this edition, the 'tercera parte' of this chronicle exists in a group of MSS, *C*, *F*, *H*, *L*, and *R*.[14] The *Vulgata* is demonstrably a reworking of the material, though its sources may not have differed from those of the *PCG*. The most obvious difference involves the arrangement of material, in that the *Vulgata* transfers back to the reign of Alfonso II the four chapters (= *PCG*, chs 649-52) dealing with Bernardo's prowess against the Moors and against Bueso, and his exile by the King. This has various results, not all of them good. It is more satisfactory that the King who imprisons San Díaz should be the one whom Bernardo repeatedly asks to free him and the one who eventually exiles Bernardo in impatience; it could be argued that this exile is a better explanation of Bernardo's absence from the pages of the chronicle for twenty-five years than the only half-believed speculation in the *PCG* that perhaps he was campaigning elsewhere in Europe with Charlemagne.

Yet it must be admitted that this rearrangement of material has the effect of isolating in a far from satisfactory way the concluding two chapters (= *PCG*, chs 654-55) which deal with Bernardo's campaign against Alfonso III and its tragic outcome, the too-long delayed release of his father. We are asked to accept the suspension of the Bernardo story in the middle of his campaign against Alfonso II, with the words 'duraron

---

[13] The *Crónica Abreviada* of don Juan Manuel seems at this point to be following the *PCG* version of the narrative, although, as so often, it gives insufficient detail for us to be able to classify the lost *Manuelina* with the 'versión regia' or the 'versión vulgar'. Nor does the *Abreviada* contain any of the distinguishing marks of the 'Crónica Fragmentaria'. See BN MS 1356, fols 89r-90r and 92r-93v; cf. the edition by Grismer, pp. 118-19 and 122-24.

[14] See pp. 152-53 for details of MSS, and Catalán, *De Alfonso X*, pp. 188-93 for an account of the *Vulgata* family. The details cited in the following paragraphs are, with minor exceptions, identical in the MSS to the printed version. Catalán regards the version of the 'tercera parte' published by Ocampo as being quite different in its origins and relationship to other chronicles to that used by Ocampo in the 'cuarta parte'; he suggests the name *Vulgata* for the former and *Ocampiana* for the latter.

aquellas guerras que ouo entre el rey e Bernaldo muy gran tiempo (Ocampo, fol. 230r); then, when he reappears (fol. 236r) he is presumably reconciled with the King (Alfonso III) since 'en todas estas batallas . . . fue Bernaldo del Carpio con el muy nobre rey don Alfonso el Magno . . . faziendo tan grandes mortandades en los moros' (fol. 236r). However, on being denied the release of his father, 'fuese para Salamanca assi como fiziera en el tiempo del rey don Alfonso el Casto e començo a correr la tierra del rey don Alfonso' (ibid.).

Apart from this major change, the *Vulgata* makes other alterations, some of them similar to the explanations found in the 'Crónica fragmentaria' MSS. Like that text, the *Vulgata* denies the possibility of Timbor being Bernardo's mother, but in a more categorical and less reasoned manner.[15] It also mentions Alfonso's oath (see above, note 12) at the point when San Diaz is imprisoned: 'por end vos juro et prometo que nunca en toda vuestra vida salgades de las tierras de Limia' (*PCG*, p. 351a4 variant; Ocampo: 'Lunia', fol. 225r). In the chapter in which Bernardo learns of his father's identity and imprisonment, the *Vulgata* dispenses with the rather unsatisfactorily explained game of *tablas* (*PCG*, p. 354b11-43) and simply has the two women tell Bernardo the facts at the instance of Velasco Melendez and Suero Velasquez (Ocampo, fol. 227r); it goes a stage further than the other chronicles at this point by telling us that until then Bernardo 'sienpre touo . . . que era fijo del rey don Alfonso' (ibid.); the compiler, however, appears to forget almost immediately that Bernardo has been disabused of this belief, adding again, after saying that the King always continued to treat Bernardo well (cf. *PCG*, p. 355a23), 'por lo qual sienpre penso Bernaldo que era fijo del rey don Alfonso' (ibid.). Then again, when Alfonso III finally exiles Bernardo, the *Vulgata* puts the following words into his mouth: 'Yd vos a Françia al rey Carlos cuyo pariente sodes' (Ocampo, fol. 237r). Now, this can be explained only in terms of a source which accepted Timbor as Bernardo's mother, and we have seen that the *Vulgata* categorically denies this (see above, note 15).

All in all, the *Vulgata*, drawing it would appear on essentially

---

[15] 'Mas esto non podria ser. Por ende non son de creer todas las cosas que los omes dizen en sus cantares, et la verdad es assi como auemos ya dicho segun que fallamos en las estorias verdaderas las que fizieron los sabios' (Ocampo, fol. 225v); cf. note 11 above.

similar material to the sources of the *PCG*, handles them differently and less well. The organisation of the material may at first sight seem to be more thoughtful, but it creates new problems of balance by isolating the final episode as it does. Moreover, the handling of contradictory sources is in reality even more uncertain than in the *PCG*, despite the categorical tone adopted by the later chronicle.

Of the remaining principal chronicle which contains this story, little need be said. This is the *Crónica de 1344* (*Cr1344*),[16] which has a detailed account only of the second part, that is of the events corresponding to the reign of Alfonso III in the *PCG*. The detailed narrative whose source is the *PCG* begins in the *Cr1344* with the reign of Ramiro I (821-28 A.D.). His immediate predecessors, including Alfonso II, are listed in the previous chapter with some information about their descendants but no information as to the events of their reigns;[17] the first part of the story of Bernardo, comprising his birth and exploits at Roncesvalles, is therefore absent from the *Cr1344*. The second part, corresponding to chs 649-56 of the *PCG*, is fully narrated, and in terms which differ hardly at all from those of the *PCG*. Despite the fact that the absence of the earlier events makes much of what follows obscure—the *Cr1344* follows the *PCG* in telling of Alfonso's stubborn refusal to release Bernardo's father—only in one instance is there any hint of a link with something which has happened in the past. This is when Alfonso explains his refusal to release the count 'por que non queria quebrantar la jura que fiziera al Rey don Alfonso el Casto' (MS *Q*, fols 111v-112r). This may be a misreading of the phrase 'la yura que el rey don Alffonso el Casto fiziera' (*PCG*, p. 372a4-5), which is correctly translated in the Portuguese original of the *Cr1344* and in the other major Castilian MS, *M*;[18] indeed, it is probably right to see this as a simple error rather than as an attempt to provide a link with the earlier material, since no such link is hinted at elsewhere,

---

[16] The *Crónica de Veinte Reyes* begins with the reign of Fruela II and therefore contains neither part of the Bernardo legend.

[17] The most succinct summary of the structure and sources of the early sections of the *Cr1344* is to be found in the edition of the text by Catalán and Andrés, I, xxx.

[18] '. . . a jura que fezera el rei dom Afonso, o Casto' (Lindley Cintra, *Crónica*, II, 434, 11. 26-27; cf. MS *M*: 'la jura quel rrei don Alfonso el casto fiziera' (fol. 65v); the Galician-Portuguese version of the *PCG* is confused here: 'a jura que del Rey dom Alfonso o Casto fezera' (MS *A*, fol. 10v).

either when the dead Count is finally produced or when Bernardo goes off to exile in France. Indeed, the incident with donna Timbor's son (see above, note 3) is retailed as if we already knew the varying stories about Bernardo's ancestry. In short, *Cr1344* makes nonsense of the story by telling only half of it, and no attempt is made to explain the essential background.

Finally, one may look at an interesting derivative version of the *Cr1344*. This is the so-called *Refundición Toledana* (*RefTol*) (otherwise known as the *Arreglo Toledano* and the *Estoria de los Godos*). The structure and content of this mid-fifteenth century version show it to be based on the *Cr1344*. In this instance, for example, it contains, like that chronicle, only the second part of the story. Unlike the *Cr1344*, however, it shows a greater concern for producing a coherent and self-contained narrative. Thus, when Bernardo makes his first appearance, at the battle of Benavente (= *PCG*, ch. 649) he is introduced as 'vn su cauallero llamado Bernaldo del Carpio' (MS *M*, fol. 80v); and the first mention of his imprisoned father is accompanied by the explanatory note 'que el [rey] de ante sobre çiertos casos tenia preso' (MS *M*, fol. 81v). This is later expanded slightly: 'ca gelo entragaran asy preso por parte del rrey don Alfonso el Casto. E el [rey] la rrespondio que el non quebrantaria la jura del Rey don Alfonso el Casto . . .' (MS *M* fols 81v–82r; MS *S* fol. 110r). The difference from the *Cr1344* is that some need is felt to explain, however briefly, these loose ends deriving from an earlier story which we must assume to have been no longer accessible to the author of the *RefTol*.

The tidying-up process may also take the more negative form of omission. Thus, there is no mention of any relationship between Bernardo and the French warrior Bueso (cf. *PCG*, p. 371a25-27); nor is there any account of Bernardo's visit to the French court and subsequent campaigning in the Pyrenees (cf. *PCG*, pp. 375b16-376a33). Both these details depend on Bernardo's supposed descent from Timbor, and with mention of this omitted the subsequent events are also dropped.

Indeed, it may be no accident that both the details discussed in the previous paragraph were mentioned in the *PCG* (and the *Cr1344*) as juglaresque in origin; they thus fall into the category of what has been called above the scaffolding of historiography, the desire to mention all available sources even when their veracity is in doubt. The *RefTol* dismantles this scaffolding, retaining only what is relevant to the main story being told.[19] It thus represents a significant change in the respect for sources which, in the case of this legend, caused so much difficulty for the earlier compilers. The sources were so contradictory that none of the early versions reconciled them satisfactorily; the *RefTol*, with its disregard for such niceties, is a more self-confident and consistent narrative. And, since we are dealing with basically legendary material, perhaps we ought not to judge too harshly a version whose criteria seem to be those of fiction rather than of historiography.

[19] One other point at which the *RefTol* omits references to such sources is the story of San Diaz being bathed and mounted on horseback, ascribed in the *PCG* to 'romances' and 'cantares' (p. 375a27-28). The *RefTol* has the story, but without the ascription (MS *M*, fol. 83v). Compare also the statement in the *PCG* (p. 373b29) that the authority for the extent of Bernardo's raids on Alfonso's territory is 'segund dize la estoria por el latin'; the *RefTol* mentions the extent of the raids, but with no such reference (MS *M*, fol. 83r).

Chapter 2
FERNÁN GONZÁLEZ

The story of Fernán González differs in a number of respects from that of Bernardo del Carpio. For one thing it is substantially longer, for another its sources are known; and, not least, it has a greater foundation in historical fact.

These last two factors necessarily affect one's approach to the subject: most important, its 'pre-history' is clearer and, perhaps, of less interest. The most extensive source used by the chronicles for the story of the first Count of Castile is the thirteenth-century *clerecía* poem known as the *Poema de Fernán González*[1] (*Poema*) supplemented by Latin histories such as those of the Toledano and the Tudense. Only in a few cases (which will be discussed below) do the chronicles introduce details not found in these sources.

This is not the place to examine in any detail the merits of the *Poema*, its possible origin in a *cantar de gesta* or its more distant antecedents.[2] The poem, in *cuaderna vía*, consists of some 760 stanzas and is incomplete; it is estimated that a further hundred stanzas are missing from the end. The chroniclers appear to have used a complete manuscript, but did not prosify the introductory section, some 170 stanzas summarising the history of Castile before Fernán González's accession. What is left deals with three main themes. First, the Count's campaigns against Almanzor, whom he defeats first at Lara (stanzas 191-285) and later at Hacinas (386-573), on each occasion with divine help. Second, his relations with the Navarrese, whom he defeats at Era Degollada (286-385) but by whom he is later treacherously imprisoned, to be released by the Navarrese *infanta* (586-696); he subsequently captures the Navarrese King but releases him unharmed (697-768). The third theme— most of which corresponds to the lost section of the poem—

---

[1] A convenient edition of the *Poema* is that in Menéndez Pidal's *Reliquias*, pp. 34-180, where the corresponding passages of the *PCG* are printed at the foot of the page.

[2] The subject is well summarised by Deyermond, *The Middle Ages*, pp. 36-38. See also J. P. Keller, 'The Structure of the "Poema de Fernán González"', *HR*, 25 (1957), 235-46, Avalle-Arce, 'Clerecía y juglaría', and the important work by Cotrait, *Fernán González*.

is that of his relations with the King of León, Sancho I, with whom he makes a bargain for the sale of a horse and a hawk at accumulating compound interest (574-85); the lost part of the poem, if the chronicles are a reliable guide, told how the King imprisoned the Count, how he escaped by a ruse and claimed the delayed payment for the sale of horse and hawk: the sum had mounted so astronomically that it could not be paid and—the climax of the story—the King granted Fernán González the independence of Castile in lieu of payment. It is highly probable that the poem also recounted the hero's death and burial at Arlanza, the monastery with which the prophecies and miraculous intervention in the Moorish campaigns are associated; indeed, it was a monk of Arlanza who recast the poem, doubtless with the interests of his monastery at heart, in the thirteenth-century *cuaderna vía* form in which we have it.[3]

It is hard to assess how much of this is fictional. Certainly Fernán González fought against the Moors during his lifetime, and his relations with other Christian monarchs were by no means smooth. It is possible that he founded Arlanza (so the Toledano tells us);[4] however, his various imprisonments are not confirmed, at least by the Toledano or the Tudense, and certainly the poem contains a good deal of legendary material. The prophecies and divine intervention are clearly linked with the ecclesiastical origins of the poem, and the motif of the horse and hawk (or other property) whose price increases so much by compound interest that only the independence of a people can pay for them is a folkloric motif of Gothic origin.[5]

There does exist confirmation of one episode, the imprison-

---

[3] See Deyermond, *Epic Poetry and the Clergy*, pp. 106 and 190, and J. P. Keller, 'The Hunt and Prophecy Episode of the "Poema de Fernán González" ', *HR*, 23 (1955), 251-58.

[4] 'Monasterium Sancti Petri in ripa Aslantiae fluminis aedificavit' (Toledano, V. 2, p. 99).

[5] See W. J. Entwistle, 'The Liberation of Castile', *MLR*, 19 (1924), 471-72, and Helen V. Terry, 'The Treatment of the Horse and Hawk Episodes in the Literature of Fernán González', *Hisp(Am)*, 13 (1930), 497-504; other folkloric motifs in the poem are discussed in Deyermond and Chaplin, 'Folk-Motifs', pp. 43-45 and 47-48; see also Deyermond, *Epic Poetry and the Clergy*, pp. 89-91, and von Richthofen, *Estudios épicos*, pp. 24-31. There is a slight danger—best exemplified by von Richthofen—of regarding as significant motifs what are no more than themes of universal validity such as exile, imprisonment, vengeance, and so on. Indeed, such themes may well have been a fairly faithful reflection of contemporary life and therefore be best seen as having historical rather than literary significance.

ment of the Count by the King of Navarre and his release by the latter's daughter; an account of this is found in the *Crónica Najerense* of c. 1160.[6] There we find a story which has the elements of stanzas 586-650 of the *Poema* (corresponding to chs 709-10 of the *PCG*).[7] As Menéndez Pidal pointed out, the *Najerense* breaks new ground by its reflection, on occasion, of popular sources, and it may be that here it is drawing on a *cantar* which was also to be the source of the later *Poema*.[8]

It will be recalled that in the case of Bernardo del Carpio the Alphonsine chroniclers found great difficulty in reconciling a fictional career with the more factual account of the Toledano and Tudense. Here, where at least the hero is a real one, even if all his deeds are not, the task is easier. They accomplish it by taking from the Latin chronicles (especially the Toledano) their basic chronological framework and the bulk of the account which they give of Fernán González's part in various succession struggles for the Leonese throne. The *PCG*, for instance, tells in chs 679, 684, 686, and 692 of his ancestry, his election as Count and his rôle in the Moorish wars of Ramiro II; in chs 703, 705, 707, and 708 he appears playing a part in the struggles for the succession which followed the deaths of Ramiro and of the next king, Ordoño III; and finally, in chs 725 and 728, under Ramiro III, we read of his last struggles against the Moors and his death.[9] Into this framework, which spans thirty-nine years and

[6] This text was first published by Cirot in 1909-11 under the title 'Chronique léonaise'. In 1923 Menéndez Pidal pointed out its Riojan rather than Leonese provenance and dated it at c. 1160 ('Relatos poéticos', pp. 330-34). Ubieto inclines to a slightly earlier date (between 1142 and 1157 (pp. 21-25 and 30 of his edition); D. W. Lomax, 'La fecha de la *Crónica Najerense*', *AEM*, 9 (1974-79), 405-06, argues for a date between 1174 and 1233.

[7] 'comes Fredenandus Gonzaluet fuit captus et filii eius in Cironia, in ecclesia Sancti Andree apostoli, a predicto rege Pampilonensis Garsea Sanctii, et transmissus Pampilonie, inde Clauillum inde Tubiam: unde cum Sanctia eiusdem regis Garsee sorore . . . habens nesciente fratre colloquium liberatus est dato prius eidem sacramento, quod si eum educeret, eam duceret in uxorem. Quod et fecit' (*Crónica Najerense*, II. 58, pp. 77-78). The *Najerense* also refers to Fernán González as the liberator of Castile: 'qui castellanos de sub iugo Legionensis dominationis dicitur extrasisse' (III. 3, p. 90).

[8] Menéndez Pidal says: 'con la *Crónica Najerense*, aparece otro tipo de historia más amplio y comprensivo, de espíritu castellano . . . La historia deja de ser una mera adulación cortesana . . . para fijarse . . . en otros personajes influyentes en la vida patria . . . esta nueva manera de concebir la historia procede evidentemente de que la *Crónica Najerense* toma de fuentes poéticas sus noticias referentes a los nuevos personajes' ('Relatos poéticos', pp. 335-36; he mentions the case of Fernán González at p. 337.

[9] Toledano, chs V. 2 (election as Count); V. 6-7 (Arab conquests with Ramiro);

the reigns of four Leonese kings, the chronicler inserts five large blocks of material taken from the *Poema*. Chapters 687-691 tell of the first campaign against Almanzor (*Poema*, stanzas 191-285); his victory over Sancho of Navarre is in chs 694-96 (*Poema*, 286-385) and his second campaign against Almanzor in chs 698-700 (*Poema*, 386-573); chs 709-716 tell of his later Navarrese adventures (*Poema*, 574-768); and, finally, chs 717-20 contain the material of the lost ending of the *Poema*, culminating in the independence of Castile.[10]

Of the relationship between poem and chronicle little need be said here. The differences have been analysed by K. Sneyders de Vogel ('Le *PFG* et la *Crónica General*'), who aptly concludes that they are on the whole due to 'la nature de la Chronique, qui ne veut pas donner un poème en prose mais une histoire d'Espagne' (p. 168). By far the greater number of these differences involve the chroniclers' abridgement of poetic features and are essentially stylistic. Such details as epithets, synonymous pairs, comparisons, and other interpolations find no place in the chronicle, and much else is paraphrased. Sneyders de Vogel also draws attention to a few cases where the chronicler appears to expand on the poetic text. This may be for the sake of explanation: compare stanza 649c 'el conde don Fernando non podia andar', to which the *PCG* adds 'por los fierros que eran muy pesados' (p. 413b29-30); or it may bring in extraneous material such as the digression on the size of a legion (*PCG*, p. 392a22-26) or the supposed etymology of the name Almanzor (*PCG*, p. 395a26-36), neither of which features in the poem. A further element, according to Sneyders de Vogel, may reflect changed social assumptions: after Fernán González's harangue to his men before the battle of Era Degollada, the *PCG* adds the sentence 'Estonces le dixieron que farien todo lo que el mandasse et quel ayudarien assi como uassallos buenos et leales fazen a sennor' (p. 397a24-26). Sneyders de Vogel sums up: 'Dans cette adjonction perce l'esprit féodal du chroniqueur qu n'admet pas l'obéissance aveugle que le Poema semble préconiser' (p. 168).

Not all the points made by Sneyders de Vogel can be accepted

V. 9-10 (Leonese succession struggles); and V. 12 final campaigns and death); pp. 98-105.

[10] For an analysis of problems caused by the harmonisation of historical and poetic sources, see Chalon, *L'Histoire et l'épopée*, pp. 460-62.

without qualification. Some of the features regarded by him as expansions made in the process of prosification are in fact found only in the 'versión regia' of the *PCG* represented by MS *E*. This is true, for instance, of the expansion of 227d of the poem, 'fuxo a un ermita, metios tras el altar', which in the chronicle becomes 'fuxo por una hermita que auie y *en essa montanna, et entro*, et metiose tras el altar', where the words in italics are found only in MS *E* (p. 393b2-4 and variant); a similar explanatory note at p. 406a16, 'Et es de saber que la hermita era aquella a que agora dezimos el monesterio de Sant Pedro de Arlança', is similarly lacking from MS *T* and others of the 'versión vulgar' (ibid., line 14 variant).

At least some of the differences, then, between the published texts of poem and chronicle must be ascribed to the tendency of MS *E* of the latter to expand verbally and add explanatory detail. This is in line with what we have seen in the case of the Bernardo del Carpio story, where MS *E* appears consistently to depart further from its sources than the relatively concise 'versíon vulgar' (cf. pp. 16-17 above). It was there stated that the difference was essentially stylistic, and up to a point the same is true here. A number of cases are found, however, where the difference between the two chronicle versions is more significant.

We may dismiss as of relatively little importance—hardly more than stylistic—such cases as those noted in the last paragraph; the first of these is a logical deduction from what is in fact a poetic narrative abbreviated in the interests of speed of movement, and the second is an example of the cross-referencing technique which is a feature of the chronicles. Not dissimilar are two points noted by Diego Catalán. In ch. 709, when the Count is besieged in a hermitage by the King of Navarre, the chronicle, following the poem, tells how the Count's squire could help his master only by throwing his sword in at the window (MS *Z*, fol. 238v, quoted by Catalán, *De Alfonso X*, p. 137; cf. *Poema*, stanza 600, quoted ibid., p. 136). MS *E* alone explains as follows:

> ...metieronse en una hermita que estaua y *de cerca, et descendieron de sus cauallos, et subieron luego en ellos sus escuderos. Et aquellos escuderos tenien las espadas del conde et de los otros caualleros, cada uno la de su sennor; et apartaronse de los del rey percebidos et mientesmetidos que si el rey alguna cosa quisiesse fazer de los caualleros, ellos que se le saliessen*

> de mano et se fuessen pora Castiella; ca de alcançarlos ninguno, non se temien. Et el conde metiose en aquella hermita cuedandose alli defender, et cercaronles bien la puerta. Et el escudero del conde . . . echoles las espadas por una finiestra . . . (p. 411a6-22).

All the italicised words are missing from both *Poema* and 'versión vulgar' and represent a clarificatory addition of the 'versión regia'.[11] Another sort of clarification is also noted by Catalán in ch. 696, where a passing reference to Judas Maccabeus (*PCG*, p. 398b23) is followed in MS *E* alone by the statement 'que fue obispo et buen cauallero darmas et muy grand lidiador et lidio muy bien et defendio muy bien de los enemigos el regno de Judea en quanto el visco' (*De Alfonso X*, p. 141).

Other such cases are the intercession by the Castilians on behalf of the Countess donna Sancha for her father García of Navarre, imprisoned by Fernán González (ch. 714). The passage reads as follows in the *PCG*:

> dixieronle: 'Sennor, pedimosuos *por uuestra mesura que nos oyades. Rogamosuos sennor, et pedimosuos* por merced que dedes el rey don Garcia a su fija donna Sancha, yl mandedes sacar de la prision; et faredes en ello grand mesura, et quantos uos lo sopieren teneruos lo an a bien, ca bien sauedes uos quamanno algo fizo ella a nos et a uos. Et sennor, si al fazedes non uos estara bien'. *Et tanto trauaron dell et tantol dixieron de buenas razones et debdo que auie y, quel fizieron otorgar lo que agora dira aqui la estoria, et complirlo. Et dize assi*: Respondioles alli estonces el conde que pues que ellos lo tenien por bien *et lo querien, et aunque fuesse mayor cosa,* que lo farie muy de grado. Et mandol luego sacar de los fierros; *et dalli adelant fizieron muchos plazeres et muchos solazes al rey don Garcia el conde Fernand Gonçalez et la condessa donna Sancha, su fija, et los nobles cauolleros de Castiella. Et en tod aquello* guisol *el cuende* muy bien *a el et a su compaña,* de pannos et de bestias et de quanto ouo mester . . . (pp. 416b26-417a4)

in which all the italicised sections are peculiar to MS *E*. Similarly, in the escape of Fernán González from prison in his wife's clothes (ch. 718), MS *E* has a more complex narrative:

> Et el conde mudado desta guisa fuesse pora la puerta en semeiança de duenna, *et la condessa cerca dell et encubriendose quanto mas et meior pudo; et quando llegaron a la puerta* dixo la condessa al portero quel abriesse la puerta . . . El portero cuedando que era la duenna *et que saldrie ella,* abriole la puerta et salio el conde; *et la condessa finco dentro tras la*

---

[11] Menéndez Pidal thought that the poem was defective at this point (*Reliquias*, pp. 125-26), but Catalán accepts Marden's proposed emendation and argues that MS *E* is here simply expanding in its usual way (*De Alfonso X*, p. 137 and n. 14).

puerta encrubiendose del portero, de guisa que nunqua lo entendio. Et el conde, pues que salio, non se espidio nin fablo, por que por uentura non fuesse entendudo en la boz et se estoruasse por y *lo que ell et la condessa querien;* et fuesse luego derechamientre pora un portal, *de como le consennara la condessa,* do estauan aquellos dos caualleros suyos *atendiendol con un cauallo.* Et el conde, *assi como llego,* caualgo en aquel cauallo quel tenien *presto, et començaronse de yr,* et salieron de la uilla muy encubiertamientre, et dieronse a andar quanto mas pudieron *derechamientre poral logar do dexaran los caualleros* (p. 421a11-39).

Once again, italics signify the extent of the narrative expansion felt necessary by the compilers of the 'versión regia'.

The next series of points made by Catalán to illustrate differences between the two versions are much more significant for our purposes. He calls them 'retoques ... para perfeccionar la historia del libertador de Castilla' (p. 142). They include such details as the moral commentary made by the compiler on Fernán González's behaviour in supporting the infante Sancho against his son-in-law Ordonno III (ch. 703). Both versions tell how Ordonno thereupon divorced Fernán González's daughter, but only MS *E* adds:

Et segund aquel fecho que el conde fiziera en ayudar a aquel con quien non auie debdo, et uinie contra ell que era su yerno, en que se mostro por so enemigo, dexole la fija por ende et con razon (p. 407b19-24).[12]

It even appears that the compiler of the 'versión regia' invented incidents. At the end of Fernán González's lifetime the chronicle, following the Toledano, tells how Castile was invaded by the Moors, causing great devastation (ch. 725). The 'versión vulgar' simply says 'E el conde non podiendo defenderseles, presieronle Simancas ...' (MS *Z*, fol. 244r, quoted by Catalán, *De Alfonso X*, p. 145); the 'versión regia' expands this in such a way as to exonerate Fernán González or at least to explain his passivity:

Et el cuende, non teniendo guisado de salir a ellos solo, estonces non podiendo mas, dexolos andar, faziendo el mal que podien. Et ellos entraron et prisieron daquella uez en esse anno, assi como cuenta la estoria, la uilla de Sietmancas ... suffriendo esto todo el cuende Fernand Gonçalez,

---

[12] Catalán quotes MS *Y* at this point (*De Alfonso X*, pp. 144-45), which is in fact rather confusing here: 'la que ell tomara por meter paz entre los castellanos et los leoneses, por amor de su suegro el cuende que fallara por su enemigo. Et caso con otra duenya'; the *CVR* is clearer: 'la qual tomara por meter paz entre los castellanos e los leoneses, por que entendio que el conde era su henemigo e le desamaua. Caso luego con otra duenna' (MS *N*, fol. 5v).

esperando tiempo en que pudiesse ende alcançar derecho et uengança (p. 424b19-28),

and follows this up in ch. 728 with an account of this vengeance which has a place in no other chronicle:

En aquella sazon . . . Fernand Gonçalez conde de Castiella otrossi oyendo tantos dannos et astragamientos como los moros fazien en el regno de Castiella, pesol et fue ende muy sannudo, et salio et llamo todas sus yentes, et apoderose lo mas et lo meior que el pudo, et fue et lidio con ellos; et tan atreuudamientre los firio, que los moros fueron uençudos, et mato muchos dellos ademas et catiuo muchos, et a los otros segudo de la tierra matando en ellos. Et desta guisa se torno bienandant el cuende Fernand Gonçalez desta uez a Burgos. (p. 425b32-45).

Menéndez Pidal referred to this as probably a 'deducción del compilador' (*PCG*, p. clviii), but deduction seems hardly the right word for what is, as Catalán says, more a necessary rehabilitation of a hero.[13]

The 'versión regia' in this section is therefore characterised by something more than stylistic amplification (though this is certainly one of its features); it represents a first step towards the departure from source material for reasons of moral comment and exemplary exaltation of a hero.

The concise version represented by the MSS of the 'vulgar' family is also to be seen in the *Vulgata*, and it is reflected in Juan Manuel's *Crónica Abreviada*. As for the latter, the lost text of which it is a summary appears to have been very similar to the version preferred in MSS *G*, *T*, *Y*, and *Z* of the 'versión vulgar', although with some peculiarities.[14] The *CVR* and the *Vulgata*, however, although they generally agree with each other and with the 'versión vulgar' against the expanded version of MS *E*, form a separate family within the concise version. They do this most strikingly through their chronology and organisation of this section. The *PCG*'s system (common to 'regia' and 'vulgar' versions) was outlined above: how the five blocks of material from the *Poema* were inserted into a frame-

[13] '. . . el formador del texto regio sintió la imperiosa necesidad de inventar una última entrada del conde por tierra de moros que le rehabilitase de su espectacular fracaso anterior' (*De Alfonso X*, p. 146).

[14] The *Crónica Abreviada* omits mention of the chapter corresponding to ch. 711 of the *PCG*, though its numeration jumps from 255 to 257 (fol. 99v; cf. the edition by Grismer, p. 131). It also runs together chs 727 and 728 and makes Fernán González rather than Gonçalo Sánchez responsible for the defeat of the Normans (fol. 101r; cf. the edition by Grismer, p. 133). Both of these are presumably errors, either in the original chronicle or in the summary.

work provided by the Toledano covering the 39 years from 901 (first year of the reign of Ramiro II) to 939 (third year of the reign of Ramiro III). In the *CVR* the framework remains similar, though it is compressed in that the first mention of Fernán González (his election as Count) comes not in the first but the fifteenth year of Ramiro's reign (A.D. 915). The first three poetic episodes are inserted at quite different points: Fernán González's early campaign against Almanzor (chs 687-91), which in the *PCG* falls in the reign of Ramiro II (in A.D. 904-05) is put back in the *CVR* to that of his successor Ordonno III (in A.D. 921-22); the first involvement with the Navarrese (chs 694-96), A.D. 908 in the *PCG* (under Ramiro II) is also postponed until Ordonno's reign (A.D. 924), while the second campaign against Almanzor (chs 698-700 in the *PCG*, = A.D. 910) is in the *CVR* placed even later, under Sancho I in A.D. 927. There it is immediately followed by the fourth poetic episode, the second involvement with the Aragonese (A.D. 928, as in the *PCG*), and the order and chronology of the two chronicles is once more in accord from this point.

The *Vulgata* follows the same system as the *CVR*.[15] However, it abbreviates the reign of Ramiro II so much as to make no mention of Fernán González and thus has no account of his election. Thereafter it follows the order of the *CVR*, though it abbreviates once again considerably at the end of Fernán González's life and omits entirely the Moorish invasion (= *PCG* ch. 725) which so engaged the attention of the compiler of *E* (see above, pp. 29-30).

These structural differences apart, the *CVR/Vulgata* version is essentially similar to the concise 'vulgar' version of the *PCG*. In all the instances quoted above, pp. 27-30, the *CVR* (and the *Vulgata* where it has the corresponding chapter) is close to the 'versión vulgar'.[16] The relatively few cases in which the two families do not agree can be explained individually.

In one instance, euphemism appears to be a factor: when the wife of the imprisoned Count arranges to spend the night with

---

[15] The *Vulgata* version is best consulted in Ocampo's edition, fols 240v-253v. The manuscripts do not offer significant variants.

[16] The corresponding folios of MS *N* of the *CVR* are as follows: 7r (stylistic expansion); 16r (cross-reference to Arlanza); 17v (Count and squire); 11r (Judas Maccabeus); 21v (release of García); 24v (F. G. released from prison); 5v (F. G.'s daughter divorced by Ordoño); and 26v (F. G.'s passivity in face of Arab invasion). For minor peculiarities of this version, see Chalon, *L'Histoire et l'épopée*, pp. 467-70.

him (ch. 718), the 'versión vulgar' provides the most explicit account of her request to the King of León, his captor:

rogaua mucho, como a sennor bueno et mesurado, que mandasse sacar al conde de los fierros, diziendol que el cauallo trauado nunqua bien podie fazer fijos. Dixo el rey estonces: 'si Dios me uala, tengo que dize uerdad', et mandol luego sacar de los fierros et *que les fiziessen muy buen lecho*. Et desi yoguieron toda la noche amos en uno (*PCG*, p. 420b46-421a5 and variants).

(It should be noted that MS *E*, perhaps for similar reasons, omits the italicised phrase.) The *CVR/Vulgata*, however, replace the earthy reference to the horse ('diziendol . . . fijos') with the phrase 'demientra que ella con el estaua' (*CVR*, MS *N*, fol. 24v; also Ocampo, fol. 252v).[17] On rare occasions one or other chronicle may elucidate or expand stylistically in a way similar to that which is such a regular feature of MS *E*: so, at *PCG*, p. 393b10, when Fernán González leaves his horse to pursue the boar, the *Vulgata* (but not the *CVR*) inserts 'et arrendo el cauallo porque non sel fuesse' (ibid., variant).

More complex are the varying accounts of Fernán González's election as Count of Castile. In the 'versión regia' this is related at *PCG*, p. 390a8-26; there is no reference to any approval sought from or granted by the King of León. The 'versión vulgar' adds the note 'et fizol conde el rey don Ramiro' (p. 390a30 variant), and the *Crónica Abreviada* also notes 'e diol el condado depues el rey don Rramiro' (fol. 76v, cf. the edition by Grismer, p. 127). Two chapters later (ch. 686) there is in both versions an obscure reference to a grievance held by the King against the Castilians ('non se quiso membrar del mal quel fizieran los ricos omnes de Castiella'; *PCG*, p. 391b14-15). The *CVR* explains this: not only does the text have no earlier reference to royal approval, it explains the grievance:

[17] This same tendency is seen even more strikingly in the *Versión Interpolada*, where a different motive is given for the Countess's request: 'que aquellos fierros para los robadores e matadores convenyan' (MS *V*, fol. 194r); this version goes on to omit any reference to beds or to the couple sleeping together. Another possible case of euphemism concerns ch. 711, where the Count and doña Sancha have to kill a lecherous Archpriest who has designs on the *infanta*. At the climax of the action, MS *E* reads: 'La infant . . . trauo del a la boruca, et diol una grand tirada contra si' (*PCG*, p. 414a37-40). *Boruca* may mean 'testicles' (see Corominas, *DCELC*, s.v., and cf. another 'regia' manuscript, *I*: 'trauo de sus uerguenças et tiro contra si reziamente' (ibid., variant)). The *CVR* and the *Vulgata*, however, paraphrase: 'trauo del muy esforçadamente' (*CVR*, MS *N*, fol. 19v; Ocampo: 'atreuidamente', fol. 250r). It is conceivable that bowdlerisation may explain the absence of this entire episode from the *Crónica Abreviada* (see above, note 14).

el mal que le fizieran los Ricos omnes de Castilla en alçar conde sin su mandado, e demas que lo non podien ellos fazer con derecho por sisse mesmos: ca ninguno non puede sseer conde ssi el Rey non le faz (MS *N*, fol. 4r).

Moreover, at the end of the same chapter, the *CVR* takes steps to regularise the situation, in that it adds, at a point corresponding to *PCG*, p. 391b28:

Los castellanos metieronsse estonçes a la mesura del Rey por el conde que fizieran et el Rey otorgoles al conde Ferrand Gonçales. E defendieron esos Ricos omnes de Castilla cosas sennaladas de alli adelante que les otorgo el Rey por pleytesias que pusieron estonçes con el (ibid.).[18]

One explanation is that the original draft—the Alphonsine *borrador* perhaps—either lacked this reference to any royal part in the election or gave contradictory information;[19] the 'versión vulgar' supplied the missing detail of approval, but the revisers of the 'versión regia' saw the contradiction between this approval and the King's wrath mentioned in ch. 686, and resolved the difficulty by omitting the reference to the former. Only the *CVR* gives a consistent account with no loose ends.[20]

Indeed, this explanation accounts for the other differences between the chronicle texts so far described: that the 'versión regia' and the *CVR* (with which may be coupled the *Vulgata* for the sections therein contained) represent independent treatments of the original concise text to be seen in the 'versión vulgar'. They are, of course, very different in scope and technique: the 'regia' *PCG* amplifying widely and consistently for a number of different reasons outlined above; the *CVR*/*Vulgata* providing a new chronological framework but otherwise keeping

[18] Catalán noted without comment that one manuscript of the 'versión vulgar' has part of this second reference: 'se metieron los castellanos entonces so el señorio del rrey ca entendieron que era derecho conosçudo, pero defendieron ellos alcunas cosas senyaladas que les otorgo el rrey por pleitesias que pusieron con el' (MS *Y*, fol. 398, quoted in *De Alfonso X*, p. 143), but without the specific statement that the King confirmed Fernán González's election.
[19] It may be relevant to note that the *Poema* has no reference to any election at all, apparently assuming that Fernán González inherited the office (stanza 170), while the Toledano clearly refers to an election: 'ab universis populis Castellanis in Comitem crearetur' (V. 2, p. 98). Sneyders de Vogel ('Le *PFG* et la *Crónica General*', pp. 164 and 168) saw the difference between the *Poema* and the *PCG* as another example of the more exact feudalism of the latter (cf. above, p. 26). He did not allow for the possible influence of the Toledano on the *PCG*.
[20] As Babbitt pointed out, this is largely because the *CVR* is here following the Tudense (*Latin Sources*, p. 22).

much closer to the original text and departing from it only when it seemed incomplete or contradictory (or, in the one case noted above, where it may have offended the compilers' sense of propriety).

This is an appropriate point at which to mention a chronicle version not so far discussed. MS 1277 of the B.N., Madrid (MS *V*) was included in the discussion of the version of the Bernardo del Carpio story known as the 'Crónica fragmentaria' (see above, pp. 17-18). From the end of the reign of Alfonso IV, this manuscript changes in character (and, indeed, in scribe) and is an interpolated or expanded version of the *Crónica General 'Vulgata'* described above.[21] In the case of the Fernán González story the interpolations take the form of sententious, often religious additions, generally made to speeches of Fernán González rather than as authorial comments. Two examples must suffice. The Count's harangue to his troops before the battle of Lara contains the following passage of rhetorical expansion:

> Ca mas valen çient cavalleros buenos de vn coracon e de vna voluntad que non treziendos [sic] de diversos coraçones. Ca nunca ellos se pueden ygualar con nos en linaje ny en proeza nyn en nynguna otra cosa. Ca entre ellos ay buenos e malos e fallamos muchas vezes que por falta de los malos se vençen los buenos; e nos avemos asaz peones buenos y esforçados que nos ayudaran con ascones e dardos, e por ende vamos a ellos . . . (fol. 174r-v).

Before a subsequent battle, that of Hacinas, the Christian troops are dismayed by the apparition of a fiery serpent; on being awakened, Fernán González encourages his troops, and in *PCG* as well as in the *Poema* he does so in religious terms. Only in the *Versión Interpolada*, though, is this expanded as follows:

> . . . bien se vos devria entender quel diablo no tiene poder para nos fazer mal nynguno, e por ende encomendemonos al nuestro Redentor Jhesu Christo en quyen es todo el poder, que nos conpro por su sangre penosa derramada en el arbol de la Santa Vera Cruz por salvar el vmanal linaje; e pues el murio por nosotros, muramos nosotros por el, e pues el es podroso en todas cosas, acomendemonos a el e el nos librara de todo poderio e tenpestad mala, e de oy; mas vayase cada vno a dormyr . . . (fol. 180r-v).

Very different from all these is the *Cr1344*. This chronicle, in the 'tercera parte', normally follows the *PCG*: it will be

---

[21] See Catalán, *De Alfonso X*, p. 191 n. 58.

recalled that in the case of the story of Bernardo del Carpio, although the *Cr1344* contains only half of that story, it slavishly adheres to the *PCG* version even when this involves retaining unexplained allusions to the missing part of the story (see above, pp. 20-21). In the case of Fernán González the differences between the two versions are all the more striking. They were regarded by Menéndez Pidal as reflecting a later *cantar de gesta* or *refundición* used by the compilers of the later chronicle, a view reaffirmed by Catalán.[22] This argument is based on the insertion of a new episode unknown to the *PCG* (or to the other versions so far discussed) and should be seen in the context of a wider argument—relevant especially in the cases of the *Leyenda de los Infantes de Lara* and the *Poema de mio Cid*— as to how far narrative elaborations in a chronicle text presuppose the existence of a poetic *refundición*. This question will be examined more thoroughly in later chapters; here though, it should not be overlooked that the differences extend far beyond the insertion of a new episode, as I shall briefly show.[23]

The first thing to note is that the *Cr1344* abandons the careful arrangement by which the *PCG* reconciled chronologically material drawn from the Toledano and from the *Poema*. However it does not do so in favour of the alternative and equally careful system adopted in the *CVR/Vulgata* version. Instead its compilers resort to a simple technique of juxtaposition. After referring to the election of Fernán González in a chapter which much abbreviates ch. 684 of the *PCG*, the *Cr1344* goes on to relate *seriatim* all those chapters of the *PCG* whose source is the Toledano (chs 685-86, 692-93, 697, and 701-08). This brings the compilers to the beginning of the reign of Sancho I, whereupon they return to the *Poema* and begin to prosify it, following its exact order. At the end of this, i.e. after the liberation of Castile, the *Cr1344* returns to the other events of Sancho's reign (*PCG*, chs 721-23) and those of the beginning of that of Ramiro III, leading up to the final campaign and death of Fernán González as in the 'versión regia'.

As for the prosification of the *Poema*, it appears to be based

---

[22] Menéndez Pidal, 'Notas para el romancero', pp. 430-54. This view is reaffirmed in *Reliquias*, p. lxviii, and shared by Catalán ('Introducción' to *Romancero tradicional*, II, 5-6) and Lindley Cintra (*Crónica*, I, xxxiii and lxxxii).

[23] The text of the relevant chapters of the *Cr1344* is printed in *Reliquias*, pp. 156-70.

on the poetic text itself (either in the version which has survived or in one which differed from it only in minute details) rather than on the *PCG*. The prosification is much closer than in the earlier chronicle, often retaining phrases, lines, and even stanzas which were paraphrased or omitted in the *PCG*. Two examples must suffice. Stanza 323 of the *Poema*,

> El conde fue del golpe fiera miente llagado
> ca tenie grand lançada por el diestro costado
> llamava castellanos mas ningun fue i viado
> de todos sus caveros era desanparado

is rendered in the *PCG* as 'Otrossi cayo el conde en tierra, ca tenie otrossi muy mala lançada, et non auie y quien le acorriesse' (p. 397b10-12). The *Cr1344*, however, renders the second line more literally: 'ca tenia una lançada por el costado diestro que salia de la otra parte' (*Reliquias*, p. 159. 7-8). Line 397d, the first line of a prayer, 'Señor, tu me aguarda de error e d'ocasion', is omitted in the *PCG* (cf. p. 400b12) but rendered in the *Cr1344* as 'Señor, pidote por la tu santa piadad que me quierras guardar de los peligros e de las ocasiones e de los errores deste mundo' (*Reliquias*, p. 160. 5-6).[24]

In a far smaller number of cases the *Cr1344* departs from the poetic text to add an explanation or amplification of a point. Stanza 634 is prosified by the *PCG* as follows:

Pues que el conde ouo tod esto dicho, espidiose della et fuesse en romeria pora Sant Yague. La infante donna Sancha, *ydo el conde de Lombardia*, enuio luego una duenna con este mandado al conde Fernand Gonçalez (p. 412b38-43; the italicised words are an addition of MS *E*),

while the *Cr1344* expands as follows:

e estonçe despidiose el conde della e dixole que se le nenbrase lo que le dixera, e que non posiese en ello luenga nenguna e que faria de su pro. E estonçe se fue el conde su camino contra Santiago, e luego la ynfante enbio una dueña, en quien ella fiava mucho, para el conde don Fernan Gonçalez e contole toda aquella manera que el conde de Lonbardia dixera (*Reliquias*, p. 165. 8-11).

A similar desire to amplify may be behind the following case. In a harangue to his troops, Fernán González says:

---

[24] Other stanzas of the poem which are paraphrased or omitted completely in the *PCG* but rendered more or less faithfully in the *Cr1344* are: 234-36, 319, 383-85, 396, 415cd, 444-47, 456, 470, 475, 499, 505-08, 616, 685, 697b.

'Et non nos deuemos espantar por que ellos son muchos, ca mas pueden tres leones que x mill oveias, et matarien xxx lobos a xxx mil corderos' (*PCG*, p. 393a29-32; the *Poema* is defective at this point, stanza 223);

the *Cr1344* adds: 'ca ellos seran las ovejas e nos los leones' (*Reliquias*, p. 157. 6).[25]

A third feature of the later chronicle is an interest in proper names and family history: the knight who was swallowed up by the earth as a divine sign during the battle of Lara, unnamed in the *Poema* (stanza 256) and in the *PCG* (p. 394b21) becomes 'Pero Gonçalez ... E era natural de apar de la Puente de Fitero' (*Reliquias*, p. 157. 16-17), in the same battle, the Count's *alférez* is named as 'Pero Alvitez, que ... era natural de Trebiño' (*Reliquias*, p. 158. 5-6) and another *cabdillo* as 'Gonçalo Cuçoz ... e [era natural] de Salas de Varvadillo' (*Reliquias*, p. 158. 8-10), neither of them known to the *Poema* or the *PCG*.[26] Chalon describes this detail to a desire for 'la véracité historique' (*L'Histoire et l'épopée*, p. 473).

The later chronicle, however, does more than add detail of this kind. It also expands and clarifies. So, Fernán González's lateness in arriving at the Cortes in León (*PCG*, p. 409b30-31) is explained as follows:

Despues que el conde le vino mandado del rrei, enbiole dezir que faria su mandado en quanto a su onrra conpliese; mas que lo non culpase por non llegar tan ayna, ca el e los suyos venian muy cansados, pero que yrian lo mas ayna que podiesen para el; e enbiole contar toda la manera como pasara con Almançor e con sus grandes poderes; e ansi andudo por su camino fasta que llego a Burgos, e estovo hy tres dias. E desi endereçaron su camino contra Leon a do el rrei estava (*Reliquias*, p. 163. 27-31).

Similarly, after the Countess has released her husband by exchanging clothes with him (*PCG*, ch. 718), the *Cr1344* takes care to spell out the obvious fact that after the exchange of clothes she has to be given some new ones before she can be sent home by the King:

---

[25] Similar cases correspond to stanzas 263-64 (where a battle is described more vividly than either in the *Poema* or in the *PCG*; 484 (a prayer is rhetorically expanded); 590 (doña Teresa's letter to the King of Navarre is longer and more detailed); and 645 (the Count's promise to marry the *infanta* if she sets him free is made more explicit and twice referred to in legal terms as 'juramento e pleyto'.

[26] Cf. also *Reliquias*, p. 161. 19-20, where the 'don Lope el vizcaino' of the *Poema* (460a; 'don Lope de Vizcaya', *PCG*, p. 402a21-22) acquires a surname, 'don Lope Ortiz el vizcayno'; this may be drawn from a Portuguese source, the *Livro das Linhagens* (Lindley Cintra, *Crónica*, I, cxxiv).

mandole enbiar muy buenos paños e mucho onrrados e mando que se los vistiese (*Reliquias*, p. 167. 17-18).[27]

And the incident of the squire who threw the swords to the Count when he was besieged in a hermitage, discussed above as an example of the deductive technique of the 'versión regia', is expanded yet further in the *Cr1344*:

> E seys escuderos que venian en pos dellos, venian de cavallos e de espadas: e el uno era del conde, e los otros de los cavalleros que con el vinieran. Despues que vieron a sus señores estar en tal peligro, e vieron que les non podian acorrer que ante non fuesen muertos todos, dixo el escudero del conde a los otros: 'seguidme e yo vos dire lo mejor que podremos fazer'. Estonçes fueron contra el camino françes por donde yvan los romeros, e tomo a un rromero el escudero del conde las sus vestiduras e diole las suyas, e desi tornose e dio el cavallo a los otros, e dixoles que se fuesen para Castilla e que dixesen a los castellanos como estava el conde en una hermita donde lo tenia el rrei de Navarra çercado, e que non podria ser que non fuese luego tomado; e el que yva en aquellos vestidos que traya en logar de rromero, e que faria su oraçion e que les lançaria alla aquellas espadas (*Reliquias*, pp. 164. 33-165. 7).

The introduction of extraneous elements such as the pilgrims and the squire's disguise are further attempts to add realistic credibility to the episode.[28]

Now, it is possible that some or all of the elements mentioned in the last paragraph owe their origin not to the chroniclers but to a hypothetical poetic text which was their source. The added details, though, have nothing inherently poetic about them: rather they are marked by a somewhat naïve insistence on practicalities which is far more a quality of the chronicles than of heroic verse; it is altogether more likely that the chroniclers felt themselves free to amplify their source where desirable. This, then, is a factor to bear in mind as we

---

[27] The author of the *Versión Interpolada* also took this point: 'y mandole dar rricas tropas e todo lo que ovo menester' (MS *V*, fol. 194v), but had previously realised its implications for the scene between King and Countess: '. . . y ella muy vergonçosa por lo que avia fecho e porque tenya vestida poca rropa, que todo lo avia dado al conde con que salio de la carcel; avia verguença de pareçer antel rrey, pero con todo esso ovo de yr alla . . .' (ibid).

[28] A similar rationalisation is to be seen in the *Cr1344* at the point corresponding to stanza 648 of the *Poema*, where the release from prison is preceded by the *infanta*'s securing the keys and accompanied by a note of the need for stealth (cf. *PCG*, p. 413b 24-25 and *Reliquias*, p. 165. 19-23); the story of the lecherous Archpriest (*PCG*, ch. 711) is expanded in a variety of ways (cf. *PCG*, pp. 413a42-414a44 and *Reliquias*, pp. 165. 23-166. 2).

approach the two episodes in which the *Cr1344* differs substantially from the other texts so far discussed.

The first—and less significant—of these concerns the Count's upbringing. The *Cr1344* contains a reference lacking in the *PCG*:

> e fue criado en la montaña e criolo un cavallero bueno que era ya viejo de edad e non pudia husar de armas como conplia. E el cavallero era muy sesudo e muy de buenas mañas (*Reliquias*, p. 156. 2-4) . . . E quando morio su padre, fueron los castellanos por el a la montaña donde lo criavan e . . . fizieronlo conde (*Reliquias*, p. 156. 7-9).

Although no such idea is reflected in the *PCG*, the *Poema* does refer to Fernán González's childhood, in the lines 'furtol' un pobreziello que labrava carbon, / tovol' en la montaña una grande sazon' (177cd), and this story is developed in the succeeding stanzas, culminating like the *Cr1344* in the recognition of the new Count by his vassals (stanzas 183-84). This is a folkloric motif of some antiquity,[29] which the compilers of the *PCG* discounted, presumably as fabulous. The *Cr1344*, in accordance with its generally greater fidelity to the *Poema*, preserves some elements of it, while replacing the theft by the charcoal-burner with the less irregular if still unusual guardianship of the old knight.[30]

The final feature of the *Cr1344* to be discussed cannot be explained in this way. This concerns the granting of Castile's independence in payment of the enormous debt accumulated for the horse and hawk. While the *PCG* gives a relatively brief summary in ch. 720, the *Cr1344* has a longer account including an interview or *vistas* at Vega de Carrión during which Fernán González insults the King and showers him with water from his horse's hooves.[31] This is followed by a lengthy account of how the magnates and prelates of the kingdom mediated between

---

[29] See Deyermond and Chaplin, 'Folk-Motifs', p. 43; J. P. Keller, 'El misterioso origen de Fernán González', *NRFH*, 10 (1956), 41-44; and Avalle-Arce, 'Clerecía y juglaría', pp. 62-65 and 68-71.

[30] Avalle-Arce suggests that the 'cavallero bueno, ya viejo' may have his origins in the lost *cantar*, and that while the clerical author of the *Poema* substituted the folkloric or literary motif of the charcoal-burner, the compiler of the *Cr1344* returned to the epic source ('Clerecía y juglaría', pp. 64-65). He also draws attention, however, to parallels for the 'cavallero' in French epic and in thirteenth- and fourteenth-century Spanish manuals of knighthood (p. 68); these could presumably have inspired the compiler of the *Cr1344* as easily as could a *cantar*. Avalle-Arce's view seems to be shared by Chalon (*L'Histoire et l'épopée*, pp. 471-72; Cotrait has doubts about the existence of a *cantar* (*Fernán González*, pp. 340-44).

[31] The text may be seen in *Reliquias*, pp. 167-70.

King and Count and how at last agreement was reached. Menéndez Pidal discounted the possibility that these episodes originally formed part of the *Poema*—which, in its modern form, lacks almost the whole final story of the hero's confrontation with Sancho I—but were omitted by the compilers of the *PCG*. One reason for his doing so is that nowhere else does the *PCG* omit material:

> la prosificación del poema contenida en la Primera General, hecha verso por verso, no tiene esta entrevista ni deja lugar para ella (*Reliquias*, p. lxviii);

however, we have seen that the earlier chroniclers did omit the tale of Fernán González's mythical upbringing (as well, of course, as the whole introductory section of the *Poema*, some 170 stanzas). Menéndez Pidal went on:

> ni el monje autor del poeme podía imaginarla, pues siempre quiere presentar al conde como un modelo de virtudes, y en especial comedido, respetuoso con la persona del rey, discutiendo su pleito con éste en el terreno de la juridicidad. El episodio en cuestión responde bien a los gustos del siglo xiv mejor que a los del xiii; el vasallo insolente con el rey es tipo tardío, posterior al vasallo mesurado, cosa observable también en el cantar de las Mocedades del Cid (ibid.).[32]

This is clearly a much more valid point; were it only a question of the *vistas* at Vega de Carrión one would incline to accept Menéndez Pidal's postulation of a 'verdadero cantar de gesta' of the early fourteenth century ('Notas para el romancero', p. 448). The stumbling block to this seems to me to be the subsequent account of the mediation by 'ombres buenos' and 'perlados'. Not only is this very long, even anticlimatic in its context, at the end of the Count's struggle, it also has a very pronounced legalistic note to it. In the forty-six lines of the edition of this text in *Reliquias* (pp. 168. 32-170. 14), the word *pleytear* occurs three times (and *pleytesia* twice), *cartas* four times, *librar* five times and *trebuto* three, as well as an abundance of other such terminology (e.g. *otorgar, asmar, postura, firmedumbres, preuillegios*, and a reference to *roborar con sellos*). It may be significant that the word *estoria* is used in this section to refer to the source (*Reliquias*, p. 168. 19), which is very unusual in the section of the chronicle referring to Fernán González; it seems at least possible that the second half of this interpolated section

---

[32] Menéndez Pidal is here summarising his more extensive argument which may be seen in 'Notas para el romancero', pp. 445-48.

in the *Cr1344* may reflect not a *cantar* but a later prose rewriting of the climax of the *Poema*, done with the aim of regularising in true legal form this important, if fictional, stage in Castile's history.

The *Cr1344*, therefore, has two characteristics which set it apart from earlier chronicles in its treatment of the story of Fernán González: an attitude towards its source which is at once more faithful as regards verbal detail and more bold in its willingness to expand and rationalise some parts of the narrative; and, at the end, an acceptance of new sources which, for a variety of reasons, seem nearer to fourteenth-century taste and preoccupations than to those of Alphonsine historiography.

The final version to be discussed, the *RefTol*, keeps more closely to its model, the *Cr1344*, than in the case of Bernardo del Carpio (see above, pp. 21-22). It does, however, contrive to simplify in cases where an accretion of sources and a developed form of rationalisation have conspired to obscure an originally clear and fast-moving story. For example, the various versions of the Count's imprisonment in the hermitage by the Navarrese and the explanation of how his weapons reached him (pp. 27-28 and 38 above) are dealt with in the *RefTol* by the expedient of omitting all reference to squire or swords (MS *M*, fol. 144v); likewise, the improbabilities surrounding Fernán González's upbringing are simplified to a mere statement that 'fue criado en las montannas' (MS *M*, fol. 99r).

On the other hand, the *RefTol* does contain many instances of expansion. One straightforward one concerns the escape of the Count and the Navarrese *infanta* from prison, in which a more convincing scene involving deception of the jailer replaces simpler statements such as 'la ynfante abrio la puerta del corral' (*Cr1344*, in *Reliquias*, p. 165. 21; this in turn is more convincing than the *PCG* or other earlier versions: see note 28):

> E desque fueron amos a dos solos de fabla, llamaron ally al portero. E como el conde era de muy grand fuerça, echo mano al portero por los cabeçones, diziendo que sy non estouiesse quedo, que lo mataria, e el portero callosse. E atolo luego el conde de pies e de manos alli, e salieronse amos fuera e çerraron la puerta del castillo por de fuera e escondieron las llaues e fueron se amos a dos solos su camino ... (MS *M*, fol. 118r).

Sometimes such expansion is stylistic rather than narrative. Thus the mention of the Count's standard-bearer at Hacinas, one Orbita, in the *Cr1344* slightly expanded from the *Poema*,[33] is here lengthened still further: he is called a 'yunque de ferrero', his hands are 'betunadas en la vara ferrada con el amor e lealtad que al conde auia', and the author concludes:

> Pero non era esta mucha marauilla, ca bien sabia el conde onde y en que tierra la vara de su estandarte senbro, e porque luego fue ençepada en rrayzes de lealtad la qual non le podia turar menos entre las manos quel anima en el cuerpo le turasse (MS *M*, fol. 109v; cf. MS *S*, fol. 132v).

The legalistic tone of the end of the story is yet more marked in the *RefTol*. As well as much of the specialised vocabulary referred to above, this text uses formulae such as 'libre e desenbargademente', 'para el e para todos sus herederos por sienpre jamas', and 'libres e quitos el vno del otro e el otro del otro' (MS *M*, fol. 128r).

All in all, this text has its idiosyncrasies;[34] like the *Cr1344* but perhaps to a greater extent, it reflects changing attitudes towards history which show us how far we have come from the original Alphonsine respect for sources and desire to harmonise them to the best of the compilers' ability. Here narrative fluency and authorial preoccupations—with style, with legalism—are more important.

---

[33] *Poema*: 'Orbita su alferez, el que traia la seña, / non sofria mas golpes que si fues una peña' (518 ab); *Cr1344*: 'E Arbita, que era alferez del conde, e traya la su seña, tantos golpes sofria de lanças e de espadas e de maças e de saetas que seria mucho para los sofrir una piedra, pero todo lo el avia de sofrir con gran bondad que en el avia' (*Reliquias*, p. 162. 27-29).

[34] I quote two others which are worthy of note. When Fernán González and the Navarrese *infanta* are discovered by the Archpriest, the immoral suggestion, which in all other versions comes from the cleric, is, in the *RefTol*, presented as an 'enganno' of doña Sancha (MS *M*, fol. 118v). Another feature, noted by Menéndez Pidal, is its attempt to play down the haughty treatment given by the Count to the King at Vega de Carrión: his fiery exit is explained by a desire not to stay and, presumably, do something he might regret: 'e por que la su yra del conde se yua ençendiendo e non errase contra Dios, boluio el conde las rriendas a su cauallo e diole de las espuelas; e el cauallo, con el grand contorrno que dio, leuanto muchas aguas por ençima del Rey e quedo toda la cabeça e el cuerpo del Rey lleno de agua' (quoted by Menéndez Pidal, 'Notas para el romancero', p. 446, as MS *M*, fol. 164; in the modern foliation it is fols 127v-28r).

Chapter 3
THE INFANTES DE LARA

Of all the epic material of mediaeval Spain, only the *Poema de mio Cid* has become better known than the story of the seven *infantes* of Lara (or Salas).[1] It is a tale whose considerable literary merit and interest have assured its continued popularity and its survival in a number of versions, some from the Golden Age. What is more, the early chronicle versions of it have received far more critical attention than those of any other epic legend. Menéndez Pidal published the first version of his study of the legend in 1896, and most of his early work on the chronicle manuscripts was undertaken with this study in mind. A result of this early attention and much subsequent work is that all the relevant chronicle texts have been published and the relationship between them has been the subject of a certain amount of study. In the present chapter, unlike the remainder of the book, I have no unpublished material to adduce; yet to have omitted consideration of this particular legend would clearly be inappropriate given its central importance in any theory on the genesis and evolution of the epic. I will, though, limit myself to summarising the traits of the different versions and discussing some previous views on them, taking up again the wider issues of epic and historiographical development in a concluding chapter.

A preliminary point to be made is that, unlike all the material so far discussed, the story of the *infantes* finds no place in the Latin historiography of early mediaeval Spain. Neither the Tudense nor the Toledano mentions the *Infantes de Lara* and even the *Crónica Najerense*, so prone to accept vernacular literary sources, does not do so in this case. The reason would appear to be that this is an essentially private story, involving Count Garci-Fernández only peripherally, while other legends deal either with rulers and their families (Fernán González, the Condesa Traidora, Fernando I and his sons) or heroic figures of

[1] All early chronicle texts use the name 'Infantes de Salas'; the alternative 'de Lara' seems to have come into use in the fourteenth century: see Pidal, *La leyenda*, p. 179, and *Romancero tradicional*, II, 89.

national importance (Bernardo del Carpio, the Cid). And while the *Najerense* was innovatory in its acceptance of vernacular versions of history, its compilers' conception of what was proper material for a historical narrative was restrictive and excluded material of such a kind as the *Infantes de Lara*.[2] The material in the *PCG* and other vernacular accounts comes, therefore, entirely from poetic material (or, one may speculate, from the compilers' invention in some cases). It is true that the background has been shown to be historical, and one central event, the death of the *infantes* and the intrigue which brought it about, has been linked by Menéndez Pidal and others to events of the late tenth century.[3] We are, however, dealing with an essentially fictional legend, with numerous literary and folkloric motifs,[4] as a brief outline of the chronicle prosification will show.

The simplest version is that found in the 'versión vulgar' of the *PCG*.[5] The story begins in ch. 736 with the wedding in Burgos of Ruy Blásquez and doña Lambra; at the *tablado* which forms part of the festivities, rivalry develops between Alvar Sánchez, a kinsman of the bride, and the seven *infantes*, nephews of the groom. Alvar Sánchez is killed by Gonzalo González, the youngest of the brothers, and Ruy Blásquez intervenes only to be affronted. A general mêlée is prevented only by the intervention of Count Garci-Fernández and Gonzalo Gustioz, father of the *infantes*. Trouble flares up again at Barbadillo where there ensues a sequence of events whose culmination is the throwing of a blood-filled cucumber and the

---

[2] 'Las más antiguas crónicas regias latinas se ocupaban sólo de los hechos que atañían directamente a los reyes (Sampiro, Silense) o todo lo más llegaron a interesarse por la historia de los condes autónomos de Castilla (Najerense); sólo cuando las crónicas en romance ampliaron su radio de visión, en el siglo XIII, pudo entrar en ellas la leyenda referente a una familia de Salas, y esto por excepción, debido a la singular fuerza trágica del tema' (*Romancero tradicional*, II, 85); cf. W. J. Entwistle, 'Remarks concerning the Order of the Spanish Cantares de Gesta', *RPh*, 1 (1947-48), 113-23 (pp. 117-18), and see above, p. 25 and n. 8.

[3] Pidal, *La leyenda*, pp. 11-16, 451-66, 503-13; see also Ruiz Asencio, 'La rebelión de Sancho García', esp. pp. 53-67, and Chalon, *L'Histoire et l'épopée*, pp. 482-99.

[4] For a discussion of some folkloric motifs, see Deyermond and Chaplin, 'Folk-Motifs', at pp. 42-43, 46, 47 and 48.

[5] Pidal had earlier preferred the 'regia' version of MS *E*, published in *La leyenda*, pp. 207-43 and subsequently included in *PCG*. The difference is discussed in *La leyenda*, p. 492 and (in Catalán's additions to the revised edition of 1971) pp. 553-54; see also *Reliquias*, p. liv.

murder of doña Lambra's servant by the *infantes* when he is clinging to her for protection. Ruy Blásquez seeks to avenge this insult by a complex plot. He sends Gonzalo Gustioz to Córdoba with a letter to Almanzor in which he asks that its bearer be beheaded: he also advises the Moor to send his army to Almenar, where the seven *infantes* will be delivered into his hands. Almanzor does not execute Gonzalo but puts him into prison, sending a Moorish noblewoman to serve him; they fall in love and she becomes pregnant. Meanwhile, the *infantes* and their tutor, Muño Salido, are lured by Ruy Blásquez to Almenar; the ensuing battle with the Moorish kings Viara and Galve is described in detail, together with the treacherous dealings of Ruy Blásquez. Despite superhuman efforts involving the killing of over five thousand Moors, the *infantes* are finally killed and their heads taken to Córdoba. There Almanzor has Gonzalo Gustioz identify them, which he does. The Moorish woman comforts him and tells him of her pregnancy; he leaves her half a ring as a token whereby if a son is born he will be able to identify himself to his father, and after his departure a son— called Mudarra—is duly born. The story is then broken off (ch. 743).

The sequel, in ch. 751, tells how Mudarra journeys to Salas to avenge his half-brothers' death: he kills Ruy Blásquez and in due course also takes vengeance on doña Lambra by burning her alive.

The differences between the 'versión vulgar' and the 'versión regia' in this story are small, apart from a certain degree of difference in the forms of proper names and in numbers.[6] On the whole the differences are stylistic and are comparable to those already described in the cases of the legends of Bernardo del Carpio (see above, p. 17) and Fernán González (pp. 27-29 although there are no instances of narrative elaboration of the kind seen in the latter case and discussed at pp. 29-30). Diego Catalán has described one instance of this, taken from ch. 751. The 'vulgar' version of Mudarra's departure from Córdoba reads:

Et pues que Mudarra Gonçalez la ovo tomada, fue espedido de la madre et fuesse pora Almançor et dixol commo querie yr ver su padre. Et dixol

[6] The 'versión regia' has the seven *infantes* alone responsible for the death of 10,060 Moors (10,700 in one MS), the 'versión vulgar' for that of only 2,060 or less (*Reliquias*, p. 194. 11 and variant).

Almançor que lo tenie por bien et quel plazie. Et el estonçes espidiosse del et de todos los otros moros poderosos, et fuesse su via; et segunt cuenta la estoria llevo consigo muy grant cavalleria;

while MS *E* expands as follows:

Et Mudarra Gonçalez, pues que ouo recabdada la sortija et tomada espidiose de su madre et fuesse pora Almançor et dixol como querie yr uer su padre, si el por bien lo touiesse. Respondiol Almançor que lo tenie por bien et quel plaze por tan buen fecho como aquel que yua fazer; et cumpliol estonces Almançor de caualleros et cauallos et armas et de auer et de quanto ouo mester por que fuesse bien acompannado et onrrado, et segund la estoria cuenta otrossi diol de christianos que tenie catiuos caualleros et otros christianos muchos. Et el, pues que se uio tan bien guisado, espidiose del et de todos los otros moros poderosos, et fue su uia; et leuo consigo muy grand caualleria et grand companna (*De Alfonso X*, pp. 139-40).

Very similar is the tendency of MS *E* to cross-reference to a greater degree than the manuscripts of the 'versión vulgar'. Thus Ruy Blásquez's complaint against the *infantes* of 'lo que fezistes a mi muger doña Lambla quandol matastes otrossi el omne delante' is, in the manuscripts of the 'regia' family only, expanded to 'lo que fezistes a mi muger doña Lambla quando le sacastes el omne de so el manto e ge lo matastes delante e le ensangrentastes los paños e las tocas con la sangre del' (*Reliquias*, p. 192. 26-27 and variant), and the letter which Ruy Blásquez sends with Gonzalo Gustioz to Almanzor is only in these same manuscripts referred to as 'la carta que dixiemos quel fiziera el su moro' (*Reliquias*, p. 187. 9 variant).

The *CVR* and *Vulgata*[7] appear to tell basically the same story as the *PCG*, though they both alter the chronology, placing the action between the fourth and fourteenth years of Bermudo II of León (= A.D. 965 and 975) instead of the twenty-third year of Ramiro III (A.D. 959) and the ninth of Bermudo (A.D. 968).[8] More significant are certain divergences of detail. If we consider first the *CVR*, the departures from the *PCG* generally take the form of omission: of Gonzalo González's threat to kill Muño Salido when the latter insists that the omens are unfavourable for the expedition against the Moors (cf. *Reliquias*, p. 188.

[7] The *Crónica Abreviada* also follows the *PCG* and does not alter the chronology as do the other two versions: MS fols 102r-103v, cf. the edition by Grismer, pp. 134-36 (also edited in Pidal, *La leyenda*, pp. 244-47).

[8] See Pidal, *La leyenda*, p. 68 and note 2; Babbitt, *Latin Sources*, pp. 31 and 33; Chalon, *L'Histoire et l'épopée*, pp. 499-500.

26-28 and *CVR*, MS *N*, fol. 35r); and of the detail that Mudarra kills Ruy Blásquez by cleaving him 'bien por medio del cuerpo' (cf. *Reliquias*, p. 198. 12 and *CVR*, MS *N*, fol. 41r). The incident in the orchard at Barbadillo, where doña Lambra is affronted by Gonzalo González's appearing semi-clothed in her presence (*Reliquias*, p. 184. 10-14) is recounted as follows in the *CVR*:

entraron los infantes en vna huerta que y avie por folgar y a la sonbra de los arboles. Gonçalo Gonçalez tomo estonces su açor e començo de lo bannar. Donna Lanbra quando lo vio, como auie del gran pesar e lo desamaua de coraçon, dixo a vn so omne 'toma agora un cogonbro . . .' (MS *N*, fol. 33v).

The point of the scene is therefore lost, perhaps, as Menéndez Pidal surmised, out of a sense of prudery (*La leyenda*, p. 69). On the two occasions on which Gonzalo González kills men —first Alvar Sánchez, then Gonzalo Sánchez—the compilers of the *CVR* insert the phrases 'e algunos dizen' and 'e avn dizen' (MS *N*, fols. 32v and 36r respectively). Finally, the *CVR* includes a detail not in the *PCG*, the baptism of Mudarra at the instance of his father at the end of the legend:

. . . lo fizo batear su padre e tornole Christiano ca antes moro era (MS *N*, fol. 41r)

The *Vulgata* (that is, Ocampo's chronicle and the related MSS *C*, *F*, *H*, and *R*) has in common with the *CVR* all the features just described.[9] It differs from it in that it has some additional details. It tells us that Mudarra had a facial resemblance to his half-brother Gonzalo González and that for that reason he became a favourite of his stepmother, Gonzalo Gustioz's wife,[10] and that the Mooress sent to console Gonzalo Gustioz was possibly Almanzor's sister,[11] both details not found in the *CVR* or in the 'vulgar' *PCG*, though there is a reference in the 'regia' *E* MS to Almanzor's love for Mudarra being because 'era muy su parient' (*Reliquias*, p. 197. 1 variant). Menéndez Pidal saw the features which the *CVR* and *Vulgata* versions have

[9] Ocampo, fols 263v (threat against Muño Salido), 267r (death of Ruy Blásquez), 262r (incident in the orchard at Barbadillo), 261v and 263v (doubts as to Gonzalo González's killings) and 267r (baptism of Mudarra); the MSS are all very similar (MS *L*, ending in the reign of Alfonso II, does not contain this episode).

[10] 'E donna Sancha quisol siempre bien porque paresçiera en todos sus fechos a Gonçalez Gonçalez, su fijo el menor' (Ocampo, fol. 267r).

[11] 'Fizol Ahnançor cauallero, ca lo amaua mucho porque dezien que aquella mora cuyo fijo el era era su hermana' (Ocampo, fol. 266v).

in common as proceeding from a lost 'abreviación' of the 'versión vulgar' (*La leyenda*, pp. 68-69) while the peculiarities of the *Vulgata* version were seen as due in part to its compiler's pretensions as a story-teller, in part as reflecting the 'second' or fourteenth-century epic poem.[12] It will be wise to postpone discussion of this latter point until we have looked at other later versions, though it might be stated now that Pidal's hypothesis of a compiler who prized his story-telling ability seems sufficient to explain most of the *Vulgata*'s innovations; moreover, in at least one case which is less easily explicable (the supposed relationship between Mudarra and Almanzor) the compiler may have known of the 'versión regia' and expanded and clarified its somewhat cryptic reference to a relationship.

As for the 'abreviación', its existence was called into question by Babbitt who held that the simpler version of the story told in the *CVR* was quite simply an indication of the earlier date of that chronicle.[13] While there is in general much sense in Babbitt's theory and while there is no doubt that the *CVR* is considerably earlier than Menéndez Pidal thought in 1896, an abbreviation seems to be the best explanation of some of the peculiarities of the *CVR* and the *Vulgata*.[14] The scene in the orchard at Barbadillo, as we have seen above (p. 47) makes much less sense in the *CVR/Vulgata* version, and the motives suggested by Menéndez Pidal for some of the other omissions in these versions are equally convincing.[15] Abbreviation, in short, seems an appropriate name in this case for what has more generally been called, by Diego Catalán, the 'versión crítica'.[16]

[12] '[La 3ª Crónica general] añade varios pormenores extraños a la primera redacción y altera mucho sus palabras, en lo cual se echa de ver que el formador de esta Crónica preciábase un poco de ameno narrador, y, confiado en su habilidad, no se limitaba siempre a copiar ese original, hoy perdido, de que arriba hablamos, sino que se permitía alterar el lenguaje de su modelo para dotarlo de más viveza y animación, y aun añadir al relato fugaces rasgos, de los cuales alguno procede seguramente de la 2ª Gesta de los Infantes, que nuestro copista habría oído con atención varias veces' (*La leyenda*, pp. 69-70). Chalon appears to accept this view (*L'Histoire et l'épopée*, p. 500).

[13] 'Observations', p. 208 n. 26, and 'Twelfth-century Epic Forms', passim; see also *Latin Sources*, pp. 17 and 161.

[14] See Lindley Cintra, *Crónica*, I, cccxi-cccxiii, and Catalán, *De Alfonso X*, pp. 122-23 and 178-88.

[15] He suggests that the excision of Gonzalo Gustioz's threats may be due to the compiler's dislike of 'cosas que . . . parecían ya indecorosas o bárbaras', and that the account of Ruy Blásquez's death is suppressed 'por inverosímil' (*La leyenda*, p. 69 and n.).

[16] *De Alfonso X*, pp. 178-93 (especially pp. 188 and 192-93) and 202-03 and 'El taller historiográfico alfonsí', esp. pp. 373-75.

It must, however, be stressed that the differences between this 'abbreviation' and the *PCG* are less marked than would appear from Menéndez Pidal's remarks of 1896, when he was taking the 'versión regia' of the latter as one point of the comparison. The relationship between the 'vulgar' *PCG* and the *CVR/ Vulgata* version is adequately explained by Lindley Cintra's hypothesis, subsequently accepted by Catalán: that the 'abreviación', prepared from the same *borrador* as gave rise to both 'versión regia' and 'versión vulgar' was used first in the formation of the *CVR* and subsequently in the elaboration of the *Vulgata*.[17]

The remaining chronicle texts to be discussed tell much more notably different versions of the legend. They are the *Versión Interpolada* of the *Vulgata*, the *Cr1344* and the *Refundición Toledana*. The first of these, while following the Vulgata version in broad outlines, expands and amplifies the narrative in several respects. Some of these additions at least may be regarded, in Pidal's words, as 'invención del cronista' (*La leyenda*, p. 74 n. 2): so we find expansion and clarification, as when the placing of the *infantes* under Ruy Blásquez's tutelage is expanded to explain that this is for the purpose of punishment (*Reliquias*, p. 186. 4-6); and when the infantes see the Moorish standards approach at Almenar (*Reliquias*, p. 191. 4-9) Ruy Blásquez's reply is more complex and deceitful.[18] Another trait of this text is the introduction of pious motives: so Gonzalo González prays when Almanzor's host appears (cf. *Reliquias*, pp. 190. 31 and 201),[19] and a similar tendency may lie behind one case

[17] Lindley Cintra, *Crónica*, I, ccx-ccxvi, ccxix-ccxx and cccxiii-cccxiv, summarised by Catalán, *De Alfonso X*, pp. 101 and 121-23. Pidal regarded the so-called *Cuarta crónica general* (or *Estoria de los fechos de los godos* or *Traducción interpolada del Toledano*) as an independent descendant of the same 'abreviación' (*La leyenda*, p. 71); subsequent work by Lindley Cintra and Catalán has modified this view, as summed up by the latter: 'Cintra . . . mostró ya que la obra se basaba, para los capítulos referentes a los infantes, en la propia *Crónica de Veinte Reyes* (y no en la **Abreviación*); posteriormente Catalán . . . ha examinado con detenimiento cómo la *Estoria* combina, en toda esta sección histórica, el *Toledano Romanzado* y la *Crónica de Veinte Reyes* (la leyenda de los infantes, ignorada por el Toledano, procede íntegramente de la segunda fuente)' (*La leyenda* [3rd revised edition], p. 558).

[18] In the first instance the *Versión Interpolada* says 'e metieronse los siete ynfantes en mano y poder de don Rodrigo, su tio, que les diese la pena quel mandase' (*Reliquias*, p. 200); in the second, Ruy Blásquez says 'aquellos moros astrosos traen muchas señas, por dar a entender que son muchos, e ellos non llegan a mill . . .' (ibid., p. 202). These and other examples are discussed in my 1979 article 'Legendary Material'.

[19] Other cases may be seen in *Reliquias*, pp. 191. 17-18 and 202 (Muño Salido

of narrative expansion, when Mudarra is offered an escort by Almanzor on his departure for Castile and requests that it be composed of Christian knights held prisoner (cf. *Reliquias*, pp. 197. 3-4 and 216).

The most striking features of the *Versión Interpolada*, however, come towards the end of the story. First, Gonzalo Gustioz's lament over his sons is expanded from the laconic summary of the *PCG* ('tomava las cabesças una a una e retraye e contaua de los infantes todos los buenos fechos que fizieran'; *Reliquias*, p. 195. 25-26 variants) to an extended lament over each head in turn, which has unmistakable signs of assonance (*Reliquias*, pp. 205-11); second, the final chapter involving Mudarra's revenge is much expanded, and the sequence of events it contains altered and made more complex. In brief, Mudarra pursues Ruy Blásquez, defeats him in single combat at Castro and takes him back to Bilbestre for execution. He then hounds doña Lambra out of the court and she dies in the Sierra de Mena (*Reliquias*, pp. 215-36). This chapter too has numerous signs of being based on an assonanced poetic text and since in many features it coincides with the account found in the *Cr1344* (see below), Menéndez Pidal's conclusion was that both chronicles drew independently on a fourteenth-century *refundición* of the *cantar de gesta*. Writing of the *Versión Interpolada* he says:

> ... altera por completo, en la parte relativa a los Infantes, el texto de su original en vista de una redacción poética de la leyenda, que no es otra sino el 2º Cantar de Gesta ... cuyos versos copia a ratos, en tal abundancia y tan fielmente, que muchas páginas de esta Crónica aparecen del todo rimadas (*La leyenda*, p. 74).

This hypothesis is maintained by Diego Catalán in *Romancero tradicional* (II, 93) and it has been generally accepted until recently.[20] It has, however, been challenged by J. G. Cummins ('The Chronicle Texts'), who draws attention to the fact that the *Versión Interpolada* follows the *PCG* (or, to be accurate, follows the *Vulgata*, which he does not discuss) far more closely than does the *Cr1344*. He sums up:

exhorts the *infantes*); 192. 5-7 and 202 (Diego Gonzalez's exhortation to his brothers is given a more religious note); and 194. 24 and 203 (the *infantes*' death is marked by the prayer 'Dios les aya las almas').

[20] For example, E. von Richthofen, *Tradicionalismo épico novelesco* (Barcelona, 1972), pp. 39-53 and 55-65.

A close examination of the texts suggests that the epic version behind most of *ITCG* [= *Versión Interpolada*] may have been much closer to the version behind *PCG* than to that behind *1344*. The *1344* version includes numerous episodes which figure in neither of the other accounts, and virtually all the new (i.e. non-*PCG*) elements of the story are in the *1344* account, which represents a considerable expansion of the version behind *PCG*. In contrast, the story-line of the *ITCG* version follows almost exactly that of *PCG*, and practically every element of the content of *ITCG* is already present in *PCG*, in condensed form. The main exception is Mudarra's chase of Ruy Velázquez at the end, which has all the appearance of being a late appendage borrowed from the *refundición* represented by *1344* ('The Chronicle Texts', p. 102).

He therefore sees all of what one might call the non-structural innovations of the *Versión Interpolada* as being due to a difference in prosifying technique between that chronicle and the *PCG*. In particular, the lament of Gonzalo Gustioz may in Cummins' view have formed part of the original legend but have been drastically condensed in the original Alphonsine prosification.[21] The *Versión Interpolada*, therefore, may be a text which in some places departs from its sources to expand, to add circumstantial detail and pious motives; and in others eschews the terseness of the earlier chronicle to recall the direct speech of the poetic tradition.[22]

As for the 'appendage' of which Cummins speaks, it should be noted that in at least two details the join is visible. The *Versión Interpolada* account contains passing references in its final chapter both to Mudarra's laying waste of Ruy Blásquez's town of Barbadillo (*Reliquias*, p. 229) and to doña Sancha's dream of drinking Ruy Blásquez's blood (ibid., pp. 231-32); these two events, however, are fully described only in the *Cr1344* version.

If we now turn to that version, we will find a yet more complex story. The additional complexity takes three main forms. First, there is a considerable amplification of detail, some of

[21] 'The *PCG* prosification of the thirteenth-century version is characterized by concision and usually by careful concealment of epic line-structure. Condensation is achieved partly by summarizing in reported speech passages which in the epic probably consisted of longer utterances and conversations in direct speech ... The most extreme case of this condensation of direct speech may well be the lament' ('The Chronicle Texts', p. 109).

[22] Apart from the Lament, other cases in which the *Versión Interpolada* introduces dialogue are in doña Lambra's complaint to Ruy Blásquez (*Reliquias*, p. 200, cf. *PCG*, ibid., p. 185. 25); and in the words of comfort addressed by the Moors to Gonzalo Gustioz (*Reliquias*, p. 212, cf. *PCG*, ibid., p. 196).

which coincides with what we have already seen in the case of the *Versión Interpolada*. Gonzalo Gustioz's lament over his sons' heads, for instance, is similar in the *Cr1344* and the *Versión Interpolada*, though by no means identical (*Reliquias*, pp. 205-11 confronts the two texts as well as attempting to reconstruct the poetic version which Pidal saw as underlying both of them). Other details are also expanded, of which one example must suffice. The omens which Munno Salido sees at Almenar are in all the versions so far discussed, including the *Versión Interpolada*, simply referred to as bad. Only *Cr1344* expands:

> El primero aguero que ouieron fue vna corneia diestra, e sobre ella vna syniestra, e desy vieron vna aguila cabdal ferir la que estaua encima de vn pynedo. E quando esto oyo Nunno Salido, pesole mucho de coraçon e dixoles: 'Fijos, tornemos nos para vuestra madre donna Sancha e folguemos y algunos dias fasta que estas aues corrijan, ca ellas non vos muestran synon todo mal sy las pasamos.' E ellos dixeron que non quisiese Dios, ca los atendia su tio dos dias auia, e que por las aues non curasen nada, ca non fazia a ellos aquello synon al mayor de la hueste con que todos yuan. Entonçe fueron adelante e vieron venir vn aguila cabdal por el ayre dando muy grandes gritos e vino posar en vn pinar por donde todos yuan, e estouo ay vna grande pieça dando muy grandes bozes; e desy a la çima tomose por la garganta con amas las manos e degollose e dexose caer muerta en tierra al pie del pino. (MS *Q*, fol. 154v; cf. MS *M*, fol. 127r-v, and *Reliquias*, p. 201. 5-14),

and each of these omens is expanded in detail.

Second, the story is less self-contained in the sense that Count Garci-Fernández is tied into it to a greater extent and its events are invested with a greater degree of political significance. So the wedding of Ruy Blásquez to doña Lambra which opens the story is a favour granted by the Count for Ruy Blásquez's help in the siege of Zamora (*Reliquias* p. 199);[23] and at a later stage Ruy Blásquez's treacherous plot against the *infantes* is seen as part of a rebellion against the Count. This at once helps to explain how the villain remains immune from punishment (as an outlaw) until Mudarra appears, and makes him a yet more reprehensible character by adding treason to his crime.[24]

---

[23] The *Cr1344* also integrates the story into the general historical narrative by separating its beginning (the marriage of doña Lambra) from the rest of the story, placing it before the account of Count Garci-Fernández's marrriage to doña Argentina (see below, ch. 4).

[24] Doña Lambra is also made to seem more reprehensible: in particular, her reaction to Alvar Sánchez's success at the *tablado* makes her seem more shameless:

The third way in which *Cr1344* differs from *PCG* is that, as with the *Versión Interpolada*, the ending of the story is considerably expanded. The changes, however, are more far-reaching. Gonzalo Gustioz's amorous encounter with the Mooress (Almanzor's sister) and Mudarra's conception is placed after the lament over the *infantes*' heads and not when Gonzalo Gustioz is first cast into prison (but see below, note 30); Mudarra's decision to leave Córdoba for Castile comes about as a result of a quarrel and an insulting slight on his parentage; on arriving in Castile, Mudarra sacks Ruy Blásquez's stronghold of Bilbestre; the vengeance he then takes on Ruy Blásquez and on doña Lambra is similar to the extended story of the *Versión Interpolada*, but with many further details, chief among them the prophetic dream of doña Sancha (the *infantes*' mother), her acceptance of Mudarra as a son, owing to the resemblance he bears to Gonzalo González, and her forgiveness of her husband's adultery.

This is no more than an outline of the salient points of the *Cr1344* version.[25] It has generally been taken as reflecting a fourteenth-century poetic *refundición*: so, even Cummins, who sees many of the details found for the first time in the *Versión Interpolada* as being from the original poem, has no doubt that a *refundición* is necessary to explain the innovations of the *Cr1344*.[26] There are a number of respects in which this is almost certainly a fair hypothesis. As Cummins points out, the structural innovations have the effect of making the lament 'the fulcrum of a see-saw in which Mudarra's weight at one end just about balances that of the seven *Infantes* at the other' ('The Chronicle Texts', p. 109). He also draws attention to the extension of thematic scope involved in making Ruy Blásquez 'not just a wicked uncle, but a rebel against Garci-Fernández' (ibid.), and he analyses the other elements whose purpose seems to be the improvement of overall cohesion (the theme

'dixo ... que non vedaria su amor a ome tan de pro si non fuese su pariente tan llegado' (*Reliquias*, p. 199); in Pidal's words this has the effect of accentuating 'los rasgos odiosos en la fisionomía de la orgullosa y vengativa dueña' (*La leyenda*, p. 23).

[25] Detailed comparisons may be seen in Lathrop, *The Legend*, pp. 37-42, and Cummins, 'The Chronicle Texts', pp. 103-08; see also Pidal, *La leyenda*, pp. 23-35.

[26] 'At some point before the compilation of *1344*, this version underwent a sweeping *refundición*' ('The Chronicle Texts', p. 109); 'The poem, then, underwent a major *refundición*, probably after 1289, and certainly before 1344. The result is prosified in *1344*' (ibid., p. 110); cf. the reference from p. 102 quoted above (p. 51).

of blood, the idea of Mudarra as a re-incarnation of Gonzalo González, the motif of the hawk) (ibid., p. 110).[27]

It is not beyond doubt that all these factors owe their origin to a poetic *refundición*; we have seen in other cases how chronicles too amended and strove to give unity to their narrative. The extent of narrative invention in this case, however, as well as the remnants of assonance to be found with some frequency in the closing sections, make a poetic *refundición* a reasonably firm hypothesis in this case.[28]

The version of the *Infantes* legend found in the *Refundición Toledana* has also been described and analysed at length, this time by Lathrop (*The Legend*, pp. 42-75). It would be idle to repeat or paraphrase his full and interesting analysis. Suffice it to say that on the whole the changes made by the author of the *RefTol* are not structural; rather, they affect narrative technique and style. Events are never anticipated: cross-references to later events are regularly excised. Dialogue in particular is rewritten so as to make speeches more persuasive and arguments better constructed.[29] Other characteristics are the tendency to intensify moral distinctions: thus Ruy Blásquez's actions are on repeated occasions made more reprehensible (*The Legend*, pp. 49-50, 54, 56, 58-60, 61 and 72), and the same is true of doña Lambra (ibid., pp. 47 and 74); conversely, reservations we might have about Gonzalo Gustioz's rape of the Moorish princess (as he does in the *Cr1344*; see *Reliquias*, p. 213. 10-15) are removed by rewriting the scene between them and making it a story of mutual love and comfort rather than of lust.[30] Similarly, Mudarra's action in laying waste

---

[27] Sponsler, *Women*, points out that the *Cr1344* version is also of interest in the enhanced role it gives to the *infantes'* mother (p. 25).

[28] The only critic seriously to have questioned this hypothesis is A. Monteverdi, 'Il cantare degli Infanti di Salas', *Studi Medievali* (Nuova Serie), 7 (1934), 113-50, who held that the differences between the *PCG* and *Cr1344* versions could be due simply to differences in compilatory technique: that the authors of the first abbreviated and compressed to a far greater extent. Without being totally implausible, this seems to assume a much greater degree of confidence on the part of the *PCG* compilers, who were apt to put in doubtful details rather than omit them (compare the treatment of the legends of Bernardo del Carpio (ch. 1) and the Infante García (ch. 4)). See also Pattison, 'Legendary Material', especially pp. 179-80, and Chalon, *L'Histoire et l'épopée*, pp. 507-09, who argues convincingly in favour of the existence of a second *cantar* as a source for the version prosified in the *Cr1344*.

[29] Lathrop (*The Legend*) cites examples of the elimination of anticipatory references on pp. 43, 44, and 69, and of stylistic elaboration of dialogue on pp. 45, 46, 48-49, 51-52, 54-55, 57-58, and 73.

[30] This same incident shows how the *RefTol* clears up some of the inconsistencies

Bilbestre is given better justification (*The Legend*, p. 67). The tendency of the poetic *refundición* to regard Mudarra, the new hero of the climax of the story, as a reincarnation of Gonzalo González, the most prominent hero of its first part, is given added point by the *RefTol*'s having him rebaptized with the same name as his half-brother and thereafter being referred to as Gonzalo for the rest of the narrative (*The Legend*, pp. 70-72). Lathrop is unwilling to see a poetic text as responsible for any of these innovations in the *RefTol*. He examines the possibility of assonance being found in the prose text (pp. 16-19) but finds no firm traces. Indeed, he seems amply justified in his conclusion that all the innovations are 'literary devices used to polish, improve and make more dramatic and intense the legend of the *infantes*' and 'a conscious effort by an expert story teller to justify actions, create drama and heighten intrigue in his narrative' (p. 75). It is fair to recall that in 1896 Menéndez Pidal, who devoted a few pages to the *RefTol* (which he called *Estoria de los godos*), referred to its 'galas de estilo y . . . alardes de crítica' (*La leyenda*, p. 60); he went on, however, to deplore its departure from the sober simplicity of Alphonsine prose (ibid., p. 61), and elsewhere referred to its style as one of 'enfadosa palabrería' (ibid., p. 105).

This becomes, then, a question of taste: Lathrop has amply demonstrated that the *RefTol* is, on its own terms, a coherent and well-thought-out narrative. That these terms are not those of Alphonsine historiography is plain enough, but the basic structure of the narrative is taken from the *Cr1344*, which also provides a starting-point for some of the detailed innovations. Without being strictly an extension of the thirteenth-century historiographical tradition, the *RefTol* is in this instance a logical descendant of that tradition.

left in the *Cr1344*. The latter chronicle takes from the *PCG* the story of the Mooress coming to the prison cell, and at that point refers to Mudarra's conception and his future role as avenger (*La leyenda*, p. 262. 15-22); it also takes (presumably from the poetic *refundición*) the notion that the conception took place later, between Gonzalo Gustioz and Almanzor's sister, after the Lament (ibid., pp. 286. 14-287. 1; cf. *Reliquias*, p. 213. 10-15). The *RefTol* simply omits any suggestion of a sexual relationship in the first encounter in the prison cell: 'mando a vna mora suya que lo syruiese e procurase bien de todo lo que menester oviese, tanto que preso estouiese' (MS *M*, fol. 138r; Lathrop, *The Legend*, p. 108).

Chapter 4
THE CONDESA TRAIDORA AND THE INFANTE GARCÍA

(a) *The Condesa Traidora*

The last section of the *tercera parte* contains two further episodes of interest, the stories usually called the *Leyenda de la condesa traidora* and the *Romanz del Infante García*.

The first of these deals with the unfortunate marital affairs of Garci-Fernández, second Count of Castile and son of Fernán González. The so-called *Leyenda* is in fact a more complex one than its short title suggests, the motif of the treacherous countess being only one of the stories found in this section. It will be convenient, as before, to begin with a brief account of the *PCG* version of the story, as the most accessible text. Chapters 729-32 tell how Garci-Fernández's first wife, the French doña Argentina, ran off with a visiting French count; how her husband pursued her in disguise and was able to kill her and her lover with the aid of the latter's daughter, who returned with him to Castile to become his second wife. This doña Sancha proved no more satisfactory than her predecessor: in the second part of the story (chs 763-64) we learn how she brought about her husband's death by feeding his warhorse unsuitably, with the result that it failed him in battle against the Moors, leading to his death. Nor was this the limit of her treachery: wishing to marry a Moorish king, she plotted to kill the new Count, her son Sancho, by poisoning his wine. The plot was discovered and revealed by her maid, and Sancho forced his mother to drink the proffered cup herself. So died the Condesa Traidora—or rather the second one, since the title could also be applied to doña Argentina, Garci-Fernández's almost equally unsatisfactory first wife.

I have given here only the outlines of a complex story whose details may be seen in the *PCG*. It will be useful, however, to point to a few of them before looking at the other available versions of the story.

Garci-Fernández's first marriage is preceded by an account of a miraculous happening: during a battle against the Moors at Vado de Cascajares an unnamed knight whose devotion to the Mass caused him to miss the battle was miraculously represented in it by an angel who fought valiantly in his guise. This story clearly has little to do with that of the Countess, but it appears to be equally fictional and may have formed part of the same poetic source.

At the end of the story there is a certain amount of circumstantial detail as to how doña Sancha's plot against her son came to fail. The maid who saw her mistress mixing the poison was in love with one of the Count's squires and it was through him that the news of his mother's plot reached Sancho; this squire is said to be the ancestor of the Monteros de Espinosa, hereditary bodyguards of the Kings of Castile.[1] Finally, we are told that after the death of his mother, don Sancho, 'con pesar et crebanto por que matara a su madre', founded the monastery of Oña as her burial place: the name is explained as an abbreviation of Mionna, a name by which the lady was known (*PCG*, p. 454b5-10.)

Menéndez Pidal analysed this collection of stories, arguing that it had more of the 'cuento versificado' than of the 'canto épico' ('Condesa traidora', p. 9). In other words, it is essentially novelesque and contains a whole series of non-historical elements: 'salvo la muerte de Garci Fernández en lucha con los musulmanes, todo lo demás es o parece fabuloso' (ibid).[2] Indeed, even without corroborative evidence one would have a strong suspicion that this was so. The miracle at Vado de Cascajares has clear hagiographical origins;[3] the errant wife pursued by her disguised husband, the discontented stepdaughter and the ritual

---

[1] Later versions of the story add the detail of the Count's regularising the relationship between maid and squire by marrying them, a marriage from which descended the Monteros. This is in the *A* (Galician) MS of the *PCG* which is generally of the same type as the 'regia' *E*; it is also in the *Cr1344*. Menéndez Pidal took the view that MS *E* was abbreviating its source at this point ('Condesa traidora', p. 8 n.). I prefer to see this as a later improvement to the story: see below, p. 67.

[2] For further discussion of the nature of the primitive source as 'cantar' or 'cuento' and its relation to history, see Chalon, *L'Histoire et l'épopée*, pp. 519-31, especially 529-31 and the same author's 'La historicidad de la Leyenda de la Condesa traidora', *JHP*, 2 (1978), 153-63; see also Ruiz Asencio, 'La rebelión de Sancho García', especially pp. 45-53, and C. Guerrieri Crocetti, *Il Cid e i Cantari de Spagna* (Florence, 1957), pp. 68-71.

[3] Plumpton (*Historical Study*, pp. 37-38) suggested a particular source for this episode in one of Alfonso's *Cantigas de Santa María*; see the edition by Walter Mettmann (facsimile edition, 2 vols., Vigo 1981), I. 278-81 (no. 65).

avenging of outraged marital honour are further literary or folkloric motifs; and the same could be said, as Pidal has also pointed out, of such other elements as the would-be poisoner forced to drink first from the fatal cup.[4]

The earliest and simplest version of part of this story is to be found in the Latin *Crónica Najerense* of c. 1160.[5] The sections corresponding to chs 763-64 of the *PCG* tell how the (unnamed) wife of Garci-Fernández was tempted by the hope of becoming Almanzor's queen and resolved to betray her husband. This she did first by feeding the warhorse on scraps instead of on proper fodder, then by advising her husband to let his knights enjoy Christmas at their homes; she then advised Almanzor who attacked on Christmas day, and Garci-Fernández, his weakened horse failing him, was fatally wounded.[6] Almanzor's campaign continued against the new Count, Sancho, who was forced to take refuge at Lantarón with his mother and sister and achieved peace only by offering the latter to Almanzor. The story continues basically as in the *PCG*, with the Countess's plan to poison her son, the maid (here 'sarracenula') who tells the Count, and the Countess forced to drink the fatal draught.[7]

[4] 'Condesa traidora', pp. 23-26; cf. also the same author's 'Relatos poéticos', pp. 339-40, and von Richthofen, *Estudios épicos*, pp. 75-88. A summary of the folkloric elements involved is given by Deyermond and Chaplin ('Folk-Motifs', pp. 49-51, who conclude: 'the plot is largely made up of folk-motifs' (p. 51). See also Plumpton, *Historical Study*, especially pp. 490-93; Chalon, *L'Histoire et l'épopée*, pp. 521-22, and W. P. Shepherd, 'Two Assumed Epic Legends in Spanish', *MLN*, 23 (1908), 146-47, who pointed out similarities between the final scene of the poisoner forced to drink from the poisoned cup and elements of Lombardic legend.

[5] For the *Crónica Najerense*, see above, p. 25 and note 6.

[6] 'Interea ad comitissam, comitis Garsiez Ferrandez uxorem, per numtium uerba amoris dolose dirigit et an comitissa esse, an in reginam uelit prouehi, callidis sciscitatur. Quibus uerbis illecta et uiro interfecto, reginam se fore arbitrans, quomodo uirum intercifi faciat, querit sollicita, unde quo uiri per noctes singulas, ordeum subtrahens, saluiatum, ut hora deficeret necessaria, ministrabat. Quid plura?. Instante Dominice Natiuitatis festo uirum ammonuit et induxit, ut ad tante festiuitatis gaudia cum suis uxoribus et filiis habenda, suos milites ad loca propria ire permitteret et mandaret. Profectis ergo ad uoca loca militibus, statim ad Almazor que fecerat nuntiauit. Qui mox ipsa Natiuitatis Dominice die, electam militum copiam misit ad perdendam terram in qua comes Garsia Ferrandus festum deuotissimus celebrabat. Quibus ille cum paucis qui secum remanserant audacter obuians, deficiente sibi equo, captus et lanceatus a sarracenis in rippa Dorii inter Alcozar et Langa, quinta die expirauit era M^a. XXX^a. III^a., quarto kalendas ianuarii; qui, ductus Cordobam, sepultus est in Sanctos tres, deinde translatus est Caradignam. Tunc rex Almazor omnem hoc christianorum terram sibi subiciens, fecit tributariam, tunc in Hyspania omnis diuinus cultus omnis christianorum gloria, omnes ecclesiarum thesauri funditus perierunt' (*Crónica Najerense*, II. 80, pp. 85-86).

[7] 'Supradictus autem Almazor uirga furoris domini super christianos nequaquam

It will have been noted that, apart from the major omission of the entire first episode—the miracle at Vado de Cascajares, the adultery of doña Argentina and Garci-Fernández's revenge —this narrative is in some respects simpler than that in the *PCG*. There is, for instance, no squire involved in the dénouement, and no mention of the Monteros de Espinosa for whose ancestor he is claimed. Other circumstantial detail is also lacking: while in the *PCG* Sancho forces his mother at swordpoint to drink the cup, the *Najerense* has no such detail; nor is the Countess's death linked with the foundation of Oña. On the other hand, the *Najerense* gives a more complex account of doña Sancho's first treachery (the Christmas leave granted at her instance to weaken the Count's army is not mentioned in the *PCG*, which charges her instead with sowing discord between Garci-Fernández and his son); it also has an episode unknown to the later chronicle, the handing over of Sancho's sister to Almanzor as a part of peace terms.

Menéndez Pidal saw in the *Crónica Najerense* an account closer to historical fact than the later versions. Although recognising the novelesque character of many aspects of it (the false counsel of the Countess and the motif of the poisoner forced to drink her own poison: see above, note 4), he points out that the story of Sancho's handing over his sister to Almanzor is wholly consistent with what we know of the latter's habitual political strategy. He also speculates more generally that the original of doña Sancha may be Garci-Fernández's historical

a perditione et persecutione christiana desistens, sed et totam fere Castellam depredando, Castelle munitiones diruendo,. perambulans in tantum eam afflixit, quod eius terrore percussus comes Santius Garsie cum comitissa matre sua et sorore et cum omnibus suis in Plantaronem se mittere est coactus; sed cum nec etiam ibi assiduas incursiones et assultus undique graues posset sustinere, causa pacis cum eo habende, sororem suam, habendam illi dicitur tradidisse. Mater autem eius comitissa spe nubendi cum Almazor, non contenta quod patrem occidi fecerat, ut inanis glorie cupiditatem saciaret et sue libidini liberius deseruiret, filium ex quo solo salus totius pendebat Hyspanie necare potionibus attemptauit, sed Dominus qui consilia hominum dissipat impiorum, contra que non est consilium, qui omnia scit ante quam fiant, malignantis matris malignum consilium dissipauit. Aduentum enim de quodam assultu comiti quaedam sarracenula facti non ignara Deo disponente obuia, morte potu paratam et ut a tali scipho omnino abstineret, rem per ordinem propalauit. Ingressus itaque palatium de equo descendit scanno resedit militum sedente corona pre nimia lassitudine potum ex more quesiuit. Quem statim sibi uase porrectum argenteo, matri quasi causa honoris ipse exhibuit et ipsam ut prior biberet inuitauit. Cumque diutina et mutua inuitatione contenderent, tandem ipsa compulsa in primo haustu animam exalauit, cadens in laqueam quem tetendit' (*Crónica Najerense*, II. 83, pp. 86-87).

wife, the Ribagorzan doña Aba, who may have been unpopular in Castile and may have advocated just such a policy of treaties and marriage alliances with the Moors—as was not uncommon in the East but alien to Castilian practice.[8] The theory of the relative historicity of the *Najerense* version is part of the more general debate on *neotradicionalismo*, with which I do not concern myself here. Suffice it to say that even in its earliest form this story obviously contains many novelesque elements. It is true that the almost certainly fictional doña Argentina has not yet made her appearance, either as adulteress or as cruel stepmother; nor are we asked to accept the miracle of Vado de Cascajares. But in the second part of the story it is hard to see the *Najerense* account as intrinsically more historical, containing as it does the literary motif of the false counsel in preparation for the attack on Christmas day. Indeed, much of what the *PCG* adds to this story—the ancestry of the Monteros de Espinosa, the foundation of Oña—can readily be explained not so much as departures from history or as poetic reworkings of it, rather as examples of the kind of accretion, always common in later chronicles, whose motive is the glorification of a family or monastery by reference to its illustrious ancestry or historic foundation.

Another relatively simple version appears in the *CVR*. Like the *Najerense*, the *CVR* omits any mention of Garci-Fernández's first marriage to Argentina and the subsequent story of adultery and revenge; nor does it contain the Vado de Cascajares miracle. It does have, at least in part, the story of doña Sancha. As in the *Najerense*, she attempts to poison her son and, the plot being revealed by her maid, is forced to drink the cup herself. It will be noted that the more elaborate details of the *PCG* version—the squire, the Monteros de Espinosa, the drawn sword—are absent; the *CVR*, however, does mention the foundation of Oña, albeit in rather obscure terms ('pusole nonbre Onna porque aquella su madre ouiera nonbre Mionna'; MS *N*, fol. 45v) which might suggest abbreviation, and it also mentions that from this episode came the Castilian habit of women drinking first.[9] More interesting, doña Sancha plays

---

[8] Menéndez Pidal, 'Condesa traidora', pp. 15-21; Plumpton, *Historical Study*, pp. 243-72 and 483.

[9] 'Agora sabed aqui que desde alli adelante fue tomado en vso en Castilla de dar primero a las mugeres a beuer' (*CVR*, MS *N*, fol. 45v).

no part in the death of her husband Garci-Fernández. He dies in battle against the Moors, who invade knowing of the dissension between the Count and his son. There is no hint (as there is in the *PCG*) that doña Sancha is responsible for this discord or for the invasion, let alone that she deliberately engineered his death by neglecting his warhorse. The *CVR*, in short, appears to be based on only part of the story known to the other chronicles.

There are considerable similarities between this (*CVR*) version and that found in two others: the 'versión vulgar' of the *PCG* and the *Vulgata*. In both of these, the fundamental line of the second part of the story (i.e. doña Sancha's treachery) is as in the *CVR*. She plays no part in the death of her husband, either by neglecting his horse or by collusion with the Moors; but she does attempt to poison her son, is betrayed by a maid (acting alone), forced to drink the poison (but not at swordpoint) and has the Monastery of Oña founded in her honour. The *Vulgata* has the *CVR*'s note about the practice of women drinking first, but this is not found in the 'versión vulgar'.

However, unlike the *CVR*, both versions do tell the earlier story of Garci-Fernández's first marriage to doña Argentina, in a way basically similar to the *PCG*. Indeed, there are very few differences from the version summarised above, except for the minor fact that the knight to whom the miracle happened at Vado de Cascajares is named, albeit variously.[10]

To sum up so far: we have two primitive versions of the second part of the legend, represented by the *Najerense* and the *CVR* (although there are substantial differences between these versions) and a number of more complex narratives containing the story of Garci-Fernández's first wife as well; of these latter one—the 'versión regia' of the *PCG*, represented by MS *E*— has details found in none of the other texts so far discussed. These are the intervention of the squire, the institution of the Monteros de Espinosa and the drawn sword. Also, the 'versión regia' tells the war-horse story—unlike all other versions discussed except the *Najerense*—and has the most carefully

[10] He is Ferrand Antolinez in most MSS of the 'versión vulgar' and in Ocampo's edition of the *Vulgata* (MSS *G*, fol. 101r, *T*, fol. 165v, and *Z*, fol. 244v, Ocampo, fol. 253v); Ferrand Armentales in MS *Y* of the 'versión vulgar' (fol. 425v); and don Antolinez in MS *C* of the *Vulgata* (fol. 24r). This last MS deforms a number of proper names: for instance, the place of the battle is given as 'Vado de Trascajal' (ibid.).

explained account of the foundation of Oña and the etymology of its name.[11]

An examination of these details in the *PCG* shows that two of them are later additions to MS *E*. The story of the war-horse (453b17-29) is written in a different hand as an addition to the account of Garci-Fernández's death; and the mention of the squire and the Monteros (454a28-36) is·likewise added to an original narrative which we may suppose to have passed directly from the maid's warning to the Countess's proffering of the cup. In its original form, *E*, the 'versión regia', seems to have been very similar to the 'versión vulgar' at this point.[12]

If one follows the basic principle that narratives become more complex with the passage of time, it must be assumed that in these episodes the *CVR* represents a more primitive stage of chronicle evolution:[13] one based in all probability on the Toledano, who in turn drew on the *Najerense*; but without the wholly novelesque episode of Garci-Fernández's first marriage, brought in only to the *PCG* and the connected *Vulgata*, and without also the details peculiar to the *regia* MS *E* of the *PCG*, which appear to be even later accretions.[14]

The three remaining versions to be examined are all later, and, in varying degrees, tell more complex versions of the story.

[11] '... et pusol nombre Onna por del nombre de su madre en la guisa que aqui agora departiremos: En Castiella solien llamar Mionna por la sennora, et porque la condessa donna Sancha era tenuda por sennora en tod el condado de Castiella, mando el conde toller deste nombre Mionna aquella "mi" que uiene primero en este nombre; et esta palabra que finca, tolluda dend "mi", que llamassen por nombre a aquel monesterio Onna, et assi le llaman oy en dia Onna' (*PCG*, p. 454b5-15); cf. the much less clear *CVR* version: '... e pusole nonbre Onna por que aquella su madre ouiera nonbre Mionna' (MS *N*, fol. 45v); the 'versión vulgar' and the *Vulgata* are similar to the *CVR*. Chalon points out that none of this is in fact true, the place being called Oña before the foundation of the monastery (*L'Histoire et l'épopée*, p. 522 and n. 11).

[12] On the composite nature of the second volume of MS *E* (Escorial MS X-1-4), see Catalán, *De Alfonso X*, pp. 19-123 and 316-23; on the folios discussed here, see especially pp. 65 and 319-20.

[13] Babbitt clearly took the view that the *CVR*, in this as in other episodes, was an earlier work than the *PCG*. Although he is guilty of overlooking the differences between the 'regia' and 'vulgar' versions of the latter (cf. Catalán, *De Alfonso X*, pp. 178-88), he makes the valid point that the complete ignorance of the doña Argentina story in the *CVR* points to its compilers' not knowing that source (Babbitt, *Latin Sources*, pp. 30 and 44); see also pp. 4-6 and 'Twelfth-Century Epic Forms', pp. 128-33 on the general principles involved.

[14] Juan Manuel's *Crónica Abreviada* throws no light on this episode. The summary is comparatively short at this point, and lacks all of the details which enable us to classify other versions. Suffice it to say that it does tell both stories, that of doña Argentina as well as that of doña Sancha (BN MS 1356, fols 101r-v and 105r; cf. the edition by Grismer, pp. 133 and 138).

The so-called *Versión Interpolada* of the *Vulgata* has the same basic version as the *Vulgata* (and as the *PCG*, 'versión vulgar') but expands at two points. The first concerns the events leading up to the meeting between the disguised Garci-Fernández and doña Sancha, daughter of the French count to whose home Garci-Fernández has pursued his erring wife (*PCG*, 427b20-42). It will be recalled that Sancha, after complaining about the unhappiness brought by her new stepmother, tells her maid to observe the poor who eat at the castle gates 'et que cates si y ha algunt omne fidalgo apuesto et fremoso quel trayas ante mi, que quiero fablar con el' (p. 427b30-3). The maid does so recognises the Castilian count as a man of quality by his beautiful hands, and after some cryptic dialogue he reveals his identity to doña Sancha and offers her marriage if she will aid him in his revenge. Her motives in giving the above instructions to her maid are unexpressed and it may have been with this in mind that the author of the *Versión Interpolada* expanded this part of the story, giving to doña Sancha a pious if not wholly convincing motive:

> Sepas, amyga, que non puedo sofrir mas esta vida atan amarga; et pidote yo de gracia que a los proves (sic) que aqui en casa de my padre dan de comer cada dia, que tu los quieras visitar et rrequerir mas que fasta aqui de aquellas cosas que ayan menester; porque es my voluntad de me adoleçer dellos porque el sennor Dios se adolezca de mi vida, et me saque desta tribulacion et pena en que bibo con my padre et con mi madrastra. E rruegote yo que los mire bien a todos et veas si entre ellos ay algun fidalgo que sea ome apuesto e de buen donayre; e aquel que tu vieres que a tus ojos parece bien, que aquel me traygas et fablare con el dos palabras en ffaz de Dios, que es my voluntad de le dar limosna por que rruege (sic) a Dios que yo salga desta vida en que bibo (MS *V*, fol. 197v).

The same chronicler clearly felt some qualms at a later stage, about don Sancho's killing of his mother by forcing her to drink the poisoned cup, he seems to feel that this needs apology or at least explanation:

> El conde don Sancho, non pensando que tanto era el mal que su madre avia de morir, ovo muy gran pesar e lloro mucho su peccado; e fizo vn notable monesterio e pusole nonbre Onna porque a la condesa su madre llamaran Mayona (MS *V*, fol. 220r).

It will be noted that this supposed remorse is also felt to be a more suitable reason for his foundation of the Monastery.[15]

[15] See Pattison, 'Legendary Material', pp. 176-77.

These attempts to tidy up motives are minor compared to the other versions not so far mentioned, the *Cr1344* and its later development the *RefTol*. The first of these has all the features of the *PCG*—including those interpolated in the *E* MS—and expands several of them as well as making other changes. Some of these are of little significance: for instance, the fact that the chapter (= *PCG*, ch. 730) which gives a brief account of Garci-Fernández, mentions that he had exceptionally handsome hands, and tells of his first marriage to doña Argentina, precedes the Vado de Cascajares miracle rather than follows it as in the *PCG*.[16] Other differences include the fact that the French count who elopes with doña Argentina comes to visit Garci-Fernández, rather than Argentina herself as in the *PCG*—thereby, perhaps, making his conduct even more reprehensible in that it involves a betrayal of hospitality (MS *Q*, fol. 151r; MS *M*, fol. 122r). Sancha, when plotting the death of her father, arranges to sleep in the same room as her father rather than simply in the same building as in the *PCG*,[17] which clearly makes more sense. The anticipatory statement at the end of the first part of the legend to the effect that doña Sancha was to turn out to be a bad wife after a period of marriage comes in the *Cr1344* at a later stage, at the beginning of the later episode: that is, when she has already become unsatisfactory (MS *Q*, fol. 171r; MS *M*, fol. 152v; cf. *PCG*, pp. 428b40-429a5). At the very end of the story the etymology of Oña appears to be based on the *PCG* explanation (see note 11 above), but is obscurely expressed.[18]

[16] In the *Q* MS of the *Cr1344* the material corresponding to *PCG*, ch. 729 forms the first part of an (unnumbered) chapter beginning on fol. 149v). The Vado de Cascajares story (in which the name of the knight is Pascual Biuas) forms the rest of this chapter and the next one (fol. 151r. The corresponding folios in MS *M* are 120v-121v).

[17] 'Donna Sancha . . . dixo que queria y esa noche dormir en la camara por amor de su padre et de su madrastra' (*Cr1344*, MS *Q*, fol. 152r; cf. MS *M*, fol. 123r); compare the *PCG* version: '. . . donna Sancha . . . enfinniose que por amor de so padre que querie esa noche albergar y en la casa con ellos' (p. 428b13-17).

[18] '. . . pusole nonbre Onna por la sennora, e por que la condesa donna Sancha era tenida por sennora en todo el condado de Castilla, mando el conde toller de aquel nonbre Mionna aquel "Mi" que viene primero en el nonbre de Mionna' (MS *Q*, fol. 172r; cf. MS *M*, fol. 154r). This appears to be an abbreviation of the much clearer (though more wordy) explanation in the Galician-Portuguese *A* MS: '. . . e posolle nume Onna por o nume de sua madre, ena guisa que agora diremos. En Castella soyan chamar Mionna por lla senora, e aquella condesa donna Sancha era teuda por senora en todo o condado de Castella; e por ende mandou o conde toller deste nume Mionna aquel "Mi" que dizia primeiro en este nume, e esta palaura que fica, tollida ende "Mi", que lli chamassem por ende a aquel moesteyro Onna' (MS *A*, fol. 66v).

All these are minor alterations which can be explained in terms of the mechanics of rewriting—especially if one bears in mind the history of the *Cr1344* composed in Portuguese using Spanish sources and then retranslated into Castilian. Two other points of the story receive greater, though still relatively minor expansion which may throw some light on the chroniclers' narrative criteria. They correspond to the two points at which the *E* MS of the *PCG* underwent interpolation—the war-horse story and the introduction of the squire and the Monteros de Espinosa. In the *PCG*, the war-horse story shows signs of hasty tacking-on to the narrative in ways other than the physical. Only after the account of Garci-Fernández's death are we told:

> Et deuedes a saber que una de las cosas por que aquel dia los moros mas prisieron et mataron al conde Garci Ferrandez si fue por que el so cauallo, que el mucho preçiaua, el qual fiara en la condessa donna Sancha so muger que gelo guardasse, et ella teniel muy gordo et muy fremoso de saluados, mas non de çeuada; et con esto enflaqueçio el cauallo en medio de la fazienda et dexosse caer en el canpo; et estonçe fue ferido et preso el conde ... (*PCG*, p. 453b18-27)

In the *Cr1344* the episode is altogether better integrated into the narrative. At the beginning of the chapter corresponding to *PCG*, ch. 763, after giving the chronology and the fact of Sancho's rebellion against his father (here, by the way, 'por consejo de su madre', thus implicating her still further in the disaster), MS *Q* continues:

> ... (en) aquel tienpo los reyes et los ricosomnes usauan syenpre sus guerras con los moros e para esto trabajauanse los moros de auer cauallos los que podian. En tal manera que los non fincaua por auer que por ellos pudiesen dar. E quando yuan en sus huestes dexauan algunos de sus buenos cauallos en sus casas et mandauanlos bien açevadar et tenianlos sienpre en sus camaras en que aluergauan con sus mugeres. E acontesçiose que este conde don Garcia Ferrandez auia vn muy noble cauallo et encomendole a la condesa donna Sancha que lo açeuadase et fartase muy bien, en tal manera que le non fallesçiese quando menester lo ouiese. E ella como aquella en cuyo coraçon reynaua toda maldat non lo quiso asy fazer mas fyzolo por el contrario, ca le non daua a comer synon saluados. (fol. 171v; cf. MS *M*, fol. 152v-153r).

And, duly, during the battle:

> E onde estua en la mayor priesa, fallesciole el cauallo de que vos ya deximos con mengua de fuerça por que non comia synon saluados. E el cauallo cayo con el en tierra de flaqueza, e el conde fue muy mal llagado, e presieronlo los moros. (ibid.; cf. MS *M*, fol. 153r).

What was in the *PCG* an afterthought, perhaps inspired by the *Najerense*, is here, as in that early chronicle, restored to its place as an integral part of doña Sancha's treachery, and in a manner wholly satisfactory from the narrative point of view.

The other addition to the *PCG*, MS *E*, that of the squire and his descendants the Monteros de Espinosa is also dealt with more smoothly in the *Cr1344*. It will be recalled that *E*, for whatever reason, tells the story as comprising three separate elements: the maid tells the squire 'que queria bien'; the squire warns the Count; and 'deste escudero uienen los monteros dEspinosa que guardan el palacio de los reyes de Castiella . . .' (*PCG*, p. 454a32-34). In the *Cr1344* (and in the Galician *A* MS of the *PCG* which may have been a source of the Portuguese chronicle) the three elements are more satisfactorily linked. After the maid learns of the Countess's plot:

E esta cobijera fazia mal de su fazienda con vn escudero del conde, e descubrierale este fecho, diziendole en como la condesa queria matar su fijo con beuer de ponçonna. E el escudero fue esto dezir al conde, e dixole la manera en como se guardase, e esto le dixo el con muy grant miedo porque le fue nesçesario de descobrir de su fecho e de la cobijera. E aquel escudero e la cobijera caso despues el conde, e de alli vienen los Monteros de Espinosa que guardan los reyes de Castilla. E esta guarda les fue dada por aquello que asy acontesçio (MS *Q*, fol. 172r; cf. MS *M*, fol. 153v, and *PCG*, MS *A*, fol. 66v).

The Monteros thus descend from both maid and squire, married by the Count, presumably partly as a reward and partly to regularise a relationship which seems to have gone beyond the 'queria bien' of the *PCG*. A touch of suspense is provided by the squire's hesitancy in warning his master, to do so being to reveal his illicit relationship with the maid. Once again, the episode is made to work better in itself, as well as contributing to the wider plot.[19]

The final version to be considered, the *RefTol*, provides the most thorough-going reworking of the narrative. Lathrop's analysis of its innovations in the Infantes de Lara story have been discussed in the last chapter. Here too its author, while

---

[19] One minor innovation of the *Cr1344* is to tell how doña Argentina, on eloping with her French lover, did so dressed as a man ('en pannos de omne'; MS *Q*, fol. 151r cf. MS *M*, fol. 122r). Chalon noted this an an indication that the *Cr1344* was inspired by 'une refonte de la légende cléricale utilisée par la *PCG*' (*L'Histoire et l'épopée*, p. 534). This seems unnecessary in the light of other instances of rewriting for purposes of verisimilitude and consistency.

patently following the *Cr1344* for the basic story line, expands and rearranges his material considerably.

We may begin by noting some of the minor alterations. A certain amount of extraneous matter is omitted where it has no relevance to the story: thus much detail surrounding the Vado de Cascajares battle is missing, such as the historical note concerning the monastery where the knight heard Mass (*PCG* 426a44-b1). Second, material may be transposed. The *PCG* narrative mentions, rather cryptically, Garci-Fernández's beautiful hands at an early stage, at the time of his first marriage, where the relevance of the detail is in no way apparent (p. 427a22-28). It becomes plain, of course, much later when it is by his hands that doña Sancha's maid picks him out from among the beggars as a man of high estate, and it to this point that the *RefTol* postpones the first mention of the hands:

Et como el conde avia muy gentyl gesto et muy gentiles manos, ca tan fermosas las tenja que avia verguença de las sacar ante presona njnguna syn guantes. Et como sacaua las manos para comer, vna seruidora que y era maraujllose mucho e mirandolo en el rrostro e en el cuerpo e como via que correspondia todo . . . (MS *M*, fol. 134r-v; cf. MS *S*, fol. 153r-v).

Third, dialogue is regularly expanded. We may take as an example the dialogue between knight and squire in the Vado de Cascajares episode. The *PCG* has a bald statement that the squire 'maltrayel et dizie que con couardia et con maldat dessi dexaua de yr alla, ca non con otra cristiandat' (p. 426b21-23) and the *Cr1344* is practically identical (MS *Q*, fol. 151r; MS *M*, fol. 121v). The *RefTol* expands as follows:

Maldesia mucho al sennor, diziendole a grandes boses que saliese de la hermita et fuese a ayudar a su sennor a la batalla, e que para que se armara. E desiale que non creya en Dios si aquello el fasia de muy Christiano, mas de puro couarde e medroso, e que non seria ya onbre para se poner delante la gente que tal sopiesen. Et destas e otras tales palabras nunca el moço cesaua de desir tanto que la batalla duraua . . . (MS *M*, fol. 133r).

Not dissimilar is the final confrontation between doña Sancha and her son over the poisoned cup. We have seen how the *PCG* added the detail of the drawn sword, but the scene is still a short one, with only one piece of reported speech: 'que si lo non beuiesse quel cortarie la cabeça' (p. 454a45-b1); again, the *Cr1344* follows the *PCG* closely. The *RefTol* version is expanded as follows:

> E rrogo el conde mucho a su madre que lo beuiese ella por su amor del. E ella rrespondio a su fijo que poco ouiera que auia beuido dello e que lo non podria beuer syn gana. Mas el conde rrogole por tantas vezes que beuiese ella primero que el por amor della beueria despues. E como tanto la aquexaua que ya donna Sancha non sabia que se fazer. Pero por ninguna manera de rruego lo quiso tan solamente allegar a la boca. E quando el conde su fijo aquello vido, creo luego que sin dubda era todo verdat lo que le auian dicho. E tyro la espada de fuera jurando a Dios que al non le consintiria saluo que de los tomase vna: S, o que beuiese aquel vino, o que muriese alli luego a cuchilladas. E quando la condesa vido enteramente la verdat del conde su fijo, e que non auia al saluo morir por vna guisa o por otra, escojo la muerte mas paçifica. E tomo la copa en la mano e començo a beuer, los ojos çerrados. E avn non era en el tercero trago quando dio el alma al diablo e cayo muerta de su estado en tierra (MS *M*, fol. 178r; cf. MS *S*, fol. 190v).

These are only a few examples of the characteristics of the *RefTol* version. The whole Vado de Cascajares episode, and not just the dialogue, is rewritten and rearranged; similarly, the episode of Garci-Fernández's warhorse is rewritten and amplified in such a way as to stress the importance of the occasion— here a single combat as the result of a challenge—and to heighten the tension of the climax by stressing the last-minute arrival of the horse.[20]

The differences between the earlier chronicles may be explained in certain more or less mechanical terms: the presence or absence of certain sources, their mistaken interpretation, an occasional detail added to clarify supposed motive or to increase verisimilitude. This tendency to tinker reaches its height in the *Versión Interpolada* (see p. 64 above), though it is also seen in the *Cr1344*. This latter chronicle, however, and to an even greater extent the *RefTol*, show a new tendency to rework whole sections of the narrative. In part this too has to do with clarity and verisimilitude. It also, however, shows for the first time an awareness of the literary aspects of narrative technique; as such, it may be said to represent a departure from the less literary and more historical emphasis of Alphonsine historiography.

---

[20] For similar examples of the *RefTol*'s amplificatory tendencies, see my article 'The Legend of the Sons of Sancho el Mayor', especially pp. 38-39. I hope to devote a more extensive study to the *RefTol* in due course.

(b) The Infante García

The last Count of Castile, son of the Sancho mentioned in the previous section, was García, whose treacherous murder at an early age provides the material for the last legend to be examined from the *tercera parte*. García is known in all vernacular sources as *infante* rather than as *conde*, despite the fact that he did succeed his father and reign, albeit briefly; indeed, at the time of his death we are told that negotiations were in progress for his being granted the title of King by the Leonese monarch.

To begin as I have done before by summarising the *PCG* version of the legend is not appropriate in this case. This is because, as will be seen, it represents a confusing and in places clumsy attempt to tell two alternative versions of the story. Instead, let us look first at the historical background and the Latin chroniclers.

A preliminary point to be made is that there is a much firmer historical basis for the outline—if not for the details—of this story than for most of those already discussed. One of Menéndez Pidal's most persuasive (and most neglected) studies of early epic is his essay on this subject ('Infant García'). In it he shows that there are considerable grounds for accepting the bare bones of the story as told by the Tudense; and that the two other principal Latin chronicles, the *Najerense* and that of the Toledano, both, if in different degrees, reflect popular sources which in turn have an indirect basis in the contemporary political background.

The Tudense tells us that when the young *infante* journeyed to León to seek the hand of doña Sancha, the King's sister, he was met by the two exiled sons of Count Vela (the family had been exiled on two occasions, the first by Fernán González, the second by García's father Sancho). The *infante* was struck down at the door of the church of San Juan Bautista, the fatal blow being struck by Diego Vela who had been the boy's godfather; many Castilians and Leonese who tried to help the prince were also killed, and the assailants escaped to the mountains. The dead *infante* was buried by doña Sancha, his betrothed, near her father in the church of San Juan Bautista. Finally we are told that the youth was barely thirteen years old at his death.[21]

---

[21] 'Obiit comes Sancius, & successit ei in ducatu Burgensium infans Garsea filius eius. Tunc Burgenses comites inito consilio miserunt ad Veremundum Regem

As Pidal says, this contains some errors of detail, notably the age of the *infante* (historically he was probably about 19 at his death in 1029) and the Christian names of his murderers; on the other hand, 'en los restantes pormenores el relato puede también pasar por histórico, y para varios de ellos encontramos confirmación en otros testimonios' ('Infant García', p. 45).

If we turn to the other chronicles, we see a perceptible accretion of detail. The *Najerense* (which is relatively early but prone to accept legendary material)[22] tells us the same story, but with the addition that the murder took place when the King and court were distracted by a tournament; that the *infante* was killed in the presence of doña Sancha; and finally that Sancho *el Mayor* of Navarre, who succeeded to the Castilian throne, avenged the murder of his brother-in-law.[23] Similar details are found in the Toledano, but so is much else: García is accompanied to León by Sancho el Mayor; the Velas (of whom there are now three) pretend to be reconciled to García and swear homage to him, thus lulling him into a false sense of security; the *infante* and doña Sancha are said to fall in love at first sight; and at his burial she is said to have wished to be entombed with him.[24] Menéndez Pidal was surely right

Legionensium, vt sororem suam Sanciam comiti Garsiae daret in coniugem, & concederet eundem Regem Castellae vocari. Rex attamen Veremundus hoc se facturum promisit. Vnde factum est, vt cum esset Rex Veremundus Oueto, venerunt Burgensium nobiles cum comite suo infante Garsia in Legionem proponentes ire Ouetum, tum causa orationis, tum vt loquerentur cum rege de matrimonio contrahendo, & Regis nomine Garsiae duci obtinendo: sed filij Velae comitis supradicti aggregantes exercitus in submontanis memores malorum, quae sibi fecerat dux Sancius, ambulantes per totam noctem intrauerunt Legionem: & tertia feria illucescente die occiderunt ipsum infantem Garsiam in porta ecclesiae sancti Ioannis Baptistae. Didacus comitis Velae filius ipsum Garsiam in baptismo de sacro fonte leuauerat, & propria manu occidit eum enormi sacrilegio perpetrato, & Dei timore postposito. Tunc occisi fuerunt multi tam de Castellanis, quam de Legionensibus, qui ad defensionem Garsiae ducis confluebant. Post haec cum iam multitudo conflueret ad vindicandam mortem Garsiae ducis, praedicti filij Velae, scilicet Didacus & Sylvester fugientes se in montibus, locis tutissimis contulerunt. Infans vero Sancia praedicta fecit planctum magnum super ducem Garsiam, & sepeliuit eum honorifice iuxta Regem Adefonsum patrem suum in ecclesia sancti Ioannis Baptistae. Puer fere tredecim annorum erat infans Garsias quando mortuus est' (Tudense, p. 90).

[22] See above, p. 25 and note 6.
[23] 'Rege Ueremundo et cuncta fere cohorte Legionensium et Castellanorum in hastiludio se ducentibus, urbem ingressi, cesis quoscumque intra urbem inuenire potuerunt Castellanis, ad palatium ubi infans Garsias cum sua infantissa erat, accesserunt, et ipsum innocuum occiderunt' (*Crónica Najerense*, II. 90, p. 89); 'Interfectores autem cognati sui infantis Garsie digna ultione interfecit' (ibid., III. 9, p. 91).
[24] '... ei obviam occurrentes, manus osculo (prout exigit mos Hispanus) se eius

in regarding most of these details as poetic in origin ('Infant García', pp. 60-62) and he subsequently made a similar point regarding the details found in the *Crónica Najerense*.²⁵

We may now turn to the vernacular chronicles. The one thing which they all have in common is that, unlike the Latin versions discussed, they are relatively extended. In particular, they share a common narrative element at the beginning—a prologue, as it were—and, with minor differences of detail, a common epilogue to the story. The prologue concerns the journey from Burgos to León, in the course of which García and Sancho surround the castle of Monzón, held by one Fernán Gutiérrez who surrenders it to them together with a number of other strongholds between the rivers Cea and Pisuerga (e.g., *PCG*, p. 470a6-24). The epilogue concerns the same castle: after the murder the Velas and their accomplice Ferrant Llaynez flee there; Fernán Gutiérrez detains them while he sends for Sancho el Mayor, and the latter, on arriving, tortures and executes them. Ferrant Llaynez, however, escapes, and it is only later that he is hunted out on the insistence of doña Sancha. She demands his capture as a precondition of her marriage to King Sancho's son, and when she has him in her power takes a personal and bloody vengeance (see *PCG*, ch. 789, p. 472a7-b35; similar stories are told in other versions, as will be mentioned below).²⁶

dominio subiecerunt, quorum hominio iam securus, et paranymphis dulci alloquio persuasis, permissus est Infans optatis solatiis delectari. Cumque se mutuo conspexissent, ita fuit uterque amore alteri colligatus, ut vix possent à mutuis aspectibus separari' (Toledano, V. 25. p. 115); 'Sponsa vero sponsi dulcedine vix gustata, ante vidua, quam traducta, fletu lugubri semiviva lacrimas cum occisi sanguine admiscebat, se occisam ingeminans cum occiso. Qui cum in Ecclesia Sancti Ioannis cum patre sponsae sepeliretur, et ipsa cum sepulto voluit sepeliri' (ibid., pp. 115-16).

²⁵ 'Relatos poéticos', pp. 340-42. After describing the *Najerense*'s version, Menéndez Pidal concludes: 'Vemos que poco más de un siglo después de ocurrido el suceso, la *Crónica Najerense* lo refiere, según relato castellano, con circunstancias poéticas no conformes a la realidad' (p. 342). For the poetic nature of the details in the Toledano and the *Najerense*, see also Chalon, *L'Histoire et l'épopée*, pp. 543-45.

²⁶ Menéndez Pidal's argument that much of this poetic material reflects history is less convincing than what he says about the Tudense's version (see above, p. 71). He argues that the taking of Monzón is a poetic representation of Sancho's incursions into León which preceded his war with Bermudo III ('Infant García', pp. 73-74). On the other hand, he admits that the vengeance exacted on the Vela family and Ferrant Llaynez is unhistorical: 'Sólo el pueblo castellano guardó fiel la memoria de su último conde, y cantó su muerte en un poema, donde buscó, aunque fuese fingida, la necesaria venganza, para castigo de los traidores' (ibid., p. 95). See also Chalon, *L'Histoire et l'épopée*, pp. 545-48 and 562.

It is in the central portion of the story—the *infante*'s projected marriage, the feigned reconciliation of the Velas, the murder and its immediate aftermath—that the *PCG* and other chronicles show most diversity. At this stage it will be convenient to look at the *PCG* version, which occupies chs 787-89. It is apparent that here is a case where the compilers are handling two divergent sources; indeed, little effort is made to resolve their contradictions. First, a story is told, with circumstantial details, which appears to harmonise broadly with the versions of the Tudense and Toledano. It includes the feigned submission of the Velas and the love-at-first-sight meeting of the *infante* and *infanta*; it goes on to relate the Velas' plot to set up a *tablado* for jousting and, in the subsequent confusion, kill the *infante* and his men. This is reminiscent of the *Najerense*'s *hastiludium*, if the details are rather different. The compilers break off this story to say:

Pero dize aqui el arçobispo don Rodrigo, et don Lucas de Tuy que acuerda con el, que antes mataron al inffante que a otro ninguno de los cavalleros; et matol Roy Vela, que era su padrino de bautismo, et era estonces ell inffante de edad de XIII annos ... (p. 471a10-18)

and continue to summarise the Toledano's version, finishing:

Mas pero que assi fue como el arçobispo et don Lucas de Tuy lo cuentan en su latin, dize aqui en el castellano la estoria del Romanz dell inffant Garcia dotra manera, et cuentalo en esta guisa ... (p. 471a31-35).

This *estoria* appears to have continued as follows: the *infante*, on hearing the tumult, dashed out and was captured, being brought before Roy Vela; doña Sancha, hearing of his capture, hurried to the scene to plead for him. But she was slapped in the face by one Ferrant Llaynez and the *infante* was killed trying to protect her. Ferrant Llaynez then took the princess by the hair and threw her down a flight of stairs. King Sancho, meanwhile, was shut out of the city and unable to help. The *infante*'s body was thrown over the wall to him, and he took it to Oña for burial. At this point we return to the Toledano, whose alternative version of the burial—at San Juan in León, with the *infanta* wanting to throw herself into the grave—is given. The sequel of vengeance has already been described. At no point do the compilers openly state that they prefer the lurid story of the *Romanz* to the account of the Latin chronicles —indeed at one point they come close to admitting the probable veracity of the latter ('pero que assi fue como el arçobispo et don Lucas de Tuy lo cuentan en su latin'); yet the story—which is in fact based primarily on the Toledano rather than the Tudense—is relegated to two passages of 'aside', and the vernacular version is clearly preferred.

The differences between 'versión vulgar' and 'versión regia' of the *PCG*, so revealing in other cases, are here much less significant. They consist of minor differences of detail, and on the whole the 'regia' version, as usual, is the longer. Thus, when García proposes to enter the city of León to see his bride and his sister the Queen, only the 'regia' MS *E* adds the detail 'et el rey don Sancho touolo por bien' (*PCG*, p. 470a48-b1); doña Sancha's grief-stricken attempt to throw herself into the *infante*'s grave is not expanded so much in the 'versión vulgar' (cf. *PCG*, pp. 471b46-472a5 and variant); and this version also lacks the moralising note that the punishment meted out to the *infante*'s murderers was appropriate 'como a traydores que mataran a su sennor' (*PCG*, p. 472a39-40 and variant); finally, the barbaric vengeance which doña Sancha takes on Ferrant Llaynez is described in all its gory detail only in MS *E* (*PCG*, p. 472b17-33 and variant).[27] Typical as these are of the basic tendency of the 'versión vulgar' to be less wordy than the 'regia', they do not compare with cases where the latter version expands in, for instance, the Fernán González story for motives of verisimilitude, or to rewrite the story in order to make its hero appear in a better light (cf. above, pp. 27-30).

Of more importance is the *CVR*, which treats the two sources —Latin chronicles and vernacular *Romanz*—in a way fundamentally different from that of the *PCG*.[28] The versions diverge at the point when the *infante* and King Sancho approach León. The *PCG* has them spending a night at Sahagún, thence proceeding to León where the *infante* camps in the Barrio de Trobajo,

[27] Lindley Cintra saw this as evidence that the compilers of the version reflected in MS *E* had access to a *refundición* of the *Romanz*: see *Crónica*, I, ccxxviii n. 155 and compare Chalon, *L'Histoire et l'épopée*, p. 555.

[28] In some details, the *CVR* seems to be closer to the 'vulgar' version of the *PCG*: so, it omits the detail of Sancho's giving approval for García's entry into León (see above, and cf. *CVR*, MS *N*, fol. 60v); Fernán Gutiérrez's promise of the castle of Monzón to the Velas as a delaying tactic until King Sancho arrives (*PCG*, p. 472a17 variant), absent from MS *E*, is found in the *CVR* (MS *N*, fol. 62r); and doña Sancha's personal motive for executing Ferrant Llaynez (*PCG*, p. 472b7-9 and variant) which conversely is in MS *E* but not in the MSS of the 'vulgar' family, is similarly lacking from the *CVR* (MS *N*, fol. 62v).

Sancho 'fuera en el canpo' (*PCG*, p. 470a29-36); according to the *CVR* there are two versions: one corresponding to the *PCG*'s story of the *infante* setting up his camp within the walls, the King outside; the other, ascribed to the Toledano, is that the *infante* left his men at Sahagún with King Sancho and went on 'con vnos pocos de los suyos encubiertamente' (*CVR*, MS *N*, fol. 60v). The *PCG*'s night at Sahagún appears to be an attempt to conflate these two. More fundamental is the *CVR*'s treatment of the differing accounts of the *infante*'s death. The primary version given is that of the Toledano, which was summarised above: it includes the meeting of the Velas with the *infante* and their false oath of loyalty, the love-at-first-sight meeting of *infante* and *infanta*, the diversion of the *tablado* and the murder of the *infante* before the church door; finally, doña Sancha buries the *infante* in San Juan Bautista near her father. After telling this story and asserting its veracity, the *CVR* gives the alternative story of the *infante*'s death according to the *Romanz*, including the ill-treatment of the *infanta* by 'Ferrant Flayno', García's body being flung over the wall and taken to Oña for burial by Sancho. This version, however, is given with less detail than in the *PCG* and, moreover, appears to be only an aside to the main story: it is introduced with words similar to those used by the *PCG* (see above, p. 73) which seem to show a belief that the Toledano/Tudense version is more likely to be true, and the veracity of the final detail of the *infante*'s burial is expressly denied: 'mas esto non semeja cosa de creer' (*CVR*, MS *N*, fol. 62r). Babbitt sums up as follows:

> It is at once evident that the *CVR* reveals a preference on the part of its compilers for the version of the Latin historians, for it is given as the main tale, so to speak, and the version of the *rromanz* is merely interjected, perhaps as being widely known, but unworthy of credence. The *PCG*, on the other hand, tells the popular story, and interrupts it to give the view of the two prelates on the matter in a very brief way. In other words, the emphasis is reversed, although both sets of compilers were familiar with the two versions (*Latin Sources*, p. 43).

The *Vulgata* follows the *CVR* in many matters of detail,[29] but is quite unlike it in its preference for the more lurid *Romanz* version; indeed, the Toledano is mentioned only once

---

[29] In each of the cases mentioned in note 28, the *Vulgata* agrees with the 'versión vulgar'/*CVR* against MS *E*: Ocampo's edition, fols 273r, 273v-274r, and 274r respectively.

and then for an incidental detail. The *Vulgata* simply tells the *Romanz* version, in terms very similar to those used in the *PCG* (pp. 470a32-471a10 and 471a35-b42); that is to say, it omits entirely the two lengthy parentheses (*PCG*, pp. 471a10-35 and b43-472a5) which summarise the alternative story taken from the Toledano. The one instance in which the Toledano is mentioned occurs as Sancho and García arrive at León. Here the *Vulgata* follows the same procedure as the *CVR*, that is, it gives two alternative versions, one that the King camped outside the walls, one that he remained at Sahagún (see above). The *Vulgata*, however, delays mention of the second version (taken from the Toledano) until a point when its inconsistency with the narrative is plain, namely when García consults Sancho before entering León:

> E el infante don Garçia fablo estonçes con el rey don Sancho. (Pero dize aqui el arçobispo don Rodrigo que quando llego el infante a Sant Facundo dexo y toda su companna con el rey don Sancho de Nauarra e que se fue con unos pocos de los suyos muy encubiertamente.) E el infante don Garçia antes que entrase en la villa fablo con el rey don Sancho . . . (Ocampo, fol. 273r)

It is as though this one demonstrable lack of veracity discovered in the Toledano influenced the compiler of the *Vulgata* to dispense with the Archbishop's version of the actual murder. If this is so, we must give him credit for a degree of confidence and consistency which the compilers of the *PCG* and *CVR*, with their respective preferences for the *Romanz* and the Toledano, did not show.

The *Versión Interpolada* (MS *V*) shows little of the tendency remarked on above (pp. 49-51 and 64) to moralise and purify the motives of characters. Virtually its only additions to the *Vulgata* version just described consist of expansions of dialogue. Whereas doña Sancha, in the *PCG* and other versions discussed, warns the *infante* against going unarmed, 'ca non sabedes quien uos quiere bien nin qui mal' (*PCG*, p. 470b29-30), she introduces this in the *Versión Interpolada* with the words 'Por Dios, Amor, syenpre mirad por vos, que non sabedes . . .' (MS *V*, fol. 227v); the Velas, when they are about to kill the *infante*, say 'Tienpo es de pagar las synrazones que vuestro padre nos fizo' (ibid.); and doña Sancha, again, at the *infante*'s death, throws herself on him with the words 'Sennor mio, ¿que ventura fue la mya que mys ojos vos viesen matar de vuestros enemigos?' (fol. 228r).

All the versions so far discussed[30] are demonstrably attempts to reconcile disparate sources, and as before we must conclude that the relation between them is not so much one of progression as of alternative and possibly contemporaneous versions of materials gathered in the Alphonsine scriptorium.

On the other hand, the *Cr1344*, here as elsewhere, follows closely the 'versión regia' of the *PCG*. This is true as much of the basic arrangement of material as of the detailed divergences listed above as dividing the 'regia' *PCG* on the one hand from all remaining early versions on the other (see p. 74 and note 28). Thus, the *Cr1344* has the detail of Sancho's authorising the *infante*'s entry into León (MS *M*, fol. 168r; MS Q^2, fol. 12r), contains the reflection that the Velas' death was fitting 'a traydores que mataran a su sennor' (MS *M*, fol. 170r; cf. MS Q^2, fol. 13r), and mentions doña Sancha's personal motive in seeking Ferrant Llaynez's death (MS *M*, fol. 175r; cf. MS Q^2, fol. 15v). It does, however, differ from all the versions so far discussed in one important respect concerning the epilogue to the story. It will be remembered that the capture and execution of Ferrant Llaynez in the *PCG* (ch. 789) was demanded by doña Sancha as a precondition to her marriage to King Sancho's son (see above, p. 72). The whole of this unhistorical chapter seems to have been taken from the vernacular *Romanz* (see *PCG*, p. clxiv), and no vengeance is mentioned by the Tudense or Toledano (the *Najerense* merely states that the King executed the murderers, without linking this in any way with doña Sancha: see above, note 23). The vernacular text, however, seems to have referred to a projected marriage with Sancho's *elder* son, García, whose name occurs in all Castilian manuscripts, 'regia' and 'vulgar' of the *PCG* at this point (*PCG*, p. 472a46 variant) as well as in the *CVR* and *Vulgata*.[31] Menéndez Pidal took this to be an error and amended the text, since the historical marriage was between doña Sancha and the king's *younger* son, Fernando (the future Fernando I), and indeed this marriage is later related in ch. 800 of the *PCG*. Of

---

[30] The *Crónica Abreviada* gives insufficient details to allow one to group it with either of the basic families mentioned: see BN, MS 1356, fol. 106v, and cf. the edition by Grismer, p. 140).

[31] *CVR*, MS *N*, fol. 62v; Ocampo, fol. 274r. The *Crónica Abreviada* refers to 'Fernando' (fol. 106v; cf. the edition by Grismer, p. 140), but we cannot know whether this reflects faithfully the lost text being summarised or whether it is a later emendation by the fourteenth-century summariser.

the early chronicles, all follow the unhistorical *Romanz* with the single and significant exception of the Galician *A* MS, supposed to have been a source for the *Cr1344* (*PCG*, p. 472a46 variant; cf. MS *A*, fol. 80r). This latter chronicle takes the emendation a stage further by postponing the execution of Ferrant Llaynez until the marriage between Sancha and Fernando which, as in the *PCG*, follows a number of digressions on Navarrese and Aragonese genealogies and other matters (*PCG*, chs. 790-99). At this point, as in the *PCG*, the marriage is arranged to bring peace between the Castilians and Leonese; and, in the *Cr1344*, it is linked back to the story of the Infante García by the princess's demand that Ferrant Llaynez be brought to justice (*Cr1344*, MS *M*, fols. 174v-175v; cf MS Q^2, fol. 15v). What may have begun as a simple attempt by the scribe of MS *A* to bring the narrative into line with history brought as its conclusion the transposition of an episode which thus becomes isolated in a not altogether satisfactory way.

The *RefTol*, finally, takes characteristic liberties with the story. First, a number of detailed alterations seem to be attempts to explain minor inconsistencies and to bring out the dramatic potential of the story. As an example of the first tendency, we may note that the taking of Monzón by Sancho and García is rationalised by making Fernán Gutiérrez a rebel: 'vn conde alçado en Castilla con ciertas fortalezas . . .' (MS *M*, fol. 184r; cf. MS *S*, fol. 195v).[32] Heightening of pathos is achieved by stressing the *infante*'s youth: 'como el ynfante era ninno e se vido asi con la rrebuelta desanparado e solo, començo de llorar, que non sabia que se fazer' (MS *M*, fol. 186v; the corresponding folio [=197] of MS *S* is missing); and an added note of tragedy is supplied by the fact that the *infante* is specifically warned of the Velas but refuses to believe ill of them on account of their false oath (MS *M*, fol. 185v; MS *S*, fol. 196v).

Second, in organisation of the basic story of the murder, the *RefTol* shows none of the vacillation which is such a feature of the earlier versions and is still to be seen in the *Cr1344*. The *RefTol* takes some features from the versions of the Tudense and Toledano—the murder outside the church, made more horrible by the fact that the *infante* is now dragged from the

---

[32] The author of the *RefTol* also clearly found it unsatisfactory that the *Count* García should be called 'infante', and ascribes this rather unconvincingly to the fact that 'con ynfanta era casado' (MS *M*, fol. 184r; cf. MS *S*, fol. 195r).

sanctuary of the building;[33] from the *Romanz* comes the maltreatment of the *infanta* by Ferrant Llaynez;[34] and the whole is knitted together with what appears to be a certain amount of free invention, as the following extract will show:

> E tomaronlo [el infante] vnas duennas de aquella posada assy desupito para lo esconder e guardar. Pero los traydores que en el carrnaje lo tenian oluidado fueronlo muy afincadamente catar a la su posada onde las duennas con temor lo encomendaron a vn su capellan que lo leuase ocultamente y metyese y çerrase en vna eglesia de Santa Martyn que y era muy çerca... (MS *M*, fol. 186v).

Finally, the epilogue of vengeance, which, as we have seen, was split into two parts in the *Cr1344*, is in *RefTol* reunited but in another and inventive way. No mention is made of any vengeance being exacted on either the Velas or Ferrant Llaynez at the end of the story; but later, as in the *Cr1344*, doña Sancha demands satisfaction as a condition of her marriage, and duly exacts a bloodthirsty vengeance on Ferrant Llaynez (MS *M*, fols 196r-198r; MS *S*, fols 204r-205r). Shortly afterwards, again as in the *PCG* and *Cr1344*, comes King Sancho's death, which in these two chronicles is referred to briefly and in rather enigmatic terms:

> andando ell rey por tierra de Asturias a sabor de si, llego un peon, et matol a traycion (*PCG*, p. 481b13-15; cf. *Cr1344*, MS *M*, fol. 175v, MS Q^2, fol. 15v).

In the *RefTol*, the Velas reappear at this point as the instigators of the King's murder: the 'peón' of the *PCG* becomes a kind of secret agent who worms his way into the King's confidence and finally kills him with a dagger in a way which foreshadows the murder of Sancho II outside Zamora.[36] The *RefTol* therefore shows yet again its tendency not merely to rewrite individual

---

[33] 'E avn el capellan con el ninno non era bien dentro en la eglesia quando aquestos dos traydores maluados Diego Vella e Ynigo Vella eran pos el e lançaronse dentro en la iglesia e tomaron al ynfante e muy cruelmente... E sacaron vn punnal e degollaron alli al ynfante, que ninguna dolor de vmanidat los pudo vençer que lo non matassen' (MS *M*, fol. 186v).

[34] '... el traydor arremetio a ella e diole vna grand punnada en su rrostro, e rrepelole todos sus cabellos e dexola por el suelo mucho ynjuriada e perdida...' (MS *M*, fol. 187r).

[35] This was ascribed to a 'fuente desconocida' by Menéndez Pidal (*PCG*, p. clxv).

[36] *RefTol*, MS *M*, fols 198v-199r, MS *S*, fol. 205r-v. The bizarre end of the story deserves to be quoted: the traitor is tracked down by the royal *monteros* and executed, whereupon 'comianlo las gentes con la rrauia que auian del, que non quedo pelo nin hueso que non fuese comido...' (MS *M*, fol. 199r; cf. MS *S*, fol. 205v).

sections in the interests of verisimilitude and internal cohesion, but also to link together disparate stories by making their characters recur. In this as in other respects it shows itself to belong to a genre more akin to romance than to historiography.[37]

[37] For the importance of recurring and interwoven structural patterns in romance, see E. Vinaver, *Form and Meaning in Medieval Romance* (MHRA Presidential Address, 1966).

Chapter 5
MOCEDADES DEL CID

Fernando I inherited the kingdom of Castile from his father, Sancho *el mayor* in 1035; in 1037 he annexed the kingdom of León on the death of his brother-in-law Vermudo III. This latter event has already been described as signifying a watershed in the organisation of the Alphonsine chronicles and those based on them. The 'Cuarta parte' brings with it a wholly new version, the *Crónica de Castilla*, and at the same time makes us reassess fundamentally the relations between other chronicles.

The period between 1037 and the end of the eleventh century is marked in Alphonsine historiography by an acceptance of popular or legendary material on a scale much larger than before. Without doubt this has much to do with the presence on the historical scene of Rodrigo Diaz de Vivar, otherwise known as 'El Cid' (*c.* 1040-1099). Of the principal texts dealing with this hero's deeds, more later. Let us look first at the reign of Fernando I.

In the *PCG* the young Cid figures only to a moderate extent in the twelve chapters (802-13) dealing with the reign of Fernando. Only in ch. 813, when the dying King divides his realms, do we find the Cid playing a major role. I shall return to this episode in the next chapter. The bulk of the reign of Fernando, in the *PCG*, is based on the histories of the Tudense and Toledano, and the story is straightforward, dealing respectively with Fernando's campaigns against his brother García of Navarra (chs. 803-04), in Portugal (chs 805-07) and in the Moorish Kingdom of Toledo (ch. 808), his foundation of the church of St Isidore in Leon, various works of piety and the collection of relics (chs 809-12 [part]); and, finally, a last campaign against the Moors (remainder of ch. 812). This last episode is taken only in part from the Latin chronicles, and Pidal surmised that it might also owe something to a lost *cantar*.[1]

The same account is found in the one manuscript of the

---

[1] *PCG*, pp. clxvii-clxviii; see also Babbitt, *Latin Sources*, p. 56.

'versión vulgar', MS *F*, which contains the 'cuarta parte'.² Like its predecessors of the 'tercera parte', it presents in places a more concise text: more accurately, MS *E*, the 'versión regia', presents one which is stylistically more amplified.³ The basic contents of these chapters remain, however, the same in both versions. The *Crónica Abreviada* reflects an essentially similar version.⁴ It is also similar in the *CVR*, though with some slight differences, which have been listed by Babbitt (*Latin Sources*, pp. 51-56); these mostly concern the use made of known sources (principally the chronicles of the Tudense and the Toledano as well as the latter's *Historia Arabum*) and are of little concern to us.⁵ The *CVR* does, however, contain one passing reference at the beginning of the section to an epic source: 'avn llamanle [Fernando] en los cantares apar de emperador' (MS. *N*, fol. 71v; MS *J*: 'las cançiones', fol. 48r), which, as we shall see, becomes relevant in the light of other, later chronicles.

These are the *CrC* and the *Cr1344*. Both amplify the reign of Fernando by adding material about the upbringing and youthful deeds of the Cid, and it is reliably supposed that they draw this from a lost epic poem which has been called the *Gesta de las Mocedades de Rodrigo*. This same poem gave rise to a later poetic reworking, the extant *Refundición de las Mocedades de Rodrigo* (otherwise known as the *Crónica Rimada del Cid* or simply as *Mocedades de Rodrigo*). The lost *gesta* and its chronicle prosification have been the subject of an unpublished study by S. G. Armistead, on which I have drawn to some extent in what follows.⁶

    ² See Catalán, *De Alfonso X*, pp. 58 n. 17 and 202 on this point: the 'vulgar' manuscripts of the 'tercera parte' either end at or before the death of Bermudo III (MSS *T*, *Y*, and *Z*) or continue with a version of the *CrC* (MS *G*).
    ³ *PCG*, p. 484a36-40 and variant: when Fernando visits his brother García of Navarre, who plans to capture him, only MS *E* has the note 'entendiolo en los bollicios que uio andar por el palacio . . . et non se detouo y poco nin mucho, e salio libremientre de la villa et fuesse pora su tierra'; cf. MS *F*: 'e el Rey don Fernando sopolo luego e salliose de la villa e fuese para su tierra' (fol. 1v); other examples are in *PCG*, pp. 485b15-31, 487a44-b2, 489a26-30, and cf. MS *F*, fols. 2r, 3r, and 4v respectively. On this point see also Gómez Pérez, 'Elaboración', pp. 242-43.
    ⁴ BN MS 1356, fols 108r-109r; cf. the edition by Grismer, pp. 142-43.
    ⁵ The *PCG* and the *CVR* begin to diverge more seriously at a point corresponding to ch. 813 of the former; this is connected with the epic material about the King's death and the partition of the kingdoms (see ch. 6 below). See Babbitt, *Latin Sources*, pp. 54-55 and Catalán, 'El taller historiográfico alfonsí', pp. 369-73.
    ⁶ Armistead, *La gesta*. Particular aspects are discussed in the same author's 'The Structure of the *Refundición*', 'The Enamored Doña Urraca', and 'An Unnoticed

I have spoken of the *Gesta*'s being prosified in the *CrC* and the *Cr1344*. In fact the position is more complex, in that the group of manuscripts which we call the *CrC* splits at this point into two main families (and one isolated and aberrant manuscript); it is also the case that there exist two versions of the *Cr1344* (the original 1344 redaction and the revised version of *c.* 1400), although the differences between their accounts of Fernando's reign are minimal.

One version of the *CrC* is represented by a group of manuscripts of which MS *G* (Esc. X-I-11) may be taken as typical.[7] The lost *Gesta* supplies the material for eleven chapters and is also reflected in certain alterations made to other chapters whose primary source is the *PCG*. The material is split into five sections which are interwoven with the existing *(PCG)* narrative of Fernando's reign outlined above. First, three chapters *(CrC,* chs 2-4) are inserted at a point after the chapter equivalent to *PCG,* ch. 802. These tell of Rodrigo's lineage; his quarrel with Count Gomez of Gormaz whom he kills; his victory over five Moorish kings; Jimena's complaint against him as her father's murderer and the King's solution that Rodrigo should marry her; and finally, the betrothal and Rodrigo's vow not to marry her until after winning five 'lides en canpo'. There follows a chapter equivalent to ch. 803 of the *PCG,* which in turn leads to the second block of material about Rodrigo, four chapters telling of the agreement to settle the dispute over the possession of Calahorra by a single combat between Rodrigo and the Navarrese champion; the hero's pilgrimage to Santiago in the course of which he is miraculously visited by St Lazarus; the actual dual for Calahorra; and the envious plot against Rodrigo by certain Castilian counts who are sent into exile as a result of it. After the material of *PCG* ch. 804 comes a third episode involving Rodrigo, who conducts a campaign against the Moors in the Duero valley. The narrative then returns to Fernando's deeds until a point part-way through ch. 810 of the *PCG* (= p. 490b49), when a fourth interpolation tells how the Moors

---

Epic Reference'. Deyermond, *Epic Poetry and the Clergy*, which is principally concerned with the extant poem *Mocedades de Rodrigo*, discusses the lost *Gesta*, especially at pp. 12-15.

[7] The others are MSS *P, B, Y,* and *V,* and parts of *Ph, Ch,* and *T*; the *Crónica Particular del Cid*, published in 1512, also belongs to this family. See Catalán, *De Alfonso X,* pp. 325-35.

paid homage to Rodrigo and gave him the title 'Cid'. After the rest of ch. 810 of the *PCG*, the *CrC* contains a further section of two chapters telling a new story of how Rodrigo and Fernando campaigned in France and Italy against the Pope and Emperor and visited the Papal court.

From this one may get a fair idea of the *Gesta*'s probable structure. Armistead saw it as bipartite, its first *cantar* telling of the Cid's vow to Jimena and its fulfillment in a series of campaigns, the second dealing with his Italian and French adventure with Fernando; to this, the account of the Cid's lineage and upbringing would have acted as a prologue.[8] (It is true that there is one major omission in all this, in that the chronicle version now being discussed mentions no actual marriage between Rodrigo and Jimena: see below, p. 86.) It appears probable that the *Gesta* also contained material relating to Rodrigo's part in Fernando's Portuguese and Moorish campaigns: although the main narrative for these follows the *PCG* (and is thus based ultimately on the Tudense and Toledano), the *CrC* interpolates or expands certain references to Rodrigo which may owe their presence to the *Gesta*. In a chapter (= [10] corresponding to ch. 805 of the *PCG*), it is remarked that at the siege of Viseo 'en todo esto fue Rodrigo de Byuar vno de los que y mas fizieron' (MS *G*, fol. 135r), at a point corresponding to p. 486b14 of the *PCG*; four chapters later (corresponding to ch. 807 of the *PCG*), the Cid's part in the capture of Coimbra is stressed. The pilgrimage to Santiago which Fernando makes before attacking the town (cf. *PCG*, pp. 486b53-487a4) is in the *CrC* made at Rodrigo's instance:

[el rrey] fuese para Santiago en rromeria, por consejo de Rodrigo de Biuar, que le dixo que le ayudaria Dios a cobrarla, et demas de torrnada que queria que lo fiziese cauallero et cuydaua rresçebir caualleria dentro en Coynbra (MS *G*, fol. 135r);

and when the town is taken, the reference to the Cid's being knighted there, brief in the *PCG* ('Et en este comedio fizo cauallero a Roy Diaz el Cit Campeador', p. 487a14-15) is expanded in the *CrC*;

Estonçe fizo el rrey don Ferrando cauallero a Rodrigo en Coynbra en la mesquita mayor de la çibdat, a que posieron nonbre Santa Maria. Et

---

[8] Armistead, *La gesta*, pp. 20-59, and 'The Structure of the *Refundición*', pp. 341-42; see also Deyermond, *Epic Poetry and the Clergy*, pp. 12-14, especially p. 13.

fizole cauallero desta guisa, çiniendole el espada, e diol paz en la boca, mas non le dio pescoçada. Et desque Rodrigo fue cauallero, ouo nonbre Ruy Diaz. Et tomo leugo el espada, antel altar estando, et fizo nueueçientos caualleros noueles. Et fizole el rrey mucha de onrra, loandolo mucho el rrey quanto bien fiziera en conqueryr a Coynbra et a los otros lugares (MS *G*, fol. 136r).

Finally, in a chapter (= [17] corresponding to ch. 809 of the *PCG*) dealing with Fernando's conquests in the West and South of the Peninsula, there is an interpolation dealing with Rodrigo's deeds at the siege of Montemayor:

Et Ruy Diaz de Biuar fizo y mucho bien en aquella çerca. Et yendo el aguardar los que yuan por la yerua et por la vianda, ouo tres lides muy grandes que vençio. Et por priesa en que se vio, nunca quiso enbiar pedir acorro al rrey. Et por esto gano muy grant prez. Et fizolo el rrey de su casa de cabo, e diole ende su poder (MS *G*, fols 136v-137r).

Almost all of what has been said about this version of the *CrC* applies equally to the chronicle published by Ocampo, which in the 'cuarta parte' ceases to be an early derivative of the 'versión vulgar', analogous to the *CVR* in some respects (hitherto called the *Vulgata*), and becomes instead a version closely linked with both the *PCG*, 'versión regia', and the *CrC*.[9] At this point it follows the latter closely, only occasionally omitting material (as, for instance, the vow Rodrigo makes to postpone his marriage until he has proved himself in battle, omitted from Ocampo, fol. 281r; this is, however, in some of the manuscript versions of the *Ocampiana*: cf. MS *Q*, fol. 3r).

The other main group of the manuscripts of the *CrC* is characterised by a tendency to concision, even to abbreviation. We may pass quickly by its main representatives, MSS *R* and *D*,[10] which do no more than condense the narrative with a minimal effect on its structure. The same cannot be said of MSS *N*, *U*, and *J* which form a distinctive and anomalous subgroup.[11] Their peculiarity is of a structural nature and involves the displacement of a series of episodes following the making

[9] A succinct description is given by Catalán, *De Alfonso X*, pp. 332-34 and nn. 29-30, summarising Lindley Cintra, *Crónica*, I, ccciv-cccviii. In the chapters which concern us, the reliance on the *CrC* is explained by Lindley Cintra as 'devido á grande quantidade de matéria estranha à *Crónica* real que nele encontrou' (*Crónica*, I, cccv), i.e. the *Mocedades* material.

[10] See Lindley Cintra, *Crónica* I, cccxx n. 7 and Catalán, *De Alfonso X*, pp. 336-39 and nn. 33-35. MS *T* also has some characteristics of this group: see Catalán, ibid., pp. 330-32 n. 26.

[11] Catalán, *De Alfonso X*, pp. 339-40 and n. 43.

of arrangements for the duel for Calahorra (= ch. [6] of MS *G*). MSS *N*, *U*, and *J* pass over the pilgrimage to Santiago, the combat itself and the counts' plot, and go straight to the subject matter of ch. 804 of the *PCG* (Fernando's defeat of García at Atapuerca). In MSS *N* and *U* the missing material comes in later, after the chapter corresponding to ch. 808 of the *PCG*—that is, in the middle of Fernando's Moorish campaigns—and is followed by an account of Rodrigo's marriage to Jimena, omitted in all other versions.[12] MS *J*, however, places the pilgrimage and the duel for Calahorra immediately after the battle of Atapuerca, postponing the episode of the counts to a later point, after the chapter equivalent to ch. 808 of the *PCG* (where it is again followed by an account of Rodrigo's marriage). The narrative in all these manuscripts then continues along the same structural lines as MS *G*, though MSS *N*, *U*, and *J* henceforth follow stylistically the 'concise' family of MSS *R* and *D*.[13]

The one remaining manuscript of the *CrC*, usually regarded as a member of the 'concise' family is MS *S*, which has individual peculiarities. It will be convenient to postpone discussion of these until after describing the other chronicle family which draws on the *Gesta* material.

This is the *Cr1344*. In general it tells the same story as the *CrC*, and like it is usually regarded as having drawn on the lost *Gesta de las Mocedades de Rodrigo*. It follows the arrangement of material which has already been described for MS *G* of the *CrC*, with only minor modifications involving the division of material into chapters.[14] In most of the narrative from

[12] Armistead notes this (*La gesta*, pp. 51 and 292), but regards it as a late addition ('a posterior arrangement of the *CRC* text', p. 51, and 'a repetition in summary of Rodrigo's "esponsales" ', p. 292); elsewhere he states: 'the crucial marriage episode is lacking also in the chronicle's prosification' ('The Structure of the *Refundición*', p. 341), and this is followed by Deyermond (*Epic Poetry and the Clergy*, p. 13). Catalán regards the existence of this episode in the manuscripts in question as 'deducido del contexto de *las Mocedades*' (*De Alfonso X*, p. 341 n. 43).

[13] MS *N*, fols 23r-41v; MS *U*, fols 13r-28r; MS *J*, fols 150v-159v. The chapter on the marriage reads as follows in MS *J*: '. . . el Rey don Ferrando, veyendo que era tienpo que Ruy Dias casase e fiziese bodas con donna Ximena Gomez; e el fuese adereşçar e vino muy honrradamente a la corte con sus parientes e amigos e vasallos e traya delante de sy trezientos cauallos e trezientos pares de armas enfiestas, e el Rey saliole a Reçebir; e fizo sus bodas muy honrradamente e el Rey le fizo muchas mercedes' (fol. 159r-v).

[14] Thus the material corresponding to chs 805-06 of the *PCG* forms a single chapter in the *Cr1344* (= ch. 38 in MS *Q*: MS *M*'s chapters are not numbered). Conversely, ch. 808 of the *PCG* is divided (= chs 40-41 of MS *Q*) and ch. 809 is combined with the first part of ch. 810 to form ch. 42; see MS *Q*, fols 42v-44v.

Rodrigo's victory over the five Moorish kings onwards (the latter part of ch. [2] in MS *G* of the *CrC*) the *Cr1344* seems to represent an independent prosification of the same poetic text or of one essentially similar to that used in the *CrC*.[15] It is at the beginning of Fernando's reign, however, that the *Cr1344*'s peculiarities are of most interest. Let us look first at the original version of that chronicle, represented by MS *M*. The reign of Fernando I opens with two chapters corresponding to ch. 802 of the *PCG*, but whereas in the latter the city and kingdom of León are surrendered to Fernando after a short siege (*PCG*, p. 483a1-15), the same event in *Cr1344* is handled differently. The Queen, Sancha, addresses the citizens of León in the following terms:

'Amigos, bien ssabedes commo sodes todos mis naturales e bien ssabedes commo non a nenguno que de derecho deva eredar el rreyno de Leon sinon yo, pues Dios tovo por bien de levar al rrey don Bermudo mi hermano, que era rrey e ssennor. E mal pecador, el morio con sobervia e con codiçia que fazia al rrey mi sennor e a mi, en tomandonos la tierra que nos, por el e por el rrey don Sancho, fuera otorgada, ansi commo vos todos ssabedes. E por esto vos vengo yo a rrogar que tengades por bien de dar el rreyno al rrey don Fernando mi ssennor e a mi. E faredes derecho e lo que devedes. E el rrey don Fernando e yo faremos vos por ello bien e merçed' (MS *M*, fol. 196v).

and this is followed by an account of a solemn council in which the citizens agree to acknowledge Fernando and Sancha as monarchs. A further detail is that García of Navarra is said to have accompanied his brother to León. At the end of this chapter and the beginning of the next, the name of Rodrigo Diaz appears, but it is not, as in the *CrC*, as the descendant of Layn Calvo. Rather, the *Cr1344* gives an extended account of how Fernando was passing through Bivar, found the ten-year-old Rodrigo and took him to his court to be brought up in his own household: there, we are told, he formed a special friendship with doña Urraca, to the extent that: '[ella] amaualo màs que a nenguno de sus hermanos' (MS *M*, fol. 198r).[16] The

---

[15] Details of the differences are given in Armistead, *La Gesta*, pp. 196-227 and 304-06.

[16] Armistead, discussing this point in 'The Enamored Doña Urraca', points out that this reference and the following sentence ('E non entendades que este amor que le ansi auia que era por nenguna otra manera que y ouiesse, nin de cuydo nin de fecho'; cf. MS *Q*: 'et non entendades que este amor que ansi auian fuese por alguna villania', fol. 29r [not fol. 129, as Armistead mistakenly cites]) — may reflect 'some inference of scandal originating in popular epic poetry' (p. 28). Cf. Sponsler, *Women*, p. 25.

narrative then continues with Rodrigo's victory over five Moorish kings; and this in turn is followed by doña Jimena's complaint against the Cid for her father's murder, and the marriage is duly arranged. This version, though it omits mention of Rodrigo's vow (fol. 198 bis r), then continues along the same general lines as the *CrC*.

It will be noticed that the *Cr1344* has another more substantial omission, in that although the sequence of events just summarised rests on Rodrigo's killing Jimena's father, that event is not explicitly included, as it is in the *CrC*. Armistead explained this as being due to a simple compilatory oversight: that in choosing to omit the material about Rodrigo's lineage (part of which had already figured in the *Cr1344* in the reign of Fruela II), the compilers inadvertently left out the immediately following episode too, namely the quarrel between Rodrigo and Count Gomez and the latter's death.[17]

The second version of the *Cr1344*, represented by MS Q, tends to expand the narrative; often this is merely stylistic, as when a reference to Rodrigo's mother is accompanied by her name 'Teresa Nunnez' and the comment 'que aun era biua' (MS Q^2, fol. 29r); sometimes the differences are of detail, involving in one case the rectification of an omission, in that MS Q does have the detail of the Cid's vow:

et fizo juramento que nunca se veria con ella en yermo nin en poblado fasta que vençiese çinco lides en canpo (MS Q^2, fol. 29v).

Finally, we may return to MS S of the *CrC*. This is normally regarded as a member of the 'concise' family,[18] and from halfway through its third chapter (corresponding to ch. 2 of MS G) it follows this family, whose structural features have been outlined above. The first two and a half chapters, however, are very different. The first tells the story of Fernando's victory over Bermudo (= ch. 801 of the *PCG*), which falls in the 'tercera parte' and does not figure in other *CrC* manuscripts, and the second is broadly similar to the first chapter of MS G (telling of Fernando's accession, qualities, and progeny). The third, instead of describing the Cid's family, tells how he was brought up at Fernando's court, and only after this—and without mentioning the death of Count Gomez de Gormaz—does

[17] Armistead, *La Gesta*, p. 198.
[18] Catalán, *De Alfonso X*, pp. 338-39 and nn. 38-39.

it rejoin the *CrC* narrative. In short, it borrows material either from the *Cr1344* or from the same poetic text as was used by that chronicle.[19] Catalán sums up:

'Indudablemente, el ms. *S* rectocó una *Crónica de Castilla*, muy análoga a *RD* . . ., con la refundición de la *Crónica de 1344* de hacia 1400 para formar una Crónica cidiana lo más completa posible' (*De Alfonso X*, p. 339 note 39).

The relationships between some of the versions discussed are comparatively easy to envisage; the mixed parentage of MS *S* of the *CrC* has just been described, and the nature of MS *Q* of the *Cr1344* is here, as it is generally, explained quite adequately in terms of its being a revision of the 'first draft' of the chronicle dating back to 1344 and represented by MS *M*.[20] As for the basic divergences between the versions found in the *CrC* and the *Cr1344*, these could reflect either a difference of sources or a conscious act of critical judgement on the part of the compilers of the former chronicle. In short, we have no positive way of knowing whether these were unaware of the material used in the *Cr1344* dealing first with the surrender of León to Fernando and Sancha, and second with the upbringing of Rodrigo in the royal household; or whether they knew of it and rejected it in favour of other sources. Were it only a question of the surrender of León, one might hold with the former explanation. After all, this episode, with no Cidian connections, probably formed part of a separate epic poem, the *Cantar del rey don Fernando*,[21] whose existence is amply demonstrated by the presence in chronicles of legendary accounts of

[19] See Cintra, *Crónica*, I, ccxlviii. An alternative explanation which Armistead originally put forward was that the *Cr1344* drew the material from 'a more complete MS of the *Crónica de Castilla* than any now known to us' ('The Enamored Doña Urraca', p. 27 note 6; see also *La Gesta*, pp. 252-56). He appears now to have changed his opinion and to accept that of Cintra (*Crónica*, I, ccxlviii); see Catalán, *De Alfonso X*, p. 339 note 39.

[20] See Cintra, *Crónica*, I, xxix-xl and Catalán and Andrés, *Cr1344*, pp. xvi-xvii. The differences in content and structure overwhelmingly concern the earliest parts of the chronicle (up to the accession of Ramiro I, = ch. 628 of the *PCG*) and in the sections which concern us they are almost entirely limited to stylistic points.

[21] Deyermond refers to the probability that 'although as time went on legends of Rodrigo's youth became almost inextricably entangled with those of Fernando I's exploits, it is by no means clear that they were linked from the beginning' (*Epic Poetry and the Clergy*, p. 10); see also Pidal, *Reliquias*, pp. lxiv-lxviii, where he seems at some points to link this poem with the *Gesta de las Mocedades* and at others to treat them separately. Catalán seems also to regard the poem on Fernando as having more to do with the fratricidal wars which followed than with the deeds of the young Cid ('El taller historiográfico alfonsí', p. 371 n. 1).

the King's death (see below, ch. 6; and compare the *CVR*'s reference to Fernando as 'apar de enperador', cited on p. 82 above), and one could speculate that this poem was used in the *Cr1344* but not in the *CrC*. This is, however, contradicted by the fact that the latter chronicle did apparently draw on the *Cantar del rey don Fernando* for the episode of the King's death and partition of the kingdoms;[22] and the fact that the innovations found in the *Cr1344* include passages on the upbringing of Rodrigo which can reasonably be supposed to come from the lost *Gesta de las mocedades* confirms one's supposition that the two chronicles do represent different treatments of fundamentally similar sources.

The reasons for the more cursory approach of the *CrC* are hard to guess: it might be that the poetic account of Fernando's accession to the Leonese throne laid too heavy a stress on his wife's rôle; it might be that the theme of Rodrigo's upbringing in Fernando's household aroused unsuitable echoes of the supposed illicit passion between the Cid and Urraca which, we have seen, appears to have troubled those chroniclers who did use this episode (see above, p. 87 and note 16). But this is and can only be speculation, and at least in the first case a simpler explanation might be that the compilers of the *CrC* were faced with a contradiction between the poetic source and one based, via the *PCG*, on the Latin chronicles, and resolved it in favour of the latter.

Finally, there is the case of the aberrant manuscripts of the *CrC*, *N*, *U*, and *J* and their rearrangement of part of the material relating to the young Rodrigo's deeds. That they alone insert an account of his marriage is not in itself surprising, forming as it does such an integral part of the story (and, presumably, of the lost *Gesta*); as for the displacement of other material, Catalán's remark that these manuscripts change sources at this point may explain the confusion which characterises them.[23]

We are dealing, therefore, with epic material whose treatment is relatively less complex than that which we have seen in the 'tercera parte'. Either the chronicles do not draw on epic

---

[22] See below, pp. 94-95.

[23] Catalán points out that these manuscripts appear to follow the full version (MSS *G*, *P*, *B*, *Y*, etc.) for the first six chapters, but switch to the abbreviated one after the lacuna (*De Alfonso X*, p. 341 n. 43).

material for the early stages of the Cid's life—the *PCG* and the *CVR*—or they do so, albeit with some slight differences of treatment, as is the case with the various versions of the *CrC* and the *Cr1344*. But there are no grounds for believing that the different prose versions we have represent different redactions of the verse legend. That legend was an epic poem which, though almost entirely unhistorical,[24] did not actually conflict with more reputable sources and could therefore be combined with them with a minimum of difficulty.[25]

[24] Deyermond, *Epic Poetry and the Clergy*, p. 14.
[25] I have chosen not to analyse here the later versions such as García de Salazar's *Libro de las bienandanzas*, Rodríguez de Almela's *Compendio historial*, and the *RefTol*. For the first two, see S. G. Armistead, *A lost version of the 'Cantar de gesta de las Mocedades de Rodrigo' in the Second Redaction of Rodríguez de Almela's 'Compendio historial'*, UCPMP 38 (Berkeley and Los Angeles, 1963), pp. 299-333, and *La Gesta*, pp. 26, 48, and 332-53; the characteristics of the *RefTol* described above in chs 1-4 are found extensively in the 'cuarta parte'.

Chapter 6

THE DEATH OF FERNANDO I AND THE FRATRICIDAL WARS

(a) The Death of Fernando I

With the death of Fernando, his division of his realms and the ensuing civil wars, we enter yet another phase of chronicle interrelationship. It is clear from a comparison of the texts of all the principal vernacular texts with each another and with the Latin historians (Tudense and Toledano) that popular sources were again used, albeit in different ways, by the various chronicles in the vernacular. Let us consider first the death of Fernando and his division of the kingdoms among his children. The chronicle versions here fall into four groups: one represented by the *PCG* and the *Crónica Abreviada*, one by the *CVR*, one by the *CrC* and the *Ocampiana* and the last by the *Cr1344* (together with its descendant the *RefTol*).

The relationship between the first two of these groups was examined by Babbitt, both in *Latin Sources* (pp. 57-63) and in 'Observations', pp. 206-07; without repeating his conclusions in detail, it may be remarked that these two versions, the *PCG* and the *CVR*, represent respectively the minimum and the maximum departure from the Latin sources, the Tudense and Toledano. These latter are followed closely by the *PCG*, whereas the *CVR* departs considerably from them to interpolate material which is apparently based on a popular source. In the *PCG*, the account of Fernando's death and the division of the kingdoms is short. The sequence of events is as follows: the apparition of St Isidore to the King (*PCG*, p. 493b12-20); the King's decision to divide his realms (not said to have been made at any particular place) and details of the division (pp. 493b27-494a3); Sancho's complaint at not inheriting the whole kingdom (p. 494a4-19); the King's move to León (p. 494a19-34) where the Cid appears and the King commends him to the *infantes* and makes them swear to accept the settlement (which all do but Sancho) (p. 494a34-50); and the King's final preparation for his death, followed by the death itself (p. 494a50-b26).

All but two elements of this story appear to derive from the Toledano: these are the complaint by Sancho and the sequence of events involving the Cid and the oath which the *infantes* are asked to swear, both of which appear to derive from popular sources.[1] The *Crónica Abreviada* reflects a version essentially similar to this; in particular, both the details just noted are present, though the second only in a highly compressed form.[2]

On problem about this account is its chronology, in that the apparent source, the Toledano (and likewise the Tudense), refer to Fernando's division of his realms as taking place some time before his death.[3] The way in which the division and the death are linked, the two interpolations, involving dialogue and prophecies of disaster, and other references to be discussed below, all lead to the conclusion that the compilers of the *PCG* did have a popular source at their disposal but that they rejected most of its features in favour of the version deriving from the Latin chronicles.

The *Crónica de Castilla* and that published by Ocampo are fundamentally similar to the *PCG* in this section, but they contain further slight but noticeable elaborations of the narrative. These take three forms: near the beginning of the story, at a point corresponding to *PCG*, p. 493b37 ('Temiendo que despues de su muerte que aurie contienda et pelea entre sus fijos, partioles el regno . . .'), the *CrC* and the *Ocampiana* insert the prophetic remark:

---

[1] See *PCG*, p. clxviii, and cf. Babbitt, *Latin Sources*, pp. 57-60. Chalon, while agreeing with Menéndez Pidal about the epic nature of these points, is generally at pains to minimise the importance of popular material in the *PCG*'s treatment of this episode: see *L'Histoire et l'épopée*, pp. 354-55.

[2] 'Mas el ynfante don Sancho, que era el mayor, non consintio en esta particion, ca tenie que todos los rregnos avien a ser suyos, pues el era el mayor. . . .' 'E fiso llamar todos sus fijos, e Rogoles que quisiesen estar por aquella particion quel avia fecho. E todos otorgarongelo; e que quisiesen creer el Cid Rroy Diaz de lo que les consejase . . .' (MS BN 1356, fol. 110r; compare the edition by Grismer, p. 144; compare also *PCG*, p. 494a4-19 and 34-50.

[3] In the Toledano, the division comes in ch. 11 of book VI (p. 126) and is followed by Fernando's campaigns against Toledo and his acquisition of certain relics (cf. *PCG*, chs 808-11); his death then follows in ch. 13 (p. 128) accompanied by no further mention either of his children or of the division of the kingdoms; the *Najerense* is essentially similar (pp. 107-09). As for the Tudense, the division of the kingdoms in that work also precedes the campaign against Toledo and the King's charitable works (cf. *PCG*, ch. 812); once again, no mention is made of Fernando's children or of their inheritance at the time of his death (pp. 96-97).

THE DEATH OF FERNANDO I   95

Mas esto que el asmo, fazialo el por bien, mas fue lo peor, porque nasçio ende grant dapno et grant mal; ca mejor fuera que los ouiera dexado al fijo mayor (CrC, MS G, fol. 140r; cf. Ocampo, fol. 288r);[4] second, after Sancho's refusal to confirm his father's decision (PCG, p. 494a16-17), these two versions insert another prophetic statement:

E a muchos del regno peso de la partiçion e a muchos plugo; mas todavia los del buen entendimiento sienpre entendieron el mal que ende avia de nasçer al cabo, asy como despues nasçio: que vino ende mucho mal (CrC MS G fol. 140v; cf. Ocampo, fol. 288v).[5]

These slight innovations may easily be explained as a new chronicler's attempt to give greater internal cohesion to his narrative by the familiar device of referring in a prophetic way to what is to come. The same cannot be said of the third innovation, which links to the minor role played by the Cid at Fernando's deathbed (PCG, p. 494a34 ff.) one Abbot or Cardinal Fernando, i.e. the supposed illegitimate son of the King, whose birth resulted from the French campaigns referred to in the last chapter. In the CrC and the Ocampiana, Fernando shares the Cid's role, in that the latter is instructed to advise the King's sons (cf. PCG, p. 494a35-37 and ff.), but:

Llamo al Cardenal don Ferrando su fijo e acomendole a Espanna (CrC, MS G, fol. 140v; cf. Ocampo, fol. 288v).[6]

This apparently gratuitous introduction of a character new to this episode can best be explained if one sees it as reflecting the popular source which to a greater or lesser degree lies behind all these versions.[7]

We may come now to the CVR.[8] In this chronicle we find a full awareness of the discrepancies between the historical and popular versions, with only a half-hearted attempt to

---

[4] CrC, MSS J (fol. 167r), N (fol. 44v), and S (fol. 14r) are similar in content, though there are slight differences in their wording.
[5] Cf. MSS J (fol. 168r), N (fol. 45r-v), and S (fol. 14r).
[6] Cf. MSS J (fol. 168v), N (fol. 46r), and S (fol. 14r-v).
[7] For minor differences between the CrC and the Ocampiana in this section, most notably in the portions assigned to the infantas Urraca and Elvira, see Chalon, L'Histoire et l'épopée, pp. 356 and 362.
[8] The relevant section of the CVR is reproduced in Menéndez Pidal, Reliquias, pp. 240-56. This is based on MS J, with variants of MSS L and N. As elsewhere in this study, I have preferred to quote from MS N, but cross-references to Menéndez Pidal's edition are also given. On the CVR version, see also Gómez Pérez, 'La EE alfonsí', pp. 502-03.

reconcile them. The account begins in a way broadly reminiscent of the *PCG* version, but with a greater precision about places: the apparition of St Isidore is at Valencia (*Reliquias*, p. 240. 4), the King then moves to León (ibid., pp. 240. 6-241. 1) and the account of his prayers there (*PCG*, pp. 494a23-34 and 494b5-7, i.e. after the partition) is anticipated (*Reliquias*, p. 241. 1-16); the *CVR* thus gives the gist of the *PCG* (i.e. Toledano/Tudense) version, adding more detail of place but omitting the actual partition of the kingdoms. There then follows an account of the partition based on popular sources whose veracity the compilers explicitly take leave to doubt. After explaining that it took place at Cabezón and beginning the story with the King's attempt to get from his sons a blanket approval of his plan before revealing its details, the *CVR* inserts a parenthesis which casts doubt on the existence of one of the principal characters:

Algunos dizen en sus cantares que auie el Rey don Ferrando un fijo de ganançia que era Cardenal en Roma, e Legado de toda Espanna, e Abat de Sant Fagunde, e Arçobispo de Santiago, e Prior de Monte Aragon . . . e avia nonbre don Ferrando. Mas esto non lo fallamos en las estorias de los maestros que las escrituras conpusieron, e por ende tenemos que non fue verdad; ca ssiquier non es derecho que vn omne tantas dignidades ouiesse (*CVR*, MS *N*, fols 81v-82r; cf. *Reliquias*, pp. 242. 13-243. 1).

The division of the kingdoms follows, but concerns only the three sons; the scene also contains the King's views on the qualities of his various subjects, generally praiseworthy but with reservations about the Portuguese (*Reliquias*, p. 243. 7-23). This is followed by another, more comprehensive, disavowal of the story being told:

Dize aqui el Arçobispo don Rodrigo de Toledo, e don Lucas de Tuy, e Pero Marcos, Cardenal de Santiago que en su salud, antes que enfermasse el Rey don Ferrando nin fuese a tierra de Çeltiberia e a Valençia assi como dixiemos, que fizo el sus cortes en Leon e que estonçes partio los Regnos a los fijos, e que dio y a donna Vrraca su fija a Çamora con la meytad del Infantadgo, e a donna Eluira la otra fija Toro con la otra meatad del Infantadgo con todos los monesterios que el y ffiziera. E que las Rogo e castigo que ssienpre en toda su vida honrrassen aquellos logares e mantouiessen castidad fasta en su muerte. E como quier que esta ssea la verdad que estos honrrados onbres dizen, fallamos en otros logares e en el Cantar que dizen del Rey don Ferrando que en Castiel de Cabeçon, yaziendo el doliente, partio los Regnos asi como dixiemos, e non dio estonçes nada a donna Vrraca su fija synon despues: e esto adelante vos lo diremos mas conplidamente (*CVR*, MS *N*, fol. 82v; cf. *Reliquias*, p. 243. 23-34).

This story follows. It tells how the Cardinal don Fernando and the Cid arrive, and the former asks why Urraca has been left out of the distribution of lands (the answer is that no one thought to remind the King about her); Urraca, summoned by Arias Gonzalo, then arrives and complains, supported by the Cid.[9] The latter suggests taking lands from all three brothers, but only Alfonso voluntarily surrenders part of his share, thereby winning his father's blessing. As soon as Zamora is settled on Urraca, Arias Gonzalo gives orders for its fortification. Next, another claimant appears in the person of don Nuño Ferrandez, the King's nephew, who, by dint of knocking down Sancho, wins from him the promise of the Kingdom of Navarre; the chronicler concludes sceptically, 'Mas esto todo non ssemeja palabra de creer' (MS *N*, fol. 87r; cf. *Reliquias*, p. 254.18).[10] Finally, the *CVR* returns to the King's death bed, his sons swearing to uphold the division of the kingdoms, and his death;[11] this is followed by a prophetic lament from Arias Gonzalo:

'Sennor, non lloro yo por vos, mas por nos mesquinos que fincamos desaconsejados, ca vos quanto quisistes fazer, todo lo acabastes, e moristes agora muy honrradamente. E, ssennor, bien sse yo que la guerra que vos soliedes dar a moros, que se tornara agora sobre nos, e matarnos hemos parientes con parientes, e assi seremos todos astragados, los mesquinos de Espanna' (*CVR*, MS *N*, fol. 87v; cf. *Reliquias*, p. 256. 7-11).

A final attempt to put together a composite version of the account deriving from the Toledano and Tudense and that from the *Cantar* is represented by the *Cr1344*.[12] This is less successful

[9] There is an interesting hint at this point that in epic tradition this was one of the origins of the enmity between the Cid and the Count García Ordóñez (and the 'bando de Carrión'): 'El conde don Garçia de Cabra, quando vio que el Çid los maltraye assi, dixole que fazie muy ssin guisa en traer mal a tanto buen fidalgo como alli era ayuntado. El Çid dixole que ssi le pesaua mucho por aquello, que non darie nada por ende. Ally sse levantaron luego los vandos, los vnos llamauan Biuar, los otros a los condes de Carrion' (*CVR*, MS *N*, fol. 84v; cf. *Reliquias*, pp. 248. 15-249. 2).

[10] The sequence of scenes outlined may be consulted in *Reliquias*, pp. 254-55. It is hard to agree with Gómez Pérez that the account is 'un relato armónico, bien construido con arreglo a todas las fuentes históricas y épicas disponibles' ('La *EE* alfonsí', p. 502).

[11] Babbitt thought the chronicler had erred in not having the King return to León to die (*Latin Sources*, p. 62); the epic may have placed the death at Cabezón. At all events, the text is unambiguous, in that the King's body is taken to León after his death (*Reliquias*, p. 256. 13).

[12] Lindley Cintra's view was that the *Cr1344* represented at this point a combination of the *CrC*—which the *Cr1344* regularly uses at the beginning of the 'cuarta

even than the *CVR*, consisting as it does of a simple juxtaposition of the two versions. Thus, it begins with the version found in the *CrC* and ●campo, containing the first two points cited above as distinguishing these two chronicles from the *PCG*: the averral that it would have been better had Fernando not divided his kingdoms and the remark that the wisest men in the realm foresaw disaster.[13] These points apart, the first part of this account is essentially parallel to that found in the *PCG* (pp. 493b11-494a17) and thus contains the division of the kingdoms among all Fernando's children, sons and daughters. However, when the scene shifts to Cabezón and the Cardinal don Fernando and the Cid appear, the *Cr1344* begins to follow a version similar to that in the *CVR* described above. These are minor differences: donna Elvira as well as donna Urraca is said to arrive to claim her share, though she takes no part in the subsequent scenes (*Reliquias*, p. 245.3-4; cf. MSS Q^2, fol. 50r and *M*, fol. 211v);[14] the *CVR*'s remark on the implausibility of the scene involving Nuño Ferrandez ('Mas esto todo non ssemeja palabra de creer') is expanded in MS Q^2 (though not in MS *M*: fol. 215r) as follows:

Mas algunos dizen en este lugar que estas palabras non suenan bien nin han semejança de ser creydas, ca otros hermanos avia y, e este don Nunno Ferrando despues duro poco (MS Q^2, fol. 52v; cf. MS *S*, fol. 21r, and *Reliquias*, p. 255.4 and variant);

and, finally, Arias Gonzalo's prophetic lament is missing, its place perhaps being taken by a more rhetorical if less dramatically effective death-bed speech from the King on the virtues he hopes his sons will show.[15]

parte'—and the *CVR*, from which the compilers took the central death-bed scene at Cabezón (*Crónica*, I, ccxciv-ccxcviii); compare Chalon, *L'Histoire et l'épopée*, p. 362.

[13] A version of this section of the *Cr1344*, based on MS *M* (with variants of MSS *Q* and *U*) was published by Menéndez Pidal in *Reliquias*, pp. 240-56. The first passage in question is very similar in both versions of the *Cr1344* to the *CrC* version quoted above (p. 95): cf. *Reliquias*, pp. 240.6-241.1 and MS *Q*, fol. 49r. The same is true of the second in MS *M* (*Reliquias*, p. 241.18-20), but MSS *Q*, *U*, and *S* expand as follows: '. . . e a los que tan bien non lo entendian non les pesaua, mas antes auian por bien todo lo que el rey auia fecho' (ibid., variant, and MS *S*, fol. 19r).

[14] See Lindley Cintra, *Crónica*, I, ccxcv.

[15] 'Por eso rruego a cada uno de vos, mis fijos, que fagades a vuestros cavalleros e a los onbres buenos e a los vuestros fidalgos de las vuestras tierras e a los otros de cada vuestros rreynos merçedes e ayudas quando vos lo fueren a demandar. [Ca non conuiene a los reyes seer avarientos.] E esso mesmo a los pueblos de las vuestras

The unsatisfactory nature of this composite version, of course, resides in the fact that the division of the kingdoms which is described—the *PCG/CrC*/Ocampo version, deriving ultimately from the Tudense and Toledano—includes the grant of lands to the two *infantas*, while the subsequent death-bed scene at Cabezón—deriving from the *cantar* or from the *CVR* —hinges on the fact that they were excluded from the division.[16]

The four groups of chronicles referred to at the start of this chapter may, then, for this section of it, be reduced to two: those which fundamentally accept the story told by the Tudense and Toledano—*PCG, Crónica Abreviada, CrC*, Ocampo—though showing an awareness of the popular version and indeed incorporating some of its minor details; and those —*CVR, Cr1344* and its derivative—which, with varying degrees of scepticism and competence, attempt to incorporate both versions into a single narrative.

What can one deduce from this about the relationships of the chronicles? Babbitt was at pains to point out that this unusual case of the *CVR* containing a more developed version of a story than the *PCG* did not invalidate his general thesis of the former being the earlier chronicle. As he points out, there is ample evidence that the compilers of the *PCG* knew a version based on popular sources, some of whose details they incorporated (see above, p. 94). What is more, references are found at later points in the *PCG* to elements of the popular story

villas e çibdades de cada uno de vos, ca todos me servieron muy bien e me ayudaron a ganar muchas villas e muchos castillos a cada uno de vos, en los rreynos que a vosotros fincan. [Sed sisudos, tenperados, muy sofridos e esforçados en las batallas, e muy francos en partir vuestro aver, e sed mesurados, de buena palabra e bien resçebientes. Onrrat los estrangeros, set muy verdaderos, castos e tenprados e fieles catolicos, fijos obedientes a la Santa Fee de nuestro sennor Ihesu Christo. Defendet sienpre bien vuestros Regnos a los moros, e tomaldes de los suyos. E amadvos todos tres e avet paz e concordia.]' (*Reliquias*, p. 255 and variant, and MSS Q^2, fol. 52v; cf. MSS M, fol. 215r and S, fol. 21v; the sections within square brackets are peculiar to the amplified version represented by MSS Q, U, and S.

[16] The *RefTol* (MS M, fols 226r-233r) has an account essentially similar to that of the *Cr1344*. There are no narrative embellishments comparable to those generally found in this version in the 'tercera parte' (see chs 1-4 above). Some minor peculiarities are: an explanation of the Cardinal Fernando's relationship to the King (fol. 227r); a remark that his father was pleased to see him 'porque le nunca oviera visto' (ibid.); and the King's remark that he has given too much to Sancho (ibid.). On the other hand, the *RefTol* tends, as usual, to omit cross-references to other parts of the chronicle, especially anticipatory ones: so there is no remark to the effect that all the King's sons save Alfonso were to break their oath (fol. 230r); and no scepticism is expressed about the intervention of Nuño Ferrando (fol. 232r).

(the division being made at Cabezón, Arias Gonzalo's lament) which do not in fact form part of the *PCG* narrative.[17] This faulty cross-referencing is stated by Babbitt to establish the fact that:

> ... the compilers of the *PCG* were working from a source which contained the *Cantar del rey Fernando* in prose form, and that, for some reason they omitted the details of the death-scene from their text, but, on coming upon the subsequent references to the prophecy of Arias Gonzalo and to Cabezón, they carelessly failed to delete them. Moreover, it seems quite probable that the compilation containing the poem was the same as that used by the authors of the *CVR*, or one very similar to it (*Latin Sources*, p. 61).

The nature of such a compilation or *borrador* can only be a subject of speculation. It is remarkable, though, that the authors of the *PCG* should have made such a poor job of reconciling their disparate sources, and it seems likely, as Catalán has pointed out, that at this point no final draft of the Alphonsine *Estoria de Espanna* was ever completed, MS *E* being only a late attempt to fill the gap. The *CVR*, on the other hand, is, in Catalán's words, the only text which,

> compilatoriamente acabada, superó la dificultad, armonizando lo armonizable y contraponiendo lo que era contradictorio en una y otra versión (con la advertencia de que sólo la de los historiadores era digna de crédito; pero sin omitir la juglaresca, por ser mucho más rica en detalles).[18]

As for the *CrC* and the *Ocampiana* (the latter almost certainly deriving from the former where the reign of Fernando I is concerned),[19] these may represent a reworking of the Alphonsine *borrador*. This was Lindley Cintra's view:

> Comparada com a *Primeira Crónica Geral*, a *Crónica de Castela* é, até à morte de Afonso VI, um resumo interpolado do rascunho original de que derivam ambas versões daquela obra [i.e. *regia* and *vulgar*] (*Crónica*, I, ccxlv).

[17] See *PCG*, pp. 497a22-27, 497b40-47, and 499b41-44 (cf. MS *F*, fols. 11r, 11v, and 13r), also quoted by Babbitt, *Latin Sources*, p. 61, and 'Observations', pp. 206-07 n. 19. The same passages are mentioned by Catalán, 'El taller historiográfico alfonsí', pp. 372 and nn. 3-7 and 373 and n. 1, together with others which are rather less conclusive.
[18] 'El taller historiográfico alfonsí', pp. 371-72; see pp. 369-73 for an analysis of the whole problem.
[19] For the relationship between the *CrC* and the *Ocampiana*, see Lindley Cintra, *Crónica*, I, ccciii-cccviii; on this point he specifies: 'Se transcreveu na íntegra o reinado de Fernando I da *Crónica de Castela*, foi devido á grande quantidade de matéria estranha à Crónica real que nele encontrou' (p. cccv); cf. Catalán, *De Alfonso X*, p. 334 n. 30.

The later *Cr1344*, in seeking to reconcile the same disparate elements which presented such problems to the compilers of the *CVR* (and, indeed, to those of the original *borrador*), represents the most ambitious—and at the same time least successful—attempt at this reconciliation.

(b) The Fratricidal Wars

With the reign of Sancho II and the fratricidal struggle that occupied so much of it, the chronicles again have recourse to popular sources, and again with varied results. The *PCG* does not here show signs of the organisational defects which were a feature of its treatment of the end of the previous reign, and it is reasonable to assume that the Alphonsine *borrador* reached a more advanced stage in this section; the compilers' task was also eased by the absence of irreconcilable contradictions between the Tudense and Toledano and the supposed legendary source—the so-called *Cantar del Rey don Sancho* or *de Sancho II*. Only on a detail of chronology—the length of the siege of Zamora, said in the *Cantar* to have lasted seven years and thus irreconcilable with the chronology adopted from the Latin histories, whereby Sancho reigned only six years in all—is there serious contradiction, which the compilers of the *PCG* simply state only to leave unresolved.[20]

Of the *Cantar* itself little need be said here. It is a subject that has been extensively studied, to a far greater extent than is the case with the majority of the other lost epic poems discussed in the five preceding chapters. As a result of the work first of Puyol y Alonso and later of Carola Reig, we have a reasonable if in places hypothetical knowledge of its content and arrangement (indeed a certain proportion has been reconstructed from chronicle texts), and it would be idle to summarise this work here.[21]

[20] 'et dizen en los cantares de las gestas que la touo cercada VII annos: mas esto non pudo ser, ca non regno el mas de VI annos segund que lo fallamos escripto en las cronicas et en los libros de las estorias desto, et en estos VI annos fizo el todo lo que auemos ya contado dell' (*PCG*, p. 509a37-43; cf MS *F*, fol. 20v. There is a detailed discussion of the whole question in Chalon, *L'Histoire et l'épopée*, pp. 279-336.

[21] See J. Puyol y Alonso, *Cantar de Gesta de don Sancho II de Castilla* (Madrid, 1911), Reig, *Sancho II*, and Fraker, 'Sancho II: Epic and Chronicle'; on points of detail see also Horrent, 'Santa Gadea', Menéndez Pidal, 'Relatos poéticos', pp. 344-50, and von Richthofen, *Estudios épicos*, pp. 130-34. See also Deyermond and Chaplin, 'Folk-Motifs', pp. 44-46 and 48-49.

In the *PCG*, the reign of Sancho II occupies 31 chapters, from 814 to 844, and to these we may add the following one recounting the accession of Alfonso VI and his oath of non-complicity in his brother's murder. Leaving aside certain linking chapters (814, 817, 828-29) which follow the course of Sancho's ambition and are broadly based on the Toledano, we may distinguish six main blocks of narrative material:

1. Sancho's campaigns in Eastern Spain, against the ruler of Zaragoza and the King of Aragón (chs 815-16);
2. His campaign against his brother García (chs 818-23);
3. That against Alfonso (chs 824-25);
4. Alfonso's exile in Toledo and subsequent return (chs 826-27 and 840);
5. The siege of Zamora, culminating in Sancho's murder (chs 830-38);
6. The subsequent challenge and duels, followed by Alfonso's accession and the oath at Santa Gadea (chs 839 and 841-45).

Generally speaking, the third and fourth of these elements—those involving Alfonso—appear to be based on the Toledano and Tudense, though with the inclusion of some material taken from the *Cantar* and from the *Historia Roderici*,[22] while the first section (Sancho's Eastern campaigns) is of unknown source;[23] the remainder—wars against García, the siege of Zamora and its aftermath—seems to be based on the *Cantar*, though, again, with details taken from elsewhere.[24] The linking of events is straightforward and the chronology, apart from the detail noted above, offers no problems. Only occasionally do the compilers show signs of difficulty in reconciling their various sources, most notably in the chapter (840) dealing with Alfonso's return from Toledo, where the Toledano and Tudense tell different stories.[25]

[22] See *PCG*, pp. clxix-clxx and clxxi, under chs 826-27 and 840.
[23] See *PCG*, p. clxviii, under chs 815-16.
[24] See *PCG*, pp. clxix-clxxii, under chs 818-25, 830-39, and 841-45.
[25] See *PCG*, ch. 840 passim. The fundamental contradiction between the Latin sources is that the Tudense says that Almemón did not know of Sancho's death, the Toledano that he did know, or at least suspected it; similarly, the Tudense tells a story of Alfonso's secret departure from Toledo, while the Toledano says that he left openly and on good terms with Almemón. See Chalon, *L'Histoire et l'épopée*, pp. 326-27.

The above description is based on the published text, i.e. on MS *E* of the 'versión regia'. Before examining other chronicles, it should be said that the 'versión vulgar', here represented by MS *F*, differs little in essential respects from the 'regia'. True, the latter contains stylistic expansions, similar to those noted throughout the 'tercera parte' (see pp. 16-17, 27-29, 45-46 above). One rarely finds here, however, narrative expansions or compilatorial interventions such as those which distinguish, for example, the treatment of the legends of Fernán González or the Condesa Traidora (see pp. 29-30 and 62-63 above). Only at two points may it seriously be claimed that the compilers of *E* are responsible for an expansion which goes beyond the stylistic: in seeking advice from his nobles on his strategy against García, Sancho is, in MS *E*, much more concerned to justify his aggression and sends a warning to his brother (*PCG*, p. 497a40-b11; cf. variant and MS *F*, fol. 12r); and, at the very end of the section which concerns us, MS *E* alone adds a short final comment on the relationship between Alfonso VI and the Cid, just soured by the oath at Santa Gadea:

Pero despues estudieron en uno, a las uezes abenidos, a las uezes desabenidos, tanto quel echo de tierra el rey; mas al cabo fueron amigos: assi lo sopo merecer el Çid (*PCG*, p. 519b32-35; cf. variant and MS *F*, fol. 29r).[26]

The *Crónica Ocampiana* can also be disposed of, as for the reign of Sancho II it ceases to follow the *Crónica de Castilla* and becomes a variant of the 'versión vulgar' of the *PCG*;[27] at all the points mentioned above and in note 26, the *Ocampiana* follows the 'versión vulgar'.[28] The *Crónica Abreviada* also

---

[26] Most of the other differences between MSS *E* and *F* are merely stylistic: cf. *PCG*, pp. 498a11-14, 34-37, 499a34-37, 500a12-13, 501b15-21, 503a34-41, 504a42-48, b3-9, 25-34, 507b21-26, 508a3-4, 32-38, b35-6, 509b35-38, 511b2-6, 512a1-4, b13-16, 20-21, 513a11-13, 19-21, 514b29-31, 515a40-46, b22-24, 516b20-22, 517a26-29, 518b36-40, 519a1-3, 25-28, 29, b7-9, 17-18, 23-24 and variants. There is one case of euphemism or bowdlerisation (*F*: 'porque yazedes [*E*: avedes de ver] con donna Urraca', p. 510a18 and variant; MS *F*, fol. 21r); and at one point (p. 500a24-28) the texts diverge where other chronicles also differ: see below, p. 112 and n. 51.

[27] In the *Ocampiana*, according to Catalán, 'El [reinado] de Sancho II se basa en la *Primera Crónica*' (*De Alfonso X*, p. 334 n. 30; and cf. Lindley Cintra, *Crónica*, I, ccciv).

[28] On the two points mentioned above in the text cf. Ocampo, fos 290r and 300r; Ocampo has the unexpurgated 'yazedes' (cf. n. 26), fol. 295v. There are two lacunae in Ocampo's text, corresponding to *PCG*, pp. 512b12-25 (cf. Ocampo, fol. 297r) and 515a1-36 (ibid., fol. 298r). The first may be explained as a haplology

follows the *PCG* in its organisation of the material into chapters (whereas, as will be seen below, other chronicles rearrange the division of events into chapters, if not their order), but as so often, the abbreviation is insufficiently detailed to allow us to decide whether the lost *Crónica Manuelina* followed the 'regia' or the 'vulgar' version.[29]

To sum up thus far: we have a group of texts—*PCG* in both versions, *Ocampiana*, *Abreviada*—which are closely interrelated and among which the differences are slight, stemming for the most part from the often noted tendency of the 'versión regia' to expand stylistically on the *borrador* which we may assume to have been its source.

To turn next, as is our usual practice, to the *CVR* would be to obscure the logical relationship between the versions, as that chronicle is much more idiosyncratic than any other in this section. Let us look first at the *CrC*. Both this chronicle and the *Cr1344*, tend as before (see above, pp. 83-85), to rearrange the material and introduce an entirely new system of chapter division. The correspondence between this and that of the *PCG* is at some times closer than at others, but in only eight of the thirty-two chapters under discussion is there identity in the contents of the chapters in the *PCG*, the various versions of the *CrC* and the *Cr1344*.[30] The permutations are so varied that it does not seem useful to analyse them here.

If we turn to the actual narrative, we find that the *CrC* follows the same fundamental order of events as the *PCG*. Where it differs it does so in three ways: it omits details found in the chronicles so far discussed; conversely, it adds details not found in them; and, finally, in one case it displaces a short section.

Two examples of the first tendency are the omission of the

(*amigos* . . . *amigos*); the second is less easily explicable, but it might correspond to one side of a folio in whatever manuscript of the 'versión vulgar' Ocampo was using (this is not the case with the sole surviving manuscript: MS *F*, fols 25r-v).

[29] One chapter—no. 29, corresponding to ch. 830 of the *PCG*—is omitted both in the *Crónica Abreviada* (fol. 112r) and in its index (fol. 14r); this seems to be a simple oversight. Compare the edition by Grismer, pp. 144-48 and 25 (for the index).

[30] The chapters concerned are those corresponding to chs 814-16, 824, 836-38, and 844 in the *PCG*. There is no apparent correlation between this factor and the subject matter or sources of the chapters concerned. See above, p. 102 and cf. *PCG*, pp. clxviii-clxxii.

PCG's remark, at the end of the first chapter of Sancho's reign, that a special relationship existed between Alfonso and Urraca (*PCG*, p. 495b2-9; cf. *CrC* MS *G*, fol. 141r); and of Urraca's threat to kill Sancho 'a furto o a paladinas' (*PCG*, p. 507b21; cf. *CrC* MS *G*, fol. 146v);[31] it might be argued that in both these cases the motive for the omission was to play down any notion of Urraca's complicity in Sancho's death.

Equally common are cases where the *CrC* expands on the *PCG* version. Sometimes such expansion is basically stylistic; so the warning to Sancho from the citizens of Zamora, which in the *PCG* reads as follows:

'Rey don Sancho, catad de coraçon esto que uos quiero dezir. Yo so cauallero fijo dalgo, et mio padre et mios auuelos por lealtad se preciaron, et quierouos desengannar et deziruos la uerdad si creerme quisierdes. Digouos que daqui de la villa salio agora un traydor que dizen Vellid Adolfo, et ua por matar a uos, et guardaduos dell . . .' (*PCG*, p. 510b1-8)

is in the *CrC* expanded as follows:

'Sennor Rey don Sancho, parad mientes en lo que vos quiero dezir, ca vos quiero desengannar. Yo soy natural de Santiago [*G*: Sayago; *R*: sangre] e aquellos donde yo vengo sienpre fueron leales e de lealtad se pagaron [*G*, *R*: preçiaron]; e yo en ella quiero beuir e morir. Digovos que de la villa de Çamora es salido vn traydor que fue fijo de Adolfo e nieto de Layno [*G*: . . . Adolfo e mato a don Nunno]. Este mato a su padre [*R*, *J*: a vn su conpadre] e echolo en el rrio, e es traydor prouado' (*CrC*, MS *S*, fol. 24r; cf MSS *G*, fol. 148v, *J*, fol. 189r, and *R*, fol. 30v).

Another, more notable, instance of stylistic expansion concerns the oath at Santa Gadea, which is presented, in MS *G* of the *CrC*, in unmistakably assonanced poetic form, easy to rearrange in lines of verse as follows:

'Rey don Alfonso, vos venides jurar por la muerte
del rey don Sancho vuestro hermano
que nin lo matastes   nin fuestes en consejarlo
Dezid: "Sy, juro", vos   e esos fijos dalgo'.
Et el rrey e ellos   dixieron;   'Sy, juramos';

---

[31] Likewise, after the incident in ch. 822 of the *PCG* in which Alvar Fannez rescues Sancho at the battle of Santarén the *CrC* omits the alternative version given by the *PCG* in which the Cid is the protagonist; cf. *PCG*, p. 501b14-20 and *CrC*, MS *G*, fol. 143v. Other omissions correspond to *PCG*, p. 498a29-35 (in which Sancho's more persuasive line of argument is omitted in the *CrC*), and p. 502a24-26 (where the *CrC* has no mention of the Cid being instrumental in García's capture). A further case, corresponding to *PCG*, p. 497a39-b20, and probably a haplology of *García* . . . *García* is found in MS *G* (fol. 141v) but not, e.g., in MS *R* (fol. 18v).

'Sy non, tal muerte murades   qual murio vuestro hermano:
villano vos mate   que non sea fijo dalgo;
de otra tierra venga   que non sea castellano'.
'Amen', respondio el Rey   e los doze fijos dalgo.

'Vos venides jurar   por muerte de mi sennor,
que nin lo matastes   nin fuestes consejador'.
Respondio el Rey   con los doze que con el eran [*P*: son],
'Sy juramos'.
'Sy non, tal muerte murades   qual murio mi sennor,
villano vos mate, ca fijo dalgo non,
de otra tierra venga   e non del Regno de Leon'.
Respondio el Rey,   mudada la color.
Tres vezes lo conjuro   el Çid Canpeador
a el e a los doze fijos dalgo   que con el son.
Respondieron 'Amen'
pero que fue muy sannudo el Rey contra el Çid e dixole:

'Varon Ruy Diaz,   ¿por que me afyncades tanto?,
que oy me juramentades   e cras besaredes mi mano'.
Respondio el Çid: 'Como me fizierdes algo,
ca en otra tierra   sueldo dan a fijos dalgo,
e Asy faran a mi   quien me quisiere por vasallo'.

Peso mucho al Rey don Alfonso desto que el Çid dixo, e desamolo de alli adelante
           (*CrC*, MS *G*, fols 152v-153r; cf. MS *P*, fol. 28r;
             with this compare *PCG*, p. 519b5-32.)[32]

Sometimes the expansion is such as to introduce new narrative elements, though not of any fundamental kind. Compare for instance, the account of how Urraca interceded for Alfonso with Sancho (*PCG*, p. 503a30-41) with the *CrC* version in which the Cid is also involved: indeed, the Cid's intercession is the clinching factor (*CrC*, MSS *G*, fol. 144v, *J*, fol. 179r, *S*, fol. 19r).[33]

---

[32] This passage is quoted almost in its entirety by Catalán, 'Poesía y novela', pp. 434-35 and in part by Horrent, 'Santa Gadea', p. 188. Other examples of stylistic expansion correspond to *PCG* pp. 496b12-20 (Sancho's exchange with Ramiro), 503b44 (Alfonso's prayer for aid in becoming ruler of Toledo), and 511b9-24 (the Cid's failure to catch Vellido Adolfo is excused at greater length).

[33] Compare also the remark that Sancho's first *cortes* (*PCG*, p. 495b22) were generous 'por ganar los coraçones' (*CrC*, MS *G*, fol. 141r), that to the effect that when the Cid returned to Sancho's camp after a temporary estrangement (*PCG*,

There are two possible explanations for these innovations. They may represent elements deriving from the *Cantar*, but rejected in earlier compilations (*PCG*, etc.): the poetic nature of the section describing the oath at Santa Gadea makes it certain that this is the explanation in that instance, and it may equally apply in others. This chronicle, after all, shows a clear tendency to use epic and novelesque sources fully and uncritically whenever they are available.[34] Alternatively, some of these innovations may equally well be compilatorial deductions, as the *CrC* shows an equally marked tendency towards elaboration of this kind.[35]

Third, there is a single instance of reorganisation of material, in that Urraca's reminder to the Cid of the ties of upbringing and friendship which bind them is placed at the end of the interview in which he is acting as Sancho's emissary to demand the handing over of Zamora, and not at the beginning as in the *PCG*.[36] It can be said to be more effective in its new position, i.e., coupled with the bad news, the rejection of Sancho's terms, and the rearrangement may once again respond to primarily literary criteria.

It is now convenient to examine this series of episodes in the *CVR*, which, as I have already remarked, presents a decidedly

p. 509a3) the Zamorans were sad 'porque con el cuydauan ser desçercados' (*CrC*, MS *G*, fol. 147v) and that at Sancho's death (*PCG*, p. 512b23 ff.) the bishops and nobles of the realm were present in order to 'meter paz entre el e su hermana' (*CrC*, MS *G*, fol. 149v). Other peculiarities of the *CrC* version are listed in Chalon, *L'Histoire et l'épopée*, pp. 336-40.

[34] 'La *Crónica de Castilla* . . . al acoger sin restricciones la historia legendaria de Castilla elaborada por la epopeya más tardía, logró una popularidad muy sostenida durante el fin de la Edad Media' (Catalán, *De Alfonso X*, p. 325). Compare the same author's 'Poesía y novela', especially pp. 431 and 433-35.

[35] See Catalán, 'Poesía y novela', especially pp. 435-41, where he talks of the preoccupation of the compiler of the *CrC* to 'revestir literariamente el relato tradicional con adiciones deducidas de la situación y del contexto' and to 'ajustar el comportamiento de los personajes históricos a unas normas de actuación ideal' (p. 436). See also my article 'The *Afrenta de Corpes*', at pp. 138-40. This tendency may affect one other case where the *CrC* differs from the *PCG*: in the description of Alfonso's leaving Toledo, the *PCG*'s version (p. 515a29-40) is improved by the addition of an account of a chess game at which Alfonso's behaviour or prowess upset Almemón to the extent that the latter said 'vete . . .' (cf. *PCG*, p. 515a29-33), which Alfonso was quick to misinterpret as a command to leave Toledo. The best reading is that of MS *S*: '. . . jugando al axedrez . . . le enojo tanto jugando fasta que le mando tres vezes que se fuese. Entonçe el Rey don Alfonso, teniendo que auia mandado del Rey para se yr porque le dixo "Vete agora", salio del palaçio e guisose como se pudiese yr' (fol. 27r). This is not in the 'concise' MS *R*, fol. 34v.

[36] It is displaced from *PCG*, p. 507a9-18 to a point corresponding to p. 508a16.

idiosyncratic view of Sancho's reign. It broadly follows the Alphonsine *borrador* on which both it and the *PCG* appear to be based, but at times does so under protest, as it were; and at some points it introduces new material or material transposed from other parts of the chronicle.

The new material consists of four more or less substantial interpolations: first, of a chapter, after the one corresponding to *PCG* ch. 814 (the first of Sancho's reign) concerning Urraca's orders for redoubling the fortifications of Zamora; this largely repeats a previous chapter found in the *CVR* during the division of the kingdoms, and in both cases it may represent a popular source.[37] Second, and immediately after that chapter, the *CVR* inserts a chapter on the Cid's lineage which appears to be based on the *Historia Roderici*.[38] It corresponds in content—though not in detail—to that found in the *CrC* and the *Cr1344* at an earlier point, in the reign of Fernando I (see above, pp. 83 and 87). The *CVR*'s expressed reason for the inclusion is 'porque atanne al fecho de nuestra estoria' (MS *N*, fol. 88v), and there is no doubt that, given the large part the Cid is to play throughout the following sections, that is a good reason for its inclusion.[39] Third, after the battle of Grados, the *CVR* digresses on the favour shown by Sancho to the Cid, including an account of his marriage. This again stems from the *Historia Roderici*, and once again fills a gap in the hero's biography which in the *CrC* and the *Cr1344* was supplied (from *Mocedades* material) in the reign of Fernando I.[40] Fourth, in the *CVR* the Cid,

[37] *CVR*, MS *N*, fol. 88r-v; cf. Babbitt, *Latin Sources*, p. 66. The repetition may be inadvertent, in that this point—when Sancho has just come to the throne and his ambitions have been stated—is the logical one for this defensive measure, the compilers overlooking the fact that (following the order of the *Cantar*?) it had already been described once. Reig does not explore this question in her study of the *Cantar*, claiming, not wholly accurately, that the *CVR* 'sigue con bastante fidelidad a la *Primera General*' (*Sancho II*, p. 79).

[38] MS *N*, fols 88v-89r; see Babbitt, *Latin Sources*, p. 66. The text of the *Historia Roderici* is in Menéndez Pidal, *España del Cid*, II, 915-16.

[39] It is significant that the *CrC* and the *Cr1344* similarly introduce this genealogical material at the point at which the Cid is about to play a major part in the narrative: in the case of these chronicles this point comes earlier because, unlike the *CVR*, they incorporate the *Mocedades* material into their account of the reign of Fernando I. As for the *PCG*, which, like the *CVR*, eschews the *Mocedades* material, the Cid's lineage is described much earlier, in ch. 678, dealing with the reign of Fruela II and the Judges of Castile, one of whom, Lain Calvo, is claimed to have been the Cid's ancestor.

[40] *CVR*, MS *N*, fol. 89r-v; cf. *CrC*, MS *G*, fol. 132r-v, and *Cr1344*, MSS *M*, fols 198v-198 bis r, and Q^2, fol. 29v; on the marriage in these chronicles, see above,

immediately after Sancho's death, challenges the Zamorans to a *reto* and fights fifteen of them (this precedes the more formal *reto* of Diego Ordonnez and its outcome). Babbitt related this to an episode in the *Historia Roderici* in which the Cid is said to have fought against fifteen Zamoran knights. It should be pointed out, though, that in the *Historia Roderici* this is explicitly stated to have taken place 'cum . . . rex Sanctius Zemoram obsederit' (Menéndez Pidal, *España del Cid*, II, 917), and is undoubtedly the source for an earlier episode in the siege (*PCG*, p. 509a46-b3, also found in the *CVR* [MS *N*, fol. 100r]). It is not therefore wholly accurate to claim, as Babbitt does, that this is a *repetition*, though there are parallels between the two episodes.[41]

These additions show the compilers of the *CVR* to have made a thorough-going revision of the materials available to them, and in particular to have been concerned to fill certain gaps in the narrative—dealing in the main with the Cid's affairs and deeds —which the *PCG* seems to overlook. Another substantial revision which the compilers of the *CVR* felt tempted to make concerns chronology, and in particular the order of Sancho's campaigns against his brothers. In the *PCG* this is unequivocal, with no hint of doubt: the campaign against García successfully over and the latter imprisoned in Luna (chs 818-23), Sancho turns on Alfonso (chs 824-25); the only other mention of García is of his death some nineteen years later (ch. 876). In fact the Latin sources are at odds on this order of events: the *PCG*'s version reflects that of the Toledano (which in turn derives from the *Liber Regum* and perhaps ultimately from the *Crónica Najerense*), while the Tudense (following an earlier *Chronicon Compostellanum*) claims that the war against Alfonso preceded that against García.[42] In the *CVR* the

pp. 86 and 88. The *PCG* for its part makes no mention whatsoever of the Cid's marriage. The first mention of Ximena comes in ch. 851, which corresponds to laisses 14 ff. of the *Poema de mio Cid* (Ximena and her daughters are left at Cardeña when the Cid goes into exile).

[41] Babbitt, *Latin Sources*, pp. 79-80; cf. *PCG*, p. clxxi, under ch. 834.

[42] Babbitt, *Latin Sources*, p. 76. As for the *Cantar*, we may assume that it too followed the order García-Alfonso (Reig seems to make this assumption, though without discussing it, no doubt on the ground that the same order is preserved in the *Najerense* (*Sancho II*, pp. 32-33) and in all the vernacular chronicles). Indeed, it may be the origin of the Latin tradition which culminated in the Toledano, as the *Najerense* is particularly prone to adopt popular sources (see Menéndez Pidal, 'Relatos poéticos', pp. 344-50, especially p. 349.

Toledano's order is preserved, but, as it were, very much under protest. A first statement is made at a point corresponding to the end of ch. 817 in the *PCG*, where we find:

> Mas comoquier que en el Cantar del Rey don Sancho diga que luego fue sobre el Rey don Garçia, fallamos en las estorias verdaderas que cuentan y el Arçobispo don Rodrigo e don Lucas de Tuy e don Pero Marques, Cardenal de Santiago,[43] que ouieron sabor de escudrinnar las estorias por contar verdaderamente la estoria de Espanna, que sobre el Rey don Alfonso fue luego que estaua en comedio; e esta fue la verdad. Mas porque vos non [sic; MS *L* omits][44] queremos contar conplidamente toda la estoria del Rey don Sancho asy como la cuentan los juglares, dexaremos aqui de contarla asy como la cuenta el Arçobispo e los otros sabios. Ca despues lo contaremos adelante bien e conplidamente e dezirvos hemos del Rey don Sancho e del Rey don Garçia (MS *N*, fol. 90v).

(In fact, as I have said, the Toledano and Tudense do *not* agree on this point.)[45] The *CVR* also follows the Tudense in holding that Sancho released García shortly after capturing him:

> Mas esto, comoquier que lo cuentan asi los joglares, non fue asi verdad. Ca fallamos en las estorias verdaderas que despues que lo priso, que lo solto luego sobre omenage que le fizo que en toda su vida fuesse su vasallo e viuiesse [MS *J*: viniese; fol. 61r] a su mandamiento cada que enbiasse por el. E avn sobre esto, que le dio arrehenes. E el Rey don Alfonso lo priso despues e lo echo en Luna assi como adelante vos lo contaremos; e vos diremos sobre que, e por qual Razon esta es la verdad (MS *N*, fol. 93v).[46]

---

[43] On Pedro Marquez or Marcos, an otherwise unknown figure, see J. Amador de los Ríos, *Historia crítica de la literatura española*, 7 vols (Madrid 1861-65), IV, 66 n. (a thirteenth-century reference to one Marcos Pérez), cited by Babbitt, *Latin Sources*, p. 59 n. 11. Another possibility may be the twelfth-century canon of Santiago, Pedro Marcio: see T. D. Kendrick, *St James in Spain* (London, 1960), especially ch. 14; I am indebted to Dr R. Fletcher for this suggestion.

[44] MS *N*, *Ñ*, and *J* all have *no(n)* (*N*, fol. 90v, *Ñ*, fol. 134v, *J*, fol. 59r; MS *L* however, omits (quoted by R. Menéndez Pidal, *Poesía juglaresca y orígenes de las literaturas románicas*, sixth edition (Madrid, 1957), p. 300; in the earlier *Poesía juglaresca y juglares* (Madrid, 1924) he discussed the textual problem at pp. 399-400 n. 3; cf. Babbitt, *Latin Sources*, pp. 68-69.

[45] The *CVR* then reminds its readers at appropriate points of its views on this subject: 'Ya vos de suso contamos que la primera guerra que el Rey don Sancho ouo con sus hermanos que fue con el Rey don Alfonso' (MS *N*, fol. 93v-94r) (at the beginning of the campaign against Alfonso); 'Despues desto fue sobre el Rey don Garçia que era su hermano, e auinole con el asi como la estoria lo ha contado de suso' (ibid., fol. 96v) (at the end of the same campaign).

[46] This theme is also taken up in the *CVR*'s account of Sancho's death-bed speech: 'Agora sabed aqui los que esta estoria oydes que ssi el Rey don Sancho touiese preso a su hermano el Rey don Garçia en el castillo de Luna assi como

Finally, in the first years of Alfonso VI's reign, the *CVR* then inserts its own version (still based on the Tudense) of García's eventual imprisonment: it contains a chapter, after that dealing with Alfonso's coronation and the oath at Santa Gadea, telling how García attacked Alfonso, was defeated by him, and imprisoned in the castle of Luna.[47]

There are a few other instances in which the *CVR* treats its sources differently from the *PCG*, of which one example must suffice. The *PCG* (and the other chronicles already described which are similar to it, the *Ocampiana* and the *CrC*) interpolate the popular story of the oath at Santa Gadea into the account of Alfonso's accession drawn from their Latin sources; it thus follows his return from Toledo, consultation with Urraca, and his receiving the homage of his non-Castilian subjects, but precedes his coronation and the traditional eulogy of his qualities (*PCG*, chs 845-46; for the sources of these elements, ibid., pp. clxxii-clxxiii). The *CVR* prefers to describe all these elements, including the coronation, in its first chapter of the reign (MS *N*, fols 108v-109v), and follows this with the oaths (ibid., fols 109v-110v); it also adds the comment: 'Agora veredes grand atreuimiento del vasallo, de querer atreuersse de juramentar su sennor tan brauamente' (fol. 110r).[48] In these rearrangements as in its interpolations, the *CVR* may be said to represent a more critical use of source materials than the *PCG*, and an unwillingness always to prefer the popular source to the learned ones, in particular the *Historia Roderici* and the Tudense.[49]

auemos contado de suso en esta estoria, que Rogara que le perdonasse como fizo a don Alfonso e mandaralo sacar de la prison. E por ende es de creer mas lo que nos del dixiemos, que le priso e le solto luego por omenaje que le fizo' (MS *N*, fol. 103r).

[47] *CVR*, MS *N*, fols 110v-111r; cf. Babbitt, *Latin Sources*, pp. 82-83.

[48] Other instances in which the *CVR* brings its own interpretation to its sources are: the statement that Ramiro was killed at Grados (MS *N*, fol. 89r.; cf *PCG*, p. 496b 48-50), where the *CVR* follows the *Historia Roderici* while the *PCG*'s sources are not known: cf. Babbitt, *Latin Sources*, p. 67 and *PCG*, p. clxviii, under ch. 816; and Alfonso's return from Toledo (see above, n. 25), where the *CVR* again blends the differing versions of the Tudense and the Toledano in its own way, which is not that of the *PCG*: cf. MS *N*, fols 104v-106r, and *PCG*, ch. 840; see also Babbitt, *Latin Sources*, pp. 81-82.

[49] Chalon, after a detailed and thoughtful analysis of this section, sums up as follows: 'L'examen du passage de la *C.V.R.* consacré au règne de Sancho II nous a permis de mettre en relief la personnalité remarquable de son compilateur: celui-ci n'hésite jamais à critiquer ses sources épiques, même quand il est le premier à en faire usage; confrontant le Tudense et le Tolédan, il ne donne pas systématiquement raison au second, mais il choisit dans chaque cas particulier la version qui lui paraît la plus plausible' (*L'Histoire et l'épopée*, p. 346).

The *Cr1344* also has its idiosyncrasies, though they are less marked and of a different kind. On the whole it follows the *CrC*, as we would expect given its general nature; it is essentially a reworking of that chronicle in the light of new sources, most notably the *CVR*.[50]

On occasion it interprets its source in an idiosyncratic way: for instance, when the Cid returns after his quarrel with Sancho (see above, note 33) and the *CrC* refers to the Zamoran's disappointment ('porque con el cuydauan ser desçercados', *CrC*, MS *G*, fol. 147v), the *Cr1344* takes a diametrically opposite view: 'E a quantos estauan en la hueste plugoles mucho de la su venida, e mas a los de Çamora, ca por el cuydauan ser descercados' (MS Q^2, fol. 60v; cf. MS *M*, fol. 226v), the implication presumably being that they misinterpreted the Cid's return as a relief expedition. On one other minor point, the Portuguese origins of *Cr1344* may be relevant; García makes a remark to his Portuguese subjects, at *PCG*, p. 500a25-27, which has disparaging overtones: 'vos avedes prez de fazer pocos sennores buenos entre uos . . .', and the *CrC* is fundamentally similar (MSS *G*, fol. 143r, *J*, fol. 174v).[51] The *Cr1344*, however, rephrases the allusion as follows: 'vos avedes pres de ardidos, e non queredes entre vos muchos sennores' (MS Q^2, fol. 55v; cf. MS *M*, fol. 219r).

Of more importance is the fact that the *Cr1344* also follows the *CVR* in some, but not all, of that chronicle's idiosyncrasies. It contains the reference to the Cid challenging the citizens

---

[50] Catalán: '[the author of the *Cr1344*] toma como narración básica la *Crónica de Castilla* . . . refundiéndola con fuentes varias' (*De Alfonso X*, p. 406); cf. Lindley Cintra: 'A *Crónica de Castela* se apresenta, em toda a sua extensão, como texto intermediário entre a *Crónica de 1344* e as suas fontes' (*Crónica*, I, ccxliv); for the part played by the *CVR* in the elaboration of the *Cr1344*, see ibid., pp. ccxcii-ccxcviii and, on the section currently under discussion, especially pp. ccxciii-ccxciv. See also note 12 above.

[51] However, MS *S* of the *CrC* omits the reference, in line with its general tendency to abbreviate (fol. 17r), and both the 'versión vulgar' and the *Ocampiana* rephrase it in such a way as to tone down its criticism: cf. MS *F*, '. . . todo el mal prez que abedes de fazer pocos con muchos sennores e buenos. . .', *PCG*, p. 500a24 ff. variant, MS *F*, fol. 13r; Ocampo, 'Ca vos auedes muchos sennores buenos entre vos . . .', fol. 291r. That both the points mentioned in this paragraph are innovations of the *Cr1344* is further indicated by the fact that neither is found in the Galician manuscript of the *PCG/CrC*, MS *A*: 'Mays bem foy tamano o pesar que ouieran os de Çamora, ca por elle coydauam seer desçercados' (fol. 112v); '. . . vos auedes preço de faser poucos senores boos . . .' (fol. 107r). On MS *A*, its sources and its relationship to the *Cr1344*, see Catalán, *De Alfonso X*, pp. 305-55 and the introduction to the recent edition of this version by Lorenzo, *La traducción gallega*.

of Zamora and fighting fifteen of them (see above, p. 109 and note 41);[52] and although it does not have the same criticisms of the accepted order of Sancho's campaigns against his brothers (see above, pp. 109-10), it does say that Sancho released García; what is more, it gives a new account of that release.

> Despues quel Rey don Garçia fue preso e metido en fierros, partiose el Rey don Sancho de Santeren para Coynbra. E en partiendo de Coynbra era primero dia de mayo. E quando llegaron a aquella fuente en que las mançebas tomauan agua para las mayas, fueron nembrados en como era primero dia de mayo. E començaron los castellanos de yr cantando las mayas; mas el Rey don Garçia que lo oya yua llorando. (There follows an account of how Urraca and Elvira intercederon for García and secured his release on his oath of allegiance to Sancho: *Cr1344*, MS Q^2, fol. 56v; cf. MS *M*, fol. 220v).

Pidal saw this as reflecting an episode from a version of the *cantar*, and this view is shared by Reig.[53] If this is so, it is hard to see why it should have left no traces in other chronicles, and it is conceivable that we are here dealing with a lyrical tradition (cf. the May ballads alluded to by Pidal in the article referred to in note 53).

This may, therefore, be a case where the *Cr1344*'s tendency to use the *CVR* to amplify the *CrC* (compare the use of *CVR* material in the Partitions sequence, pp. 98-99 above) coincided with a new detail drawn from a popular source.[54]

In the second part of this chapter, then, we have a different situation to that described in the first. There, historical and legendary sources were in clear disagreement and the attitude of the various chronicles reflects that disagreement: they omit

---

[52] MSS *M*, fol. 230r and Q^2, fol. 52v. The *RefTol*, not untypically, raises the number of the Cid's opponents from 15 to 20 (*RefTol*, MS *M*, fol. 259v).

[53] Menéndez Pidal referred in passing to 'el poema épico del Cerco de Zamora tal como lo conocía la *Crónica de 1344*' as evidence for the existence of May songs ('La primitiva poesía lírica española', in *Estudios literarios* (Buenos Aires, 1938), 181-247 (p. 214)); see also Reig, *Sancho II*, pp. 72-73; Lindley Cintra, *Crónica*, I, ccxlix and n. 217; Catalán and Andrés, *Cr1344*, p. xxviii, n. 64.

[54] Of the *RefTol*, little need be said. It tends, as usual, to amplify rhetorically: compare the following versions of a moral reflection on the fratricidal wars. *PCG*: 'Et la suerte que solien auer los moros de matarse hermanos con hermanos cayo estonces en los cristianos' (p. 502b1-4); *Cr1344*: 'La guerra que solia ser entre los moros e entre los Cristianos, tornose toda entre los Cristianos, matandose los parientes e los hermanos vnos con otros' (MS Q^2, fol. 56v); *RefTol*: 'E fueron alli muertos muy muchos gentiles onbres, hermanos contra hermanos e primos e parientes contra parientes ... Et fue tan grand la mortandad entre ellos de que non peso a los moros nin plogo a los Christianos' (MS *M*, fol. 240v).

the legendary material, though tending to refer to it indirectly (*PCG, Ocampiana, Manuelina, CrC*); or they accept it with considerable reservations (*CVR*); or they juxtapose the two versions in a rather inexpert way (*Cr1344*). Here, where there is less contradiction between the sources—the *Cantar* possibly containing more historical fact and in any case having apparently been partially assimilated into the Latin historiographical tradition (as represented by the *Najerense* and the *Toledano*), the chronicles tend to agree much more with one another, generally accepting the legendary material.[55] Only the *CVR* —and, to a much lesser extent, the *Cr1344*—appear to have serious reservations about the story they are telling.

[55] Although it has no place in the argumentation followed in this chapter, I must point to the importance of the article by Fraker, 'Sancho II: Epic and Chronicle', and in particular to his view of this episode as a (rare) instance in Alphonsine historiography of the presentation of Sancho as a figure both exemplary and tragic, with strong reminiscences of the story of Julius Caesar (pp. 494-507). If Fraker is right, then here is one instance of the way in which a good mediaeval historian would use history as more than a compilation of facts (compare my *Introduction*, p. 2 above).

Chapter 7
THE CID AS HERO

Most of the remaining legendary material in the 'cuarta parte' concerns the life and death of Rodrigo Díaz de Vivar, *el Cid*, and to a large extent this material corresponds in subject matter to the extant *Poema de mio Cid* (*PMC*). Study of this chronicle material is in one way simpler and in others more complex than is the case with almost any other of those legends discussed above. The simplification comes from the fact that the epic text concerned has survived and, though as we shall see below the matter is not perfectly straightforward, this removes one large area of uncertainty. Complications, however, derive from the Cid's very importance. As a major figure in later eleventh-century Spain, his life naturally attracted the attention of biographers. The Alphonsine chroniclers had at their disposal not merely a version of the *PMC* and possibly other legendary material but also more straightforwardly historiographical sources such as the *Historia Roderici*,[1] an Arabic history of Valencia ascribed to Ben Alcama or Ibn Alqama[2] and, as usual, the Tudense's and the Toledano's works (including the latter's *Historia Arabum*). The compilatory work was thus more complex than usual, and an analysis of the chroniclers' treatment of the Cid must take into account the existence of this wealth of historiographical material alongside the more familiar reflections of the *PMC*.

The Cid's deeds during the reigns of Fernando I and Sancho II have been dealt with in the two preceding chapters. The remaining material can conveniently be divided into three sections: the first dealing with his exile and military adventures, culminating in the siege and capture of Valencia (i.e., approximately

---

[1] The text of the *HRod* may be consulted in Menéndez Pidal, *España del Cid*, II, 919-67. See also Sánchez Alonso, *Historia de la historiografía*, I, 159-62, and A. Ubieto Arteta, 'La *Historia Roderici* y su fecha de redacción', *Saitabi*, 11 (1961), 241-46.

[2] On Ben Alcama, see R. Dozy, *Recherches sur l'histoire et la littérature de l'Espagne pendant le moyen âge*, 3rd edition; 2 vols (reprinted, Amsterdam, 1965), II, 33-54; Menéndez Pidal, *España del Cid*, II, 896-901; Sánchez Alonso, *Historia de la historiografía*, I, 198; *PCG*, p. xxxix.

corresponding to the first *cantar* of the extant *PMC* and the beginning of the second); the second with his reconciliation with Alfonso VI and the marriage of his daughters to the Infantes de Carrión, the *Afrenta de Corpes*, the subsequent *cortes* at Toledo, and the second marriages of his daughters (i.e., corresponding to the rest of the *PMC* as we know it); and the third recounting the Cid's death, the abandonment of Valencia, the preservation of his body at the monastery of San Pedro de Cardeña and various more or less miraculous happenings associated with his tomb (the so-called '*Estoria de Cardeña*' material).

(a) *The Cid's exile and the capture of Valencia*

That part of the Cid's biography with which we are concerned starts with the hero's exile, as does the *PMC*, though the doubts over the opening of the latter work make this one of the more speculative areas to be dealt with in this chapter. Chapters 849-50 of the *PCG* tell how Alfonso sent the Cid to Seville and Córdoba to collect tribute; how, when the King of Seville was attacked by the King of Córdoba, aided by García Ordóñez and other Castilians, the Cid went to the former's aid; and how, in the ensuing battle, these Castilians were captured and later released by the Cid. Subsequently Alfonso took his army to Andalusia while the Cid, back in Castile, defended Gormaz against Moorish invasion and won a great victory. Envious vassals set Alfonso against him, and the King (only too pleased to listen because of the animosity he still bore the Cid over the oath of Santa Gadea) exiled the Cid. Much of this derives from the *Historia Roderici* (*HRod*)[3] and the extent of any 'retouching' from the hypothetical, now lost, opening of the *PMC* must be a matter of speculation.[4] That the opening of the *PMC* coincided roughly with the *HRod* is argued by Pidal on the grounds of the existence of three details which are later taken up in the

---

[3] *España del Cid*, II, 917-19; cf. *PCG*, p. clxxiv.
[4] The question of the opening of the *PMC* is discussed by A. Pardo, 'Los versos 1-9 del *PMC*: ¿no comenzaba ahí el Poema?', *Boletín del Instituto Caro y Cuervo*, 27 (1972), 261-92, J. Casalduero, 'El Cid echado de tierra', in *Estudios de literatura española* (Madrid, 1962), pp. 28-58', and Hook, 'The Opening *Laisse* of the *PMC*'; as Michael admits in his edition of the *PMC*, the question is an open one. He states: 'Possible laguna: . . . Cabe la posibilidad de que los v[ersos] aparentemente perdidos contuvieran la razón del primer exilio del Cid en 1081' (Michael, *PMC*, p. 75).

Poema: the Cid's tax-gathering expedition to Andalusia; the importance of slanderers in setting the King against the hero; and the capture of García Ordóñez at Cabra.[5]

We are not here concerned with the *PMC* as such. It has been argued that the opening, as it stands, is sufficiently effective and striking to be artistically satisfactory.[6] It may also be relevant to point out that the details mentioned above from Menéndez Pidal's work, however suggestive, are not conclusive: all three could be accounted for by a semi-historical consciousness among the poem's audience who by the early thirteenth century, the probable date of its composition, might well be expected to know a good deal of more or less accurate detail about a hero as renowned as the Cid.[7] We shall return to the question later when discussing the *Crónica de Castilla*.

The simplest place to begin an account of the chronicle versions of the Cid's exile is with the *Crónica de Veinte Reyes*, for here we have a clear and straightforward case of direct prosification of the extant *PMC*. Occasionally, details are inserted which seem to derive from the *HRod* (perhaps by way of an Alphonsine *borrador*, since in every case the same details occur in the *PCG*): so the Cid's incursions into the Moorish kingdom of Zaragoza (which in the *PMC* are treated very cursorily and only as an introduction to the episode of the hero's defeat of the Count of Barcelona: see *PMC*, lines 905-06 and 935 ff.) are given a more detailed treatment including

[5] See *PMC*, lines 109-12: 'El Campeador por las parias fue entrado, / grandes averes priso e mucho sobeianos, / rretovo d'ellos quanto que fue algo ...'; line 267: 'Por malos mestureros de tierra sodes echado' (and cf. line 9: 'Esto me an buelto mios enemigos malos'); and lines 3287 ff.: '... commo yo a vós, conde, en el castiello de Cabra; / quando pris a Cabra e a vós por la barba ...'. Compare the *HRod*: 'nuntium eum per paria sua ad regem Sibiliae et ad regem Cordubiae misit'; 'causa invidiae de falsis et non veris rebus illum apud regem accusaverunt'; and 'usque ad castrum qui dicitur Capra; ... captus est igitur in eodem bello comes Garsias Ordonii'; see Menéndez Pidal, *CMC*, III, 1020-21.

[6] See the studies cited in note 4 above and the bibliography cited by Hook, 'The Opening *Laisse* of the *PMC*', p. 490 nn. 1-3; also M. Garci-Gómez, *'Mio Cid': Estudios de endocrítica* (Barcelona, 1975), pp. 44-46.

[7] It should be remembered that the extant *PMC* contains other unexplained references, such as that to the Cid and the Count of Barcelona's nephew (lines 962-63: 'Dentro en mi cort tuerto me tovo grand, / firiom' el sobrino e non' lo emendó más;') which presumably are not to anything in the lost beginning of the poem. Compare also lines 3378-80, where Asur González insults the Cid with the words: '¿Quién nos darié nuevas de Mio Çid el de Bivar? / iFuesse a Río d'Ovirna los molinos picar / e prender maquilas, commo lo suele far!', a reference to the Cid's relatively lowly origins which clearly relies for its effect on a popular knowledge of these origins (and of local geography) nowhere explained in the poem.

mention of the Cid's treaty of peace and vassalage with Almodafar of Zaragoza;[8] a similarly careful treatment of Moorish affairs, also deriving ultimately from the *HRod*, comes in the next chapter, where the enmity between the Cid and Ramón Berenguer is accounted for in terms of the dynastic struggle in Zaragoza, in which the Cid found himself supporting one of Almodafar's sons, Zuleyma, against Pedro of Aragón and the Count of Barcelona who were pressing the claims of the other son, Abenalhage.[9]

Very occasionally one finds elements in the *CVR* version which cannot be explained in this way: so, in the early part of the narrative, when the penniless Cid has to deceive the Jews of Burgos, the initiative for the ruse comes in the *CVR* from Martín Antolínez:

E Martin Antolinez dixole como non le podie el manleuar todo quanto el auia menester; mas que mandasse fenchir dos arcas de arena e çerrarlas muy bien e el que las leuaria de su parte a dos mercadores muy ricos que auia y en la çibdad . . . (*CVR*, MS *N*, fol. 114r; cf. MS *J*, fol. 72v),[10]

which may represent an early instance of the desire to attenuate the Cid's guilt shown in later chronicle versions of the episode and its sequel.[11] The whole issue of the *CVR* prosification has

[8] 'E desi a pocos de dias puso el Çid su amor muy grande con Almondafar, que era Rey de Çaragoça', *CVR*, MS *N*, fol. 120r; cf. MSS *J*, fol. 76r and *Ll*, fol. 175v. There is a lacuna in the *HRod* at this point: *España del Cid*, II, 920.

[9] 'Çulema, Rey de Çaragoça, amo mucho al Çid e metiole todo el Reno [sic] en poder e que fiziessen todo lo que el mandasse. Desy começosse grand enemistad entre Çulema e Benalhange, amos hermanos, e guerrearonsse el vno al otro. E el Rey don Pedro de Aragon e el conde Remont Bereguel de Barçelona ayudauan a Benalhange e desamauan mucho al Çid porque sse atenia con Çulema e le guardaua la tierra', *CVR*, MS *N*, fol. 120v; cf. MSS *J*, fol. 76r and *Ll* fol. 176r). See *HRod*, *España del Cid* II, 918, and *PCG*, p. 532a46-b48. The *PMC*'s brief account of the Cid's Eastern incursions, lines 951 ff., of the Count's reactions: 'Llegaron las nuevas al conde de Barçilona / que Mio Çid Ruy Díaz quel' corrié la tierra toda; / ovo grand pesar e tóvos'lo a grand fonta' (957-9), and his statement: 'agora córrem' las tierra que en mi enpara están' (964) were clearly insufficiently detailed in terms of politics and motive for the chroniclers, who filled out the detail from the Latin source.

[10] Compare *PMC*, lines 79 ff. and *PCG*, ch. 851, where the idea is clearly the Cid's: '[El Çid] apartosse con Martin Antolinez e dixol . . . que querie mandar fazer con su conseio dos arcas . . .', p. 523b36-40. See Smith, 'Did the Cid repay the Jews?', p. 536.

[11] See Smith, 'Did the Cid repay the Jews?', esp. pp. 535-38. Compare another case, corresponding to *PMC*, line 570, the Cid's approach to and besieging of Alcocer), where the *CVR*, like the *PCG*, adds the detail that the Moors would willingly have paid tribute: 'le pecharian quanto el quisiesse, e que los dexase en paz; e el Çid non lo quiso fazer, e acogiosse a su bastida', *CVR*, MS *N*, fol. 116r, cf. MSS *J*, fol. 73v, and *Ll*, fol. 170v; *PCG*, p. 526a40-44.

been thoroughly studied by B. J. Powell in his Cambridge Ph.D. dissertation, a version of which has now been published under the title *Epic and Chronicle: The 'Poema de mio Cid' and the 'Crónica de veinte reyes'*.[12] The substantial chapters of this deal with the style and language of the prosification and with the representation of the poem in the chronicle. In the first of these chapters Powell shows how the prosifiers dealt with direct speech, poetic word order, and rhetorical devices, and how they treated other distinctive linguistic features of the poem: assonance, epic epithets, physical phrases, and so on. He finds that a conscious effort to avoid assonance and other linguistic and stylistic devices means that:

the CVR remains very much the prose chronicle written in rather dull, repetitive style and language (p. 88).

In the next chapter he examines the *dramatis personae* of the chronicle version, together with the roles of the principal characters and other narrative differences including those mentioned above. One conclusion which is not without interest is that the manuscript used by the compilers of the *CVR*, while not identical with Per Abbat's, was very similar (p. 105).[13] Powell shows how the variations introduced by the chroniclers 'have reduced the heroic but human person portrayed in the poem into someone who is dull and predictable' (pp. 96-97), and how they play down the role of family affairs ('not a particularly heroic aspect of the figure of the Cid': p. 98) and add a number of compilatory deductions of the kind we shall see figuring even more prominently in later chronicle versions.[14]

Powell's general summary is worth quoting:

The chroniclers set out . . . positively to create their own version of the *PMC*, by being true to its basic story of the Cid, Alfonso, and the Infantes de Carrión, but not being tied to all the details of that story; by following the text where necessary, but by changing it linguistically to make it

[12] The narrative elements mentioned earlier in this paragraph are discussed at p. 95, and on the question of the lost opening of the poem (see above, notes 4 and 5), see p. 25.
[13] This view is shared by Chalon, *L'Histoire et l'épopée*, p. 275. His general view of the relationship between the *PMC* and the *CVR* echoes that of Powell, and he concludes as follows: 'D'une manière générale, le récit de la *C.V.R.*, comparé à celui du *Cantar*, se caractérise par son laconisme: la plupart des dialogues et de nombreux épisodes secondaires disparaissent, mais dans l'ensemble la structure du récit est identique' (p. 261).
[14] Powell, *Epic and Chronicle*, pp. 100-04.

comply with the stylistic and linguistic patterns of their chronicle prose; by positively discriminating against what did not suit them both in content and in language; and by intervening directly to amend and adapt, until there was a prose redaction which was to their liking (p. 110).

Of the other chronicle versions of the story of the Cid's exile, that offered by the *PCG* may conveniently be described next. In narrative line it departs little from the story told in the *PMC* and prosified in the *CVR*. Indeed, this is so far true that it would be idle to summarise the story line in detail. Like the *CVR*, the *PCG* complements this Cidian material with the aid of the *HRod* and also adds details on Moorish history from the Toledano's *Historia Arabum*.[15] The basic source, however, for this part of the story is recognisably a text akin to the extant *PMC*. It cannot be said with confidence that it *was* the *PMC*; Menéndez Pidal constantly referred to a *'refundición'* of the *PMC* as the Alphonsine source, basing this supposition on a general wealth of detail in the chronicle which is lacking in the poem as we know it.[16] Since Menéndez Pidal's edition and critical study of the *PCG* appeared, the question has been reexamined by Diego Catalán, who analyses in detail the discrepancies between poetic and prose versions of the narrative section in question (lines 1-1097 of the *PMC*, corresponding to chs 850-62 of the *PCG*). Of the differences which led Menéndez Pidal to postulate the existence of a later poetic *'refundición'*, some are ascribed to the process of prosification[17] and others, more significantly, to a range of criteria of a more literary or historiographical nature. To summarise briefly his analysis, he points to cases where explanatory commentary is necessary; to a desire to make explicit what is in the *PMC* indirect and suggestive; and to the chroniclers' need to ennoble the Cid's actions.[18] His conclusion is unequivocal:

[15] For example, the dates of the Moorish succession at the end of ch. 858 (*PCG*, p. 531b22-29; cf. p. clxxv). For other examples of the use of the *Historia Arabum*, see Catalán, 'Crónicas generales y cantares de gesta', pp. 288-89, nn. 46-51. On the *Historia Arabum* see Sánchez Alonso, *Historia de la historiografía*, I, 140.

[16] See *CMC*, I, 126-30. Although Menéndez Pidal admitted that the differences between this *'refundición'* and the extant *PMC* are relatively slight in the first *cantar*, he concludes roundly that 'el Cantar que hoy conocemos y el que sirvió de guía a la Crónica eran dos obras diferentes' (pp. 128-29); cf. *PCG*, pp. xlvi and clxxv ff.

[17] Catalán, 'Crónicas generales y cantares de gesta', p. 295. Catalán's view is shared by Chalon, *L'Histoire et l'épopée*, pp. 226-27 and 273-74.

[18] Examples of these three broad types of criteria are: *PMC*, lines 534-35: 'çiento moros e çiento moras quiero las quitar / porque lo pris d'ellos que de mí non digan mal', which is continued in the *PCG*, 'ca paresçrie mal de leuar moros nin moras

THE CID AS HERO 121

Después de considerar una por una todas las divergencias notables existentes entre el relato del *Mio Cid* copiado por Per Abbat y la Crónica alfonsí, me reafirmo en la creencia de que la *Estoria de España* tuvo aquí como fuente una redacción de la Gesta idéntica a la conocida (pp. 300-01).

It will come as no surprise to the reader who has followed the previous six chapters that I find myself in complete agreement with this conclusion. The compilers of the *PCG*, up to this point at least, have constantly shown themselves willing and able to expand poetic narratives in the interests of criteria which are different: more logical, more rational in terms of narratorial sequence and motivation than those of epic verse.

We may now pass on to other chronicle versions. Little need be said of the 'versión vulgar', represented here only by MS *F* (and in some respects by the *Crónica Ocampiana*, of which more later). The differences between 'regia' and 'vulgar' versions, as is generally the case in the 'cuarta parte', are minimal, never approaching the importance of those found in the 'tercera parte' (see pp. 82 and 103 above).[19] Nor need the *Crónica*

en nuestro rastro, et non nos conuiene agora, mas andar los mas afforrechos que pudiermos, como omnes que andan en guerras et en lides et an a guarir por sus manos et sus armas' (pp. 525b48-526a4); *PMC*, line 709, where Pero Vermudez's desire to attack evokes the Cid's response ' ¡Non sea, por caridad!', expanded in the *PCG* to 'Trauo estonces el Çid con ell que estidiesse quedo et non mouiesse la senna' (p. 528b 18-21); and the treatment of the banquet scene between the Cid and the Count of Barcelona, where the rather heavy, even jeering humour of the Cid of the *Poema* (lines 1025 ff.) is much attenuated, as the following extracts show: 'Conde, comet et beuet, ca esto en que uos sodes por uarones passa, et non uos dexedes morir por ello, ca aun podredes cobrar uuestra fazienda et enderençar esto. Et si fizieredes como yo digo, fare yo como salgades de la prision; et si non fizieredes como yo digo, en toda uuestra uida non saldredes de la prision nin tornaredes a uuestra tierra' (p. 533b38-46); 'Et el Çid quando esto uio, con el grand duelo que ouo dell, dixol: "conde, bien uos digo uerdad que si non comedes siquier algun poco, que nunqua tornaredes a uuestra tierra" ' (p. 534a4-8). There is no reflection of the comic treatment of the Count's eating quickly (*PMC*, lines 1049-50), of the Cid's ironic pleasure (line 1058) or of the Count's ingratiating remark, 'del dia que fue conde non ianté tan de buen grado, / el sabor que dend é non será olbidado' (lines 1062-63). On this last episode see also T. Montgomery, 'The Cid and the Count of Barcelona', *HR*, 30 (1962), 1-11 (p. 4), and R. Menéndez Pidal, 'Tradicionalidad de las Crónicas Generales de España', *BRAH*, 136 (1955), 131-97 (pp. 150-54).

[19] A short list of discrepancies between MSS *E* and *F* in the section in question would include: *PCG*, pp. 523a53, 523b7, 524a22-23, 525a30-31, 526b25-26, 527b7, 527b15-16, 528a14-15, 528a36-37, 528b33-37, 529a5, 530a45-46, 531a 35-38, 531a43, 531b4, 531b41-532a48. In every case, see the variants noted in *PCG*. Only at pp. 528b33-37 and 531a35-38 is anything of substance omitted, in the first case the words 'et fuessen todauia adelante, de guisa que acorriessen a Pero Uermudez et a la senna. Et fueron CCC caualleros de los de la parte del Çid que

Manuelina detain us: for the first part of the reign of Alfonso VI (up to ch. 895 of the *PCG*) the *Crónica Abreviada* which is our only source of knowledge of don Juan Manuel's composition seems closely to follow the *PCG*.[20]

We are left with the *Crónica de Castilla*, the *Crónica Ocampiana* and the *Crónica de 1344*. The first of these tells a story whose narrative line is basically that of the *PCG* (and hence ultimately, as I have argued, of the *PMC*). However, this version is characterised by a strong tendency to expand, particularly by way of dialogue and explanation of motives (though there are, paradoxically, some instances of compression).[21] The tendency to expand may be seen, for instance, in the scene between the Cid and Alfonso when the former is exiled:

> E el Çid quisole besar la mano mas el Rey non gela quiso dar e dixole sannudamente: 'Ruy Dias, sallid de mi tierra.' Estonçe el Çid dio de las espuelas a vn mulo en que caualgaua e salto en vna tierra que era su heredat. E dixo: 'Sennor, non esto en vuestra tierra, e ante esto en la mia.' E dixo el Rey estonçe muy sannudamente: 'Salidme de todos mis Regnos syn otro alongamiento ninguno.' E dixo estonçe el Çid: 'Sennor, dadme plazo de treynta dias como es derecho de fijos dalgo.' E el dixo que lo non faria....[22]

Another divergence concerns the Jews of Burgos (it may also be noted that in the *CrC* the ruse is planned and set in train by the Cid and Martín Antolínez *before* the departure from Vivar). In this chronicle we find the first of the moralising comments

---

fueron ferir en los moros como el mandaua . . .'; in the second, 'Et Minnaya besole las manos; desi abaxosse por besarle los pies et non quiso el rey. Desi dixo Minnaya . . .'. Both of these may be copyist's errors, as is almost certainly the case in the one remaining instance, pp. 531b41–532a48, where an entire chapter (ch. 859) is omitted in MS *F*. All other cases are merely instances of relatively concise expression in the 'versión vulgar' (MS *F*). See also Gómez Pérez, 'Elaboración', pp. 254–63.

[20] Catalán, 'Don Juan Manuel ante el modelo alfonsí', p. 38. According to Catalán, the relationship is with the 'versión vulgar' (MS *F*) rather than with MS *E* (ibid., pp. 39–40). As is often the case, the degree of abbreviation in the *Crónica Abreviada* makes it difficult to carry out any meaningful textual comparisons. It does, however, contain the chapter missing from the only extant manuscript of the 'versión vulgar' (see above, n. 19), MS *BN* 1356, fol. 116r; cf. the edition by Grismer, p. 150.

[21] So, for instance, ch. 87 of the *CrC* (MS *G*; = ch. 85 of MS *S*), corresponding to ch. 849 of the *PCG*, dealing with the Cid's mission to Seville and Córdoba, makes no mention of the Cid being called 'El Cid Campeador' from this point on (*PCG*, p. 522b49–51); similar compression is found at the beginning of the chapters corresponding to ch. 852 of the *PCG*, which states that 115 knights, including Martín Antolínez, joined the Cid as he left Cardeña; this detail is absent from the *CrC*, MS *G*, fol. 156r, MS *J*, fol. 208r, MS *S*, fol. 33v.

[22] MS *G*, fol. 155v; MS *S* (fol. 32r–v) is similar; cf. *PCG*, p. 523a43–49.

which were later to become such a feature of this episode:[23] we are told that the Jews

> ... fiauan mucho del Çid porque nunca fallaran mentira en el por cosa que les ouiese a dar ... (MS G, fol. 155v; cf. MS S, fol. 32v, which is differently worded but similar in essence).

This may be not unconnected with a slight but noticeable increase in religious and pious references in the *CrC*. Thus an extra prayer is inserted when the Cid leaves Vivar:

> 'Santa Maria, madre de todos los santos, dadme poder que pueda destruyr todos los paganos e que dellos pueda ganar como faga bien a mis vasallos e a todos los otros que comigo fueren e me ayudaren';[24]

and when Minaya is sent back to Castile after the victory over Fariz and Galve there is an extra detail, not found in the *PCG*, of the Cid's sending the Moorish standards to be placed in the Cathedral at Burgos.[25]

Numbers in the later chronicle are often exaggerated: thus, when the Cid's forces are mustered as he leaves Castile, the *PMC* mentions that he had 300 knights with him (line 419), a figure repeated in the *PCG* (p. 524b30); the *CrC* gives him 1,300 knights and 3,000 foot soldiers.[26] Similarly, the figure for which the Cid sells Alcocer back to its Moorish inhabitants, 3,000 marks in the *PMC* (line 845) and in the *PCG* (p. 530b12-13) doubles to 6,000 marks in the *CrC* (MS G, fol. 159r, MS S, fol. 37r, MS J, fol. 215v).

Finally, it may be noted that new characters are named in the *CrC*: the two knights held captive with the Count of Barcelona, unnamed in the *PMC* (line 1035) and in the *PCG* (p. 534a9-10) are here Ynnigo and Guillen Bernal;[27] not unconnected is the greater prominence given to names of knights in the lists of those who fought well in battle, for instance against Fariz and Galve. The list is basically the same as that in the *PMC* (lines 733-41), but more care is given to territorial and genealogical detail: so, Minaya is 'el que touo Aviles e Çorita'; Martín Antolínez is 'sobrino del Mio Çid e fijo de

---

[23] See Smith, 'Did the Cid repay the Jews?', pp. 52-53.
[24] MS G, fol. 156r, MS S, fol. 33r; cf. *PCG*, p. 523b25-27.
[25] MS G, fol. 158v, MS S, fol. 37r; cf. *PCG*, ch. 856.
[26] MS S, fol. 33v, MS J, fol. 208v; however, MS G mentions only 400 knights and 3,000 foot soldiers (fol. 156v).
[27] MS S, fol. 39r; MS J calls the second knight 'don Bernalte' (fol. 219v), and MS G makes the first 'don Yugo' (fol. 160v).

Ferrando Diaz su hermano . . .', and Guyllen [sic] Garcia de Aragon and Feliz Munnoz, among others, are described, in MS S at least, as 'sobrinos del Çid, non tan çercanos como los otros'.[28] Equally interesting is the reason given for including such a list:

> Porque como quier que ellos son fynados deste mundo, non es derecho que mueran los nonbres de los que bien fazen. Ca non lo terrnian por Razon los que atienden a fazer bien o lo han fecho; ca si se callase, non serian tan tenudos los buenos de fazer bien, e por ende queremos que sepades . . . (MS G, fol. 158v)

One final detail about the *CrC* must not be overlooked. Alone among the chronicles under discussion, it preserves strong traces of assonance in the scene immediately preceding the opening of the *PMC* as we have it; Minaya speaks:

> 'Conbusco yremos todos, Çid, por yermos e por poblados e nunca vos falleçeremos en quanto seamos biuos e sanos; conbusco despenderemos las mulas e los cauallos, e los aueres e los pannos; sienpre vos servyremos como leales amigos e vasallos.'[29]

This unusual feature has long been known. Indeed, it was the basis of Menéndez Pidal's reconstruction of part at least of the *PMC*'s hypothetical opening which first appeared in his edition of 1908-11.[30] Though modern editors have placed far less reliance on the chronicles than did Menéndez Pidal as evidence with which to fill any lacunae in the text,[31] the sober tone of the fragment in question makes it not improbable that it formed part of the original poem. It is, though, so far as I know, a relatively rare instance in this part of the narrative of the *CrC* being more faithful to its source than other chronicles.[32] On the whole, the distinguishing marks of the

[28] MSS G, fol. 158v and S, fol. 36v; cf. Smith, 'The Personages of the *PMC*', pp. 589-91.
[29] MS G, fol. 155v. Note that MS S recounts this in such a way as to lose the assonance: 'Çid, con vos yremos por do quier que vos fueredes, e non vos desanparemos mientra seamos biuos, e despenderemos con vos todo lo que avemos, bestias e pannos e dineros, como leales amigos e vasallos' (fol. 32v); cf. MS J, fol. 206v.
[30] Menéndez Pidal, *CMC*, II, 1024-25. Diego Catalán prints the same extract from MS G in 'Poesía y novela', p. 435.
[31] Michael, for example, rejects almost all of the isolated lines reconstructed by Menéndez Pidal on the evidence of the chronicles (see Michael, *PMC, Aparato crítico*, notes to lines 181, 442, 875-76, 935, 1937 etc.); he does not mention the case under discussion here. See also the edition by C. C. Smith (Oxford, 1972), pp. 353-59.
[32] For another instance (the 'Jura de Santa Gadea'), see above, pp. 105-06 and note 32.

CrC, as the above examples show, are cases of a progressive departure from the matter-of-fact prosification and harmonisation of sources which was the Alphonsine ideal. In Diego Catalán's words:

> ... los cronistas de los últimos años del s. XIII y primeros del s. XIV abandonaron la tradicional fidelidad a las fuentes, a lo escrito, y se creyeron autorizados a refundir la historia cronística con la misma libertad con que los juglares innovaban la historia versificada.

He concludes, with particular reference to the *CrC*:

> ... buena parte de las novedades de la *Crónica de Castilla* no son poesía prosificada, sino prosa retórica, prosa novelesca.[33]

The *Crónica Ocampiana*—that is, the 'cuarta parte' of the text published by Ocampo in 1541[34]—has been mentioned above as being basically a mixture of the *PCG* and the *CrC*. It will be remembered that in the reign of Fernando I (ch. 5 above) it generally follows the latter chronicle, returning to follow the *PCG* for most of the reign of Sancho II (ch. 6 above). For the reign of Alfonso VI the structure of the *Ocampiana* is more complex; according to Lindley Cintra, it consists of a narrative based on the *PCG*, but with the addition of a series of short passages taken from the *CrC* to 'complete' the narrative.[35]

Very few such passages are to be found in the section under discussion. Although at one point the *Ocampiana* exaggerates numbers (the number of Moors killed 'en poca de ora' during the battle with Fariz and Galve is put at 2,300, compared with 1,300 in the *PCG*), it does not do so to the same extent as the *CrC* (which at the corresponding point talks of 3,500 or 4,000, according to the manuscript, being killed).[36] Only one short and puzzling detail is shared by the *CrC* and the *Ocampiana*: when the Cid leaves Burgos for Cardeña, both chronicles tell us that he collected up and took with him the domestic beasts and fowls he could find, but that then he sent them back:

Mando el Çid . . . tomar todo el ganado que fallaron fuera e mando mouer e andar al paso de las ansares que leuaua. E asi llego a Sant Pedro

---

[33] 'Poesía y novela', pp. 430 and 441. Compare Chalon, *L'Histoire et l'épopée*, pp. 254-56.
[34] See above, pp. 85 and n. 9, 100 and n. 19, 103 and n. 27.
[35] Lindley Cintra, *Cr1344*, I, 304-05; compare Catalán, *De Alfonso X*, pp. 333-35 and n. 30, and Chalon, *L'Histoire et l'épopée*, pp. 261-66.
[36] Ocampo, fol. 305r, MS *Q*, fol. 39v; cf. *PCG*, p. 529a1, and *CrC*, MSS *G*, fol. 158r, *S*, fol. 36r (3,500), and *J*, fol. 213r (4,000).

de Cardenna do tenia su mujer e sus fijas. Et quando vio que ninguno non auia salido en pos del, mando que tornasen la presa para Burgos.[37]

The *Crónica de 1344* in the 'cuarta parte', as has been stated, is fundamentally a version of the *CrC*, via the *Versión Gallego-portuguesa*, retouched in the light of new sources. In the case of the reigns of Fernando I and Sancho II discussed above (chs 5 and 6) the most important of such sources was the *CVR*; in the section here under discussion, however, the latter chronicle—however interesting it may be to us as containing a direct and unaltered prosification of the *PMC*—had less to offer later chroniclers. The *Cr1344* is here essentially a version of the *CrC*, though with some discrepancies.

The basic identity of these chronicles may be demonstrated by the presence in the *Cr1344* of almost all the major points listed above as characteristic of the *CrC*. Thus we find the account of the meeting between the Cid and the King (*Cr1344*, MSS Q^2, fol. 69r, *M*, fol. 239r); the comment on the Cid's previous good faith with the Jews (MSS Q^2, fol. 69r, *M*, fol. 239v); the prayer for good fortune on leaving Vivar (MSS Q^2, fol. 69v, *M*, fol. 239v); the sending of the Moorish standards to the cathedral at Burgos (MS Q^2, fol. 72v, MS *M*, fol. 244r); and the naming of the Count of Barcelona's knights (here as Hugo and Guillen Bernal: MS Q^2, fol. 74r, MS *M*, fol. 247r). Numbers are exaggerated as in the *CrC*, indeed rather more so on occasion: the number of Moors killed at the beginning of the battle against Fariz and Galve is in the *Q* MS of the *Cr1344* no fewer than 10,500 (MS Q^2, fol. 72r; cf. above, p. 125 and note 36; in MS *M* the figure is 1,500, fol. 243r); when Minaya returns from Castile he brings not 200 fresh knights (as in the *CrC*, MS *G*, fol. 159v and *PCG*, p. 532a18) but 300 (MS Q^2, fol. 73r, MS *M*, fol. 243r).

The *Cr1344* does, however, have its own idiosyncrasies: it omits Minaya's speech on leaving Vivar, so strongly marked by assonance in the *CrC* (cf. MS Q^2, fol. 69r, MS *M*, fol. 239r)

---

[37] *CrC*, MS *S*, fol. 33r; cf. MS *G*, fol. 156r, and Ocampo: '... e mando tomar quanto fallo fuera de Burgos, e las ansares, e mando mouer al paso dellas ... e vio que ninguno salio empos del, e mando tornar toda la presa a Burgos' (fol. 302v; MS *Q*, fol. 35v). The manuscripts which contain this Ocampian material are all 'mixed' in nature: this includes MS *Q* (see Catalán, *De Alfonso X*, p. 333), as well as MSS *Ch, Ph, Th*, and *W* (ibid., pp. 329 and 333-34), all of which have some of the features referred to here and below (see pp. 134-35, 138 and notes 66 and 72); only Ocampo's edition has them all.

and, immediately after this point it is the only chronicle under discussion not to mention a tradition of omens deriving from *PMC* lines 11-12:

> a la exida de Bivar   ovieron la corneia diestra
> e entrando a Burgos   oviéronla siniestra.[38]

On the other hand, there are some expansions, notably in MS *Q*: the prayer on leaving Burgos referred to above (p. 123) is in fact slightly expanded when compared with the *CrC*:

> 'Ruegote mi Sennor Ihesu Christo que tu por tu merçet me des poder e saber para que yo sienpre defienda la tu Santa Fee Catolica e pueda destruyr los enemigos della. E esto me faze, Sennor, por los mereçimientos e Ruegos de la tu Santa Madre e Biendita Virgen Santa Maria que pueda dellos aver por que faga bien a los amigos; e guardame, Sennor, estos que conmigo vienen . . .' (MS Q^2, fol. 69v; MS *M*, fol. 239v is similar to the *CrC* version quoted above).

When Alvar Fánnez advises on tactics before the battle against Fariz and Galve, he ends, in the *Cr1344* only, with the words:

> 'E si aqui ay algunos que non sean confessados, luego se confiesen e arrepintan de todos sus pecados . . .' (MS Q^2, fol. 71v, MS *M*, fol. 242v).

The justification for the inclusion of the list of knights who fought well in that battle (see above, p. 124) is more rhetorically expressed here:

> Mas queremos aqui dezir quales fueron aquellos que en esta batalla ouieron la aventajen e por que fue vençida la batalla, porque los sus nobres e buenos fechos non sean oluidados: que como quier que los cuerpos son muertos, biuen las sus buenas famas. E otrosi porque todos los que han coraçones e deseo de bien fazer fallen buenos enxenplos de aquellos que esta batalla vençieron . . . (MS Q^2, fol. 72r; MS *M* (fol. 243v) is less rhetorical).[39]

When, after that same battle, the Cid sends Minaya back to Castile with gifts for Alfonso, after making the obvious remark that one must give thanks to God for the victory, the *Cr1344* is alone in having him add:

> 'E despues conoscamos sennorio al Rey don Alfonso, porque non digan en Castilla que sienpre nos dormimos' (MS Q^2, fol. 72v; cf. MS *M*, fol. 244r).

---

[38] Compare *PCG*, p. 523b21-23, *CVR*, MS *N*, fol. 114r; *CrC*, MS *G*, fol. 156r; against all these, *Cr1344*, MS Q^2, fol. 69v.

[39] The actual list of knights which follows is much plainer than that in the *CrC*, with none of that chronicle's interest in genealogy (see above, pp. 124-25); *Cr1344*, MSS Q^2, fol. 72r, and *M*, fol. 243v.

Finally this chronicle, at least in its expanded version, gives the Cid, by implication, an even greater rôle in the affairs of the Moorish kingdom of Zaragoza by referring to his putting Çuleyma on the throne, while in other chronicles his rôle is rather that of a guardian of the settlement willed by the old King, Almodafar.[40]

We have seen that the last three chronicles discussed—the *CrC*, the *Ocampiana* and the *Cr1344*—follow basically the same line as the *PCG*, though with greater or lesser degrees of divergence from it. The *Ocampiana* is the most conservative, the *CrC* and the *Cr1344*, while sharing a majority of innovating features, differ in some others; and, on balance, it is the *Cr1344* which takes us furthest from the original narrative.

In previous chapters it has been possible to explain such divergences in the light either of known sources or of the influence of one chronicle on another, as well as in terms of chroniclers' inventiveness. In the case of the story of the Cid's exile, the first two factors seem really not to apply, and the conclusions reached above about the *CrC* and its compilers' motivation should in all probability be applied equally in the case of the *Cr1344*: we are dealing, in effect, with rhetorical, novelesque prose which has its own inbuilt tendencies to complication and elaboration.

(b) *The Infantes de Carrión*

After the defeat and release of the Count of Barcelona, the chronicles, without exception, leave the narrative of the *PMC* and, for the next section of the story, follow other sources. They begin with further Eastern campaigns of the Cid (*PCG*, chs 862-65) for which the principal sources are the *HRod* supplemented by the Toledano and Tudense; continue with Alfonso's capture of Toledo and other deeds (*PCG*, chs 866-76) based principally on the Toledano, and then take up the Cid's affairs with the campaign for the capture of Valencia (chs 877-82 and 889-922). The source for these chapters, however, is not the *PMC* but the now lost Arabic history of Ben Alcama,

---

[40] Compare the *PCG*: 'Et Çulema rey de Saragoça amo mucho a Roy Diaz, et diol tudo su regno en poder et en guarda ...;... Roy Diaz ... se tenie con Çuleyma, et porquel guardaua la tierra ...' (p. 532b5-8, 15-17); and the *Cr1344*: 'E el Çid fizo luego fazer Rey de Çaragoça a Çulema ...' (MS Q^2, fol. 73v; MS *M*, on the other hand, is more like the *PCG*: fol. 245v).

supplemented here and there from the *HRod*. The chapters from 883 to 888 deal with Alfonso's affairs, including the interesting excursus on his reputed marriage to a Moorish princess, possibly based on the *Cantar de la Mora Zaida*,[41] but drawing principally, once again, on the Toledano and Tudense.

Only with ch. 923[42] does the narrative line return to that of the *PMC*. In the *CVR*, as with the previous section, the narrative is again recognisably that of the extant text, and for a detailed comparison the reader is again referred to Powell's book (see above, pp. 119-20). The other chronicles, however, present a less straightforward picture. Beginning, as is customary, with the *PCG*, it is the case that chs 923 to 948 tell basically the story of the *PMC*, lines 1221-3716: that is, the Cid's defence of Valencia against the rulers of Seville and Morocco, his reconciliation with Alfonso, the marriage of his daughters to the Infantes de Carrión, the *Afrenta de Corpes* and the subsequent *cortes* at Toledo with their sequel, the duels at Carrión; chs 950 and 951 then tell at greater length of the second marriages of the Cid's daughters to the Infantes of Navarra and Aragón, that is, what is dealt with in far more summary form in lines 3717-3725 of the *PMC*. The story told in the *PCG* is, however, patently not based directly on the extant *PMC*, and Menéndez Pidal seems to have had far more justification in claiming the existence of a *cantar refundido* for this part of the narrative than in the case of the *Cantar del destierro* (see above, p. 120 and n. 16). This may not be the only explanation for the differences, though, as we shall see. Before tackling the question, however, it will be convenient to analyse in more detail what the differences are between the poem and the chronicle versions. I have made a separate study of a central episode in this section, the *Afrenta de Corpes* itself and the events immediately preceding and following it (*PMC*, lines 2535-2900, *PCG*, chs 933-39).[43] In it I draw attention to what seem to have motivated the salient differences: the complicated narrative of the chronicle text containing more

---

[41] See *PCG*, pp. xliii-xliv and clxxx-clxxxi, also Menéndez Pidal, *España del Cid*, II, 777-79.

[42] Inevitably, the division is not so neat as this suggests. Menéndez Pidal saw reminiscences of occasional lines of the *PMC* in chs 921 and 922 (see *PCG*, p. clxxxvii).

[43] Pattison, 'The *Afrenta de Corpes*'.

explanations—and ones of a more rational kind—of characters' motives, the chroniclers' tendency to introduce new characters and to explain in detail sequences of events only hinted at in the poem. The same characteristics can be seen throughout this section of the *PCG*, as the following examples will show.

We may begin with the dramatis personae. In the chronicles, characters often act in pairs: so Pero Bermúdez joins Minaya in giving advice to the Cid in ch. 922 (*PCG*, p. 592b30; cf. *PMC*, line 1256 where Minaya alone is mentioned) and Martín Antolínez is associated with Minaya in the embassy to the King in the following chapter (*PCG*, p. 593a32-33; cf. *PMC*, lines 1270-71). A character introduced into the *PCG* who is merely alluded to in the *PMC* is the father of the Infantes de Carrión, 'el conde don Gonçalo', who is seated next to the Cid at the great feast to celebrate the reconciliation at the *vistas*.[44] New characters also appear; as well as Pero Sánchez and Ordoño, whose roles in the *Afrenta de Corpes* are discussed in my 1977 article.[45] there also appear Benito Pérez, the King's *repostero mayor* ('el qual era natural de Siguença'; *PCG*, p. 615b27-28) who is responsible for setting the hall in order for the *cortes*, and the Cid's squire Fernant Alonso ('en el que el fiaua mucho, que el le criara de pequenno'; *PCG*, pp. 615b49-616a1) who is sent to place the Cid's ivory stool in the appropriate place at the *cortes*. The judges or *alcaldes*—referred to in the *PMC* simply as 'el conde don Anrrich e el conde don Remond / e estos otros condes que del vando non sodes'[46] —are here swollen to six, named at length with their fiefs and descendants.[47] Even this pales into insignificance compared

[44] *PCG*, p. 601a6-7. In the *PMC* he is referred to as the Infantes' father in lines 2268 and 2441, is listed as present at the *cortes* in line 3008, and makes a direct intervention only to save the life of Asur González at the end of the last duel (line 3690).
[45] 'The *Afrenta de Corpes*', pp. 130 and 139.
[46] *PMC*, lines 3135-36; compare the slightly longer list of notables attending at lines 3003 ff.
[47] '... el primero fue el conde don Remont de Tolosa et de Sant Gil de Prouencia; et este conde don Remont era yerno del rey don Alfonso, casado con su fija, el qual fue despues padre del emperador don Alfonso dEspanna;— et el segundo fue el conde don Vela que poblo a Salamanca por mandado del rey don Alfonso;— el tercero fue el conde don Suero de Caso;— el quarto fue el conde don Osuero que se llamaua de Campos, et deste conde don Osuero vienen los de Villalobos et los Osueros;— el quinto fue el conde don Rodrigo que poblo Valladolit por mandado de rey et deste conde don Rodrigo viene el linaie de los Girones;— el sesto fue el conde don Munno de Lara, et deste vienen los de Lara' (*PCG*, p. 617b27-42).

with the *'mesnada'* listed as accompanying the Cid to the *cortes*. This does not correspond precisely to the list at *PMC*, lines 3063-71, which is a list of those already in Toledo who are chosen to accompany the hero to court: *PCG*, p. 615a1-25 gives the names of no less than twenty-one knights, listed with details of fiefs and the numbers of vassals and knights accompanying them.[48] Some examples of characters in this list not known to the *PMC* are 'don Dia Sanchez dArlança . . . et don Minaya Sonna que poblo Alcobiella . . . don Garçia de Roa e el Serrazin su hermano sennor de Aça . . . Gonçalo Ferrandez el que poblo Panpliga . . . Antolin Sanchez de Soria leuaua entre fijos e parientes XL^a caualleros . . . (*PCG*, p. 615a8-21).

Narrative differences also follow the expected pattern: details are 'tidied up'. The most celebrated of these is the repayment of the Jews, omitted or overlooked in the *PMC* but here to be found in ch. 923 (*PCG*, p. 594a32-b2);[49] also, the rescue of Alvar Salvadórez, captured by the Moors in the battle against Yuçef (*PMC*, line 1681) and then not mentioned again until he reappears in the list of those accompanying the Cid to the *vistas* (line 1994) is here related at the end of the battle:

. . . fue fallada vna tienda del rey de Marruecos . . . e fue fallado en ella Aluar Saluadorez que fuera preso en la espoloneada (*PCG*, p. 598a37-41)

The tendency to rationalise events is well exemplified by the account of the escape of the Cid's lion, here a complex narrative involving inattentive keepers, a rope left dangling, etc. (*PCG*, ch. 929), to be compared with the simple statement of the *PMC* that 'saliós' de la rred e desatós' el león' (line 2282).[50] A further example, this time concerning the rationalisation of a character's actions, is to be seen in ch. 927, where the Cid asks the advice of two of his vassals, Alvar Fánnez and Pero Bermúdez, about the projected marriages of his daughters to the *Infantes*, while in the *PMC* there is no hint of consultation (cf. *PCG*, p. 600a17-21 and *PMC*, lines 1931-42).

The one part of the narrative—in addition to the actual *Afrenta*, already mentioned—in which the *PMC* and the *PCG* part company most obviously is the *cortes* scene itself. In the

---

[48] See Smith, 'The Personages of the *PMC*', p. 588.
[49] See Smith, 'Did the Cid repay the Jews?', pp. 531-35.
[50] See Catalán, 'Poesía y novela', pp. 432-33 and Hook, 'The Episode of the Cid's Lion', especially p. 555.

PMC this is marked by a sober gravity and an evident relish for forensic oratory which make it in some ways the real climax of the poem. In the *PCG* all this gives way to an evident sensationalism. The threefold structure of the Cid's first speech, in which he demands the return first of his swords, then of his other property and finally of his honour in the form of a challenge of *'menos valer'* is broadly preserved in the *PCG*, chs 941-42 (cf. *PMC*, lines 3146-3269); but it includes a less characteristic threat of vengeance if justice be denied:

'yre yo a la su heredat de Carrion de que se ellos preçian, et y los prendere por las gargantas, et leuarlos he comigo presos pora Valencia o son mis fijas et sus mugeres, et y los fare yo tomar penitencia de lo que fizieron, et darles he a comer de aquellos maniares que meresçen' (p. 620a12-18).

What is more, when García Ordóñez interferes on the *Infantes'* behalf (*PCG*, p. 621a48-b11; cf. *PMC*, lines 3271-79), the response from Pero Bermúdez is a violent one:

... tan grant pesar ouo ende Pero Bermudez, que aquello le fizo oluidar el mal talante que tenie ... Et sobraço su manto, et fuesse derechamiente contra el conde don Garçia; et desque fue çerca el, et veya quel no podria errar, çerro el punno et diol vna tal ferida que dio con el en tierra. Por esta ferida ... sacaron mas de çient espadas a vna ora de las vaynas; et los vnos llamauan Cabra et los otros Grannon, et los del Çid llamauan Valencia et Biuar. A poca de ora fueron todos los condes derramados dalli; et el rey don Alfonso començo a dar muy grandes vozes ... (p. 621b28-44).

Finally, the relationship between *retos* and duels is broken: in the *PMC* it is Pero Bermúdez who challenges and subsequently fights the *infante* Fernando, and the same is true of Martín Antolínez with Diego and Muño Gustioz with Asur González;[51] in the *PCG* there are no individual *retos* as such, and when the champions for duels are decided by the Cid it appears arbitrary that Pero Bermudez should fight Diego González (although in the *PCG* it is Ordoño who has thrown in the latter's face his behaviour in the battle against Búcar), Martín Antolínez, Suer (i.e. Asur) González and Muño Gustioz, Ferrando.[52] What was a carefully constructed sequence of events has degenerated, both structurally and in terms of decorum, to a considerable extent.

What has been said above about the other chronicles

---

[51] *PMC*, lines 3306 ff., 3361 ff., and 3382 ff.
[52] *PCG*, pp. 622b44-623a3.

(pp. 121-28) is to some extent valid also for the section now under discussion. Thus, the 'versión vulgar' is often more concise in expression, though not markedly different in narrative structure;[53] the *Crónica Abreviada*, however, presents a more complex picture and shows that the *Manuelina* does not here follow the *PCG* so closely as before.[54] The *Crónica de Castilla* complicates the narrative in various ways, some of which have already been mentioned in my article on the *Afrenta de Corpes* (see above, pp. 129-30 and note 43) and by Diego Catalán.[55] A few further notes may help to indicate the nature of this chronicle's expansion of the material. Characters are again introduced, of whom the most important is Martín Peláez,[56] who plays a part in the aftermath of the Corpes episode[57] and is also mentioned in passing in chapters corresponding to *PCG*, ch. 922:

> Et en este alcançe fue muy bueno Martin Pelaez el Esturiano, asy que non ouo y tal cauallero que tan bueno fuese en armas nin tanto leuase ende de pres;[58]

and 924, where he accompanies Pero Bermúdez and others to escort doña Jimena and her daughters back to Valencia.[59] There is also a tendency to introduce details of a pious kind: so, a reference is made to the founding of churches in Valencia, notably that of Santa María de las Virtudes:

---

[53] An examination of the published variants in chs 923-47 (*PCG*, pp. 593-629) shows the differences between MSS *E* and *F* to be minimal and almost all of purely stylistic significance. Two instances where the manuscripts differ slightly more may be due to copyists' errors: pp. 601a21-23 and 621a5-6.

[54] BN MS 1356, fols 122v-126r. From the conquest of Valencia onwards, the *Crónica Abreviada*, while still structurally following the *PCG*, shows strong influence from the *CrC*. See Catalán, 'Don Juan Manuel ante el modelo alfonsí', pp. 39-43, and Pattison, 'The *Afrenta de Corpes*', pp. 136-38. Two obvious interpolations from the *CrC* are the inclusion of Martín Peláez in the escort sent by the Cid with his daughters (fol. 124r), and a chapter (130) dealing with Bucar's vow to avenge Yunes's defeat (fol. 123v). Cf. the edition by Grismer, pp. 160 and 159 and compare the *CrC*, MS *G*, fols 198v and 195r.

[55] 'Poesía y novela', pp. 433 ff.; see especially p. 438 n. 2 for the case of the escape of the Lion, and cf. Hook, 'The Episode of the Cid's Lion', pp. 557-59.

[56] Martín Peláez was introduced earlier in the *CrC* in an episode inserted into the narrative at a point corresponding to the end of ch. 915 of the *PCG*. On this episode, see Diego Catalán, 'La *Estoria de los Reyes del Señorío de Africa*', *RPh*, 17 (1963), 346-53 (p. 351 and n. 35). The episode is also in the *Crónica Ocampiana*, fols 334r-335v, and in the *Crónica Abreviada* (BN MS 1356, fol. 122v; cf. the edition by Grismer p. 158.

[57] Pattison, 'The *Afrenta de Corpes*', pp. 132-33 and 139.

[58] *CrC*, MS *G*, fol. 188v; cf. MSS *S*, fol. 72v and *J*, fol. 289r.

[59] *CrC*, MS *G*, fol. 190r; cf. MSS *S*, fol. 74v and *J*, fol. 293r.

por que era çerca del alcazar onde yua el Cid a oyr las oras mas a menudo;[60]

and doña Jimena is said to have brought with her from Castile:

muy buenas Reliquias e otras cosas sagradas que dio estonçe para onrrar la nueua iglesia de Valencia.[61]

There is also a hint of legalism, seen for instance in a reference to Alfonso granting the Cid:

buenos preuillegios de todo quanto conquiriera et de lo que conquiriese de aqui adelante, libre e quito . . .[62]

As for other differences, the King is, at the *cortes*, much more openly antagonistic to the *Infantes*; he replies to them at great length when they complain that the Cid's family was unworthy of them (cf. *PMC*, lines 3296-3300 and *PCG*, p. 620b2-24), giving what is effectively a genealogy of the Cid and concluding:

'Asy viene de la mas alta sangre de Castilla. Demas, que el Çid es tan onrrado omne e tan acabado qual non ouo otro tal en el nuestro linaje, e por ende veredes como vos defenderedes . . .'.[63]

Throughout this section the *Crónica Ocampiana* follows the narrative line of the *PCG*. As Lindley Cintra observed, the distinguishing features of the *CrC*, used elsewhere by the compiler of the *Ocampiana*, are not generally found between the fall of Valencia and the end of the *cortes* scene.[64] Diego Catalán has pointed out, however, that throughout the reign of Alfonso VI there are to be found in the *Ocampiana* isolated verbal reminiscences of the *CrC*,[65] and examples may be seen in the inclusion of Martín Peláez in the party sent to meet doña Jimena (Ocampo, fol. 339v, MS *Q*, fol. 94v; cf. *CrC*, MS *G*, fol. 190r and *PCG*, p. 595a38); in the explanation of the nickname Pero Mudo applied to Pero Bermúdez:

E Pero Mudo le dixo el Çid porque era gago vn poco que se le trauaua la lengua (Ocampo, fol. 353v; cf. *CrC*, MS *G*, fol. 206v and *PCG*, p. 621b19 ff.);

[60] *CrC*, MS *G*, fol. 189r; cf. MSS *S*, fol. 73r and *J*, fol. 290r.
[61] *CrC*, MS *G*, fol. 190v; cf. MSS *S*, fols. 74v-75r and *J*, fol. 294r.
[62] *CrC*, MS *G*, fol. 190r; cf. MSS *S*, fol. 74r and *J*, fol. 292v.
[63] *CrC*, MS *G*, fol. 205v; cf. MSS *S*, fol. 92v and *J*, fol. 333r-v.
[64] Lindley Cintra, *Crónica*, I, ccciv.
[65] 'La mezcla de una y otra crónica en la *Ocampiana* está hecha más al detalle de lo que Cintra supone; hallo en ella bastantes más párrafos o simples frases de la *Crónica de Castilla* que los consignados por Cintra' (*De Alfonso X*, p. 335 n. 30).

and in a number of other details which increase in frequency as the court scene proceeds.[66]

As for the *Cr1344*, this remains largely a slightly rewritten version of the *CrC*. It essentially contains most of the features of the latter chronicle listed above,[67] with some others. A tendency to legalism is shown, for instance, in a remark that the Cid's gift to Alfonso (after the battle against the Emperor of Morocco) was prompted 'reconosçiendo el sennorio del rey don Alfonso' (MS Q^2, fol. 107r), and a similar tendency may be seen in the end of the third duel, between Muño Gustioz and Suer González, the latter's father having accepted defeat on his son's behalf:

> E Nunno Gustius era omne bien guisado e pregunto a los fieles si era vençido por lo que dezia el padre, e ellos dixeron que non. Et el tormo luego por lo matar. Mas Suer Gonçalez, quando lo vido venir sobre si, ouo muy grant miedo e dixo 'Non me firades, Nunno Gustius, ca vençido so, e todo es verdad quanto uos dexistes . . .' (MS Q^2, fol. 121v; cf. MS *M*, fol. 321v).

Sometimes the elaboration is fundamentally stylistic, as when a fulsome speech is put into the King's mouth at the *vistas*:

> 'Don Ruy Diaz, lo por que vos enbie llamar para me ver conuusco fue por dos cosas. La primera por vos ver por los grandes e muy fermosos seruiçios que feziestes al Rey don Ferrando mi padre e mi Sennor, que Dios aya, e a mi, como quier que en comienço de mi Regnado vos oviestes sanna e yo vos echase de mi tierra por mal consejo de algunos. Pero de guisa lo fezistes vos que nunca de vos Resçeby deseruiçio, por la qual Razon yo vos so tenudo para vos fazer muchas merçedes e de vos amar sienpre . . .' (MS Q^2, fol. 108v; cf. MS *M*, fols 294v-295r).

The author of the *Cr1344* takes more care in introducing the third villain, Suero González, since when Pero Bermúdez and Muño Gustioz are set to observe the Infantes (cf *PMC*, lines 2168-73) we are told that:

---

[66] Other examples include Minaya's reply to Suer González, 'ca mas paresçen palabras de beudo que de cuerdo' (Ocampo, fol. 354r and *CrC*, MS *G*, fol. 206v); cf. *PCG*: 'ca mas son palabras de almuerzo que de fidalgo' (p. 622a40-41); and Pero Bermúdez's request to be *one* of the Cid's champions ('que me otorguedes que sea yo el vno de los que ouieren de lidiar', Ocampo, fol. 354r and *CrC*, MS *G*, fol. 207r); cf. *PCG*, 'que me otorguedes que lidie con amos los infantes de Carrion' (p. 622b 41-42).

[67] The following references are from MS Q^2: Martín Peláez (here called M. Pérez or M. Paez), fol. 103v (MS *M*, fol. 286r) and fol. 105r (MS *M*, fol. 288v); Santa María de las Virtudes, fol. 104r (MS *M*, fol. 286v); relics brought by Jimena, not in MS Q^2, but cf. MS *M*, fol. 289r; grant of privileges for future conquests, fol. 104v (MS *M*, fol. 287v); the Cid's genealogy, fol. 118r (MS *M*, fol. 315r).

muy en breue sopieron las maneras de los Infantes, porque con ellos yua el conde don Suer Gonçales, que era hermano de su padre, que los criara mal e los consejara peor. Ca ellos a todos desdennauan . . . (MS Q^2, fol. 109r; cf. MS M, fol. 295v).[68]

Finally, the court scene is even more boisterous than in the other chronicles, as may be seen from the following extract:

> E el rrey quando esto vio dio grandes bozes que non peleasen ante el, e fue muy sannudo contra Pero Bermudes e tomolo por el cabeçon e pidole el espada. E el Cid cuydo que lo queria ferir con ella, e dixole 'Sennor, non fagades, ca membraruos deue de las batallas a que uos fue bueno . . .' E entonçe lanço el Cid la mano por Pero Bermudez e tirogelo de las manos e tomole la espada e diogela . : . (MS Q^2, fol. 118v; cf. MS M, fol. 316v, which is less developed).

It is clear that the process of *novelización* is proceeding apace.

The relationship between the chronicles and the nature of their individual characteristics requires little commentary beyond what has been said both in this section and in the previous one. The process by which the *CrC* tells a more complex narrative than the *PCG*, by which the *Ocampiana* combines the two and by which the *Cr1344* takes the *CrC* and adds yet more idiosyncrasies is, if not a simple and straightforward one, still one explicable in terms of what we have seen earlier in this study of the development of historiography into what can only be called fiction. There remains the all-important question of whether the differences between the *PCG* and the *PMC* (and the *CVR*) ought to be explained in a similar way or in some other. This can conveniently be left until after we have examined the last section of the Cidian biography.

(c) *The Cid's death and its sequel.*

With one exception, the chronicles under discussion give a recognisably similar account of the Cid's death: this is the material of the so-called *Leyenda de Cardeña* or, to give it the title which appears in the chronicle version, the *Estoria del Noble Varón el Cid Ruy Diaz el Campeador, Señor que fue de Valencia*. The story is best known in its published form, that is,

---

[68] Compare *PCG*, p. 601b30 ff. In the *PCG*, Suero González is not mentioned until after the incident of the lion (p. 604b11). In the *PMC* he appears only in passing at this point (lines 2172-73) and at line 3008, but plays no positive role in the action until well into the court scene. See Pattison, 'The *Afrenta de Corpes*', pp. 131 and 138.

as it appears in the *PCG*, and it is in that version that it has been the subject of important studies by Entwistle, Russell and, most recently, Smith.[69] It will be convenient, however, to look first at the *CVR*, this being the only chronicle not to contain the material in question. The *CVR*, faithful to the *PMC* which it has used constantly as its principal source for the Cid's deeds, relates the hero's death in Valencia in the month of May in the year 1099 A.D.[70] The chronicle continues:

> Donna Ximena su muger e don Aluar Fanez Minaya leuaron el su cuerpo a Sand Pedro de Cardenna. Et porque en la su estoria sse contiene de commo murio e lo que acaesçio a la su muerte, por eso non lo pusimos aqui por non alongar [MS *J*: enbargar] esta estoria (*CVR*, MS *N*, fol. 162v; MS *J*, fol. 102r);

and goes on to deal with Alfonso's affairs. This is, as Russell has pointed out, in sharp contradiction to the heading to this chapter, which has announced its subject matter as: 'la muerte de Ruy Diaz Çid e de commo sse perdio Valençia'. Russell doubted Lindley Cintra's contention that the *estoria* of the above quotation was the *HRod*, arguing that it was more likely to be the *Leyenda de Cardeña*, and that the change of heart of the compiler may have been due to a conflict between that source and a—now lost—ending of the *PMC*.[71] I find no difficulty in accepting the first of these contentions—that the compilers of the *CVR* knew the *Leyenda de Cardeña*—but rather more in accepting the hypothesis of the *PMC*'s lost ending. This is due in good measure to the very completeness of the poem as it stands: its true narrative and thematic climax comes with lines 3724-25:

> Oy los rreyes d'España sos parientes son,
> a todos alcança ondra por el que en buen ora naçió.

Although it is not inconceivable that the copy used by the compilers of the *CVR* had as postscript a slightly more expanded form of what we know as lines 3726-30, this must be pure

[69] Entwistle, '*La Estoria del noble varon*', Russell, 'San Pedro de Cardeña', Smith, 'The Cid as Charlemagne'; see also Catalán, 'Crónicas generales y cantares de gesta', p. 306 n. 129 and 'Poesía y novela', pp. 431-33, and Chalon, *L'Histoire et l'épopée*, pp. 239-43.

[70] *CVR*, MS *N*, fol. 162v; cf. MS *J*, fol. 102r. The *PMC* mentions 'el día de cinquaesma' (line 3726), and in 1099 Pentecost fell on 29 May (Michael, *PMC*, p. 309).

[71] 'San Pedro de Cardeña', pp. 74-76; cf. Lindley Cintra, *Crónica*, I, cclxxiv-cclxxv. Chalon agrees with Russell's hypothesis (*L'Histoire et l'épopée*, pp. 260-61).

speculation. It should be remembered that the *CVR* at this stage is a shadow of the Alphonsine enterprise. While it is a version— and a unique one—which did not go the way of *novelización* like other chronicles, it is not Alphonsine either chronologically or in terms of historiographical confidence. Diego Catalán refers to it in the following terms:

'. . . de lo que hubiera sido [la *Estoria de España*] en caso de haberse realizado el proyecto alfonsí sólo pálida e indirectamenta nos lo deja entrever la *CVR*',

and he also notes that 'se aparta de la *Estoria de España* en cuanto al estilo de la redacción, pues a menudo tiende a resumir libremente lo narrado por las fuentes' ('Crónicas generales y cantares de gesta', pp. 214-15 and n. 81).

It is clear that at this point the compilers of the *CVR* were faced with a problem, a need to reconcile contradictory sources, but what those sources were cannot be known; they may have been the *HRod* and the *Leyenda de Cardeña*. At all events, the *CVR* takes for once the easiest of all ways out by effectively leaving a lacuna.

The remaining chronicles all contain the 'Cardeña' material and fall into two groups. On the one hand there is the *PCG*, together with the *Manuelina* if Juan Manuel's abbreviation may be trusted; on the other the *CrC* and the *Cr1344* (with some aspects of the *Ocampiana*), which tell versions of the story which broadly agree with one another (though with some divergences), while generally differing consistently from the *PCG*.[72]

The version found in the *PCG* occupies chs 947-48 and 951-62. Its narrative line has been summarised by Russell ('San Pedro de Cardeña', pp. 60 ff.) and as it is available in published form there seems little point in resummarising it here in any detail. Suffice it to say that it is the story of the Cid's death, preceded by an embassy from the 'Sultan of Persia' who supplied, among much else, the materials for the Cid's autoembalmment, followed by the famous story of how his corpse

---

[72] The *Ocampiana*'s hybrid nature as a blend of the *PCG* and the *CrC* (see above, pp. 125, 134 and notes 35, 64, and 65) is very apparent at this stage. For details, see Lindley Cintra, *Crónica*, I, ccciv-cccv. The *Crónica Abreviada* follows in its chapter structure that of the *PCG* rather than that of the *CrC* and the *Cr1344*, which break down the material into shorter units. Compare *PCG*, pp. 627b6-643b7; *Crónica Abreviada*, fols 125v-127v, and the edition by Grismer, pp. 162-64; *CrC*, MS G, fols 210r-219v; *Cr1344*, MS Q^2, fols 122r-128v.

was mounted for the last battle against the Moors, and culminating in the Cardeña-story properly speaking: that is, the tale of how the Cid's body was taken to the monastery and how sundry magical or miraculous occurrences at Cardeña over a period of ten years preceded its normal burial. The nature and much of the rationale behind this quasi-hagiographical account, together with its implications for the existence and details of a tomb cult have been admirably set out by Russell ('San Pedro de Cardeña', passim) and more recently Smith has pointed to definite resemblances between aspects of this account and hagiographical material dealing with Charlemagne.[73]

Only one point relevant to this study suggests itself: Russell rightly draws attention to the large amount of rationalisation involved in the *PCG*'s account. For example, the embassy of the Sultan of Persia and the story of the mysterious balsam may well be in part at least an attempt to explain in rational terms the 'unusually effective embalming' of the Cid's body (p. 61); and the complicated account of the shaped boards and cords by which the Cid's body was mounted on his horse (*PCG*, p. 637a23-45) is both incredible and faintly comic. Russell ascribes these rationalisations to the *Estoria* (pp. 61-62): where important narrative elements are introduced—as in the first of the above cases—that is probably valid; but such details as the Cid on his horse remind one irresistibly of the chroniclers' tendency to rationalise and account for details (compare the episode of the Cid's lion and many aspects of the *Afrenta de Corpes* analysed in my 1977 article: see above, pp. 129-31 and nn. 50 and 43). In short, we have little evidence on which to assert that such and such an element is due to the inventiveness either of the monastic authors of the *Estoria* or of the lay compilers of the chronicle.[74]

Let us look finally at the *CrC* and the *Cr1344*. A consistent feature of both versions, in comparison with the *PCG*, is

[73] 'The Cid as Charlemagne'. It must be said that some of the points of details where resemblance is noted seem relatively slight. The similarity to Einhard noted on pp. 513 and 516 and that to Notker on p. 514 are not convincing. However, the overall conclusion—that there exists a high probability of Carolingian influence —is amply justified.

[74] It has been pointed out that not all fantastic details in this story are necessarily pure invention. The apparently bizarre story of the black Amazons in Búcar's army (*PCG*, p. 636a48-b30) may be based on a misinterpretation, part visual, part linguistic, of actual facts: see L. P. Harvey, 'Nugeymath Turquía: *PCG*, chapter 956', *Journal of Semitic Studies*, 13 (1968), 232-40.

abbreviation. So, for instance, the list of the Cid's conquests at *PCG*, p. 628a1-4 is omitted or much shortened (*CrC*, MS *G*, fol. 210r, *Cr1344*, MS Q^2, fol. 122r, MS *M*, fol. 322v), as is the short list of the Sultan's gifts at p. 628a11-25 of the *PCG* (cf. *CrC*, MS *G*, fol. 210v, *Cr1344*, MS Q^2, fol. 122v, MS *M*, fol. 322v); Jimena and Gil Diaz are asked to bring the boxes of balsam and myrrh in the *PCG*, p. 635a3-4, but not in the *CrC* (MS *G*, fol. 214r) or in the *Cr1344* (MS Q^2, fol. 125v, MS *M*, fol. 329r).[75] The two chronicles also often agree in slight elaboration: so, in chapters corresponding to ch. 956 of the *PCG* we are told that 20,000 Moors were drowned in the pursuit (*CrC*, MS *G*, fol. 216r, *Cr1344*, MS Q^2, fol. 127v, MS *M*, fol. 329v), where the figure in the *PCG* is 10,000 (p. 638a21). The tabernacle set up to shelter the Cid's body at Cardeña (*PCG*, p. 640b30 ff.) is in the *CrC* and the *Cr1344* said to have been painted with the royal arms of Castile, León, and Navarra, and those of the Cid (*CrC*, MS *G*, fol. 217v, *Cr1344*, MS Q^2, fol. 128v, MS *M*, fol. 332r).

The same chronicles, however, contain some more substantial additions, of which two examples must suffice. The list of presents omitted at the point corresponding to the early part of ch. 947 of the *PCG* (see above) is given in much longer form in the following chapter (I quote from the *Cr1344*):

Primeramente tiro muy grant auer amonedado en oro e en plata que venia en serones de cuero enteros que trayan muy fermosas çerraduras, e despues desto mucha plata en baxillas labrada en escudillas, tajadores e bacines e ollas para fazer de comer, e todo esto era de muy fina plata e nobles labores e esta plata pesaua diez mill marcos . . .; seys copas . . . e tres barriles de plata . . . llenos de muy granado aljofar e piedras preçiosas . . .; e muchos pannos de oro e de seda. E çiento libras de mirra e balsamo en vna arqueta de oro . . . Otrosi . . . vn tablero de marfil todo plegado con clauos de oro . . . e las tablas e juegos todos eran de oro e de plata muy rricamente obrado con piedras . . . (MS Q^2, fol. 122v; the list in MS *M*, fol. 323v, is similar but less expanded; cf. *CrC*, MS *G*, fol. 210v-211r, and MS *S*, fol. 98r).

The Cid's will, contained in *PCG*, ch. 954 (p. 635b38 ff.) is also different (I here quote from the *CrC*):

---

[75] Other details correspond to *PCG*, pp. 629a15-16 (the Cid never having previously embraced a Moor); 633a32-33 (reference to the sword Tizón); 634a1-4 (reference to Cardeña, abbreviated in the *CrC* and the *Cr1344*); 635b40 (reference to the Cid's body still being at Cardeña), etc. In all these cases the reference is either missing from or abbreviated in the chronicles in question.

Primeramente mando su alma a Dios, e que el su cuerpo fuese enterrado en Sant Pedro de Cardenna. Et mando y con su cuerpo al monasterio muchos buenos heredamientos por que oy dia es muy Rico e muy seruido el lugar donde yaze el su cuerpo. Desy mando a todos sus criados e a toda su conpanna de casa a cada vno segunt meresçia . . . [amounts for different classes of followers are specified] . . . Et mando que quando llegasen a Sant Pedro de Cardenna que diesen de vestir a quatro mil pobres de estanforte, sayas e pellotes . . . (MS *G*, fol. 214v-215r; MS *S*, fol. 103r and *Cr1344*, MS Q^2, fol. 126r are similar, but abbreviated towards the end: *Cr1344*, MS *M* does not have this material).[76]

Given the evident relevance of this material to Cardeña, and perhaps specifically to relics kept and customs observed there, it seems likely that we ought to think of the *Estoria* as a text subject to constant updating, and that such *refundiciones* found their way into later chronicles. If it should seem inconsistent that I am prepared to accept the notion of *refundiciones* in this case having consistently rejected such hypotheses in the case of epic texts (see above, pp. 38-40, 50-54, 120-21), it should be said that the essential difference seems to be motive on the part of the authors: after all, the supposed *Cantar de Fernán González* was undoubtedly *refundido* into the clerical *Poema* we now have, and there is no reason to suppose the Monks of Cardeña to have been any less willing or able to use the written word to serve their interests than their brothers of Arlanza.

One final point remains for discussion. At the end of the previous section I left open the question of the source of the *PCG*'s innovations in that part of the narrative corresponding to the second and third cantares of the *PMC* (see above, p. 136). Menéndez Pidal's solution to this problem was the so-called *cantar refundido* which I joined Catalán in rejecting for the *Cantar del destierro* (see above, pp. 120-21). There is no doubt that similar arguments are insufficiently convincing to explain the

---

[76] Other relatively expanded sections of these chronicles are as follows: the Cid's parting gifts to the Sultan's emissary (cf. *PCG*, p. 630b17-28) are detailed at greater length, and 'muchas estrannas cosas' sent by the Cid are enumerated: *CrC*, MS *G*, fol. 212v, MS *S*, fol. 100v, *Cr1344*, MS *M*, fol. 326v, MS Q^2, fol. 124r; at the end of the chapter when the Cid's body is sent to Castile (corresponding to ch. 958 of the *PCG*), the *CrC* and MS *Q* of the *Cr1344* add a paragraph in his praise not found in the *PCG* (*CrC*, MS *G*, fol. 217v, MS *S*, fol. 106r, *Cr1344*, MS Q^2, fol. 128r-v, the latter being slightly more expanded (and cf. MS *M*, fol. 331v); finally, the account of Jimena's burial (cf. *PCG*, pp. 641b-642a) is concluded in these chronicles with a brief account of the subsequent fortunes of doña Elvira, doña Sol, and the bishop, don Jerónimo: *CrC*, MS *G*, fol. 218v, MS *S*, fol. 108r, *Cr1344*, MS *M*, fols. 333v-334r; there is a lacuna at this point in MS Q^2.

differences between the *PMC* and the *PCG* in the later sections. It has, however, been suggested—first by Entwistle in 1947— that the whole of the *PCG*'s version of the later history of the Cid (from the conquest of Valencia onwards) formed part of the *Estoria de Cardeña*.[77] This seems eminently likely, especially if one bears in mind that the *PCG* at this point, as preserved in MS E^2 of the 'versión regia' is a composite text of demonstrably factitious nature. From the lacuna in the Cid's conquest of Valencia onwards, the Alphonsine *Estoria de España* effectively ceases to exist: its place is taken in MS E^2 first by the *Estoria de Cardeña* under discussion and subsequently by an expanded translation of the Toledano.[78] What we have been examining in the last two sections of this chapter is at several removes from epic legend and at more than one from Alphonsine historiography.

[77] Entwistle, '*La Estoria del noble varon*', p. 210. Compare Russell, 'San Pedro de Cardeña', pp. 59-60, who tentatively accepts this view, as does Gómez Pérez, 'Fuentes y cronología', pp. 623-24; Catalán, in 'Crónicas generales y cantares de gesta' (1963) also clearly stated: 'A mi parecer, toda la materia épica relacionada con el drama de Corpes presente en la *Primera Crónica* formaba parte de la "Estoria del Cid" amañada en Cardeña; el epílogo clerical (la llamada **Leyenda de Cardeña*) buscó sustentarse, desde sus orígenes, en la arraigada tradición juglaresca' (p. 306 n. 129); however, in 1969 he continued to refer to the *Estoria* as having used as one of its sources a '**Refundición del mío Cid*' ('Poesía y novela', p. 431); cf. also the same author's 'Don Juan Manuel ante el modelo alfonsí' (1977), p. 48 n. 102. The traditional view still seems to lie behind Powell's remark in *Epic and Chronicle* 'there must have been an original poetic source behind [the *PCG Refundición*], but its total content is uncertain' (n. 43 to ch. 4, p. 173).

[78] See Catalán, *De Alfonso X*, pp. 19-93, especially pp. 64-69, and the same author's 'El taller historiográfico alfonsí', pp. 366-67, and 'Crónicas generales y cantares de gesta', pp. 209 and 304-05.

CONCLUSION

The word 'epic' has cropped up a good deal in the preceding chapters, and it seems proper to begin this conclusion with a brief discussion of Old Spanish epic in general. Not all the legendary sources referred to in this work can properly be called epics. If length is any criterion of epic nature, it is hard to see the stories of the *Condesa traidora* or the *Infante García* as epic at all;[1] what is more, the presence of a strong ecclesiastical element in both these and other stories (e.g., *Fernán González*, *Mocedades de Rodrigo*) should give one pause before accepting the traditional view of a lay and essentially popular historical genre. Of course, none of this is new;[2] nor is it nowadays at all revolutionary to point to the presence of learned elements—some clerical, such as Jimena's prayer and Bishop Jerónimo, others perhaps less so such as the strong emphasis on legalism and the written word—in the *Poema de mio Cid*.[3] It is certainly possible that we owe many of such learned features to clerical reworkings of originally popular material; such is demonstrably the case for the *Fernán González* and the *Mocedades* stories, where late and obviously clerical texts have survived. It is less clear that the *Poema de mio Cid*, with its high degree of artistry, not least in thematic structure, and its considerable inventiveness on the narrative level, can with any degree of probability be related to an earlier, more historical and less novelesque version. Nor should it be forgotten that many of the legends

---

[1] Chalon (*L'Histoire et l'épopée*, pp. 529-31) doubts whether the *Condesa traidora* was ever an epic poem; see pp. 552-53 for his slightly less sceptical judgement on the *Romanz del Infant García*. For a contrary view, see A. D. Deyermond, 'Medieval Spanish Epic Cycles: Observations on their Formation and Development', *KRQ*, 23 (1976), 281-303 (p. 298 n. 1).

[2] See, for instance, Deyermond, *Epic Poetry and the Clergy*, and the same author's *The Middle Ages*, especially pp. 37-38, 47-48 and the studies cited in notes 21 and 23 to chapter 2 (pp. 51-52).

[3] See, for instance, Russell, 'San Pedro de Cardeña', and the same author's 'La oración de doña Jimena', in *Temas de 'La Celestina' y otros estudios: del 'Cid' al 'Quijote'* (Barcelona, 1978), pp. 113-58. On the general presence of legal features in the *PMC*, see Russell, 'Some Problems of Diplomatic in the *Cantar de Mio Cid* and their Implications', *MLR*, 47 (1952), 340-49; also Colin Smith, 'El derecho, tema del *Poema de Mío Cid* y profesión de su autor', in *Estudios cidianos* (Madrid, 1977), pp. 63-85, and David Hook, 'On certain Correspondences between the *Poema de Mio Cid* and Contemporary Legal Instruments', *Iberoromania*, 11 (1980), 31-53.

concerned are fundamentally unhistorical—*Bernardo del Carpio*—or composed of such a plethora of folkloric and traditional narrative motifs—*Infantes de Lara, Fernán González, Condesa traidora*[4] —as to make it highly likely that we are dealing with a literary form, albeit perhaps one with popular elements, whose relation to history is sometimes closer than at others but which is never organically historical.

If we can trust the earliest chroniclers to give us some idea of the kind of stories told by 'los juglares en sus cantares', the view which emerges, I would suggest, is one of poems which, while set more or less firmly in what by the later thirteenth century was fast becoming a heroic past age, told stories at once familiar, pious and exemplary.

They were familiar in part because their protagonists tended to be real historical figures, and because of the mythic quality which attends a narrative dealing in basic motifs of human conduct and relationship: the tyrannical lord and the loyal, if temporarily rebellious, vassal; the exile or the bastard who makes good; the treacherous actions which need to be avenged or atoned for; the wronged husband and the adulterous wife.

Such stories were pious in their constant references to religious foundations, to vows, to divine providence and to the sure certainty with which virtue triumphs and vice is punished. Much of this is certainly part of the general religiosity of mediaeval culture, but the first element cited—the prominence given to particular churches, cathedrals and monasteries, their foundation and the famous men buried in them—strikes a specifically ecclesiastical rather than a more generally religious note. There are also a number of miraculous occurrences: the divine intervention in more than one of Fernán González's battles, the miracle of Cascajares at the start of the *Condesa traidora* story, and strange visions which appear to kings and heroes at their deaths or before some great enterprise; all of these add an undeniably pious note, not to say a hagiographical one, to many of these stories.

Their exemplary nature derives from much of what has been said in both the last two paragraphs, and can be seen more particularly in one feature which is not without importance. I refer to the legal aspect, most prominent in the story of the Cid, both in his relationship of vassalage with Alfonso and in

---

[4] See Deyermond and Chaplin, 'Folk-Motifs'.

CONCLUSION

his reaction to the dishonour brought on him by the *infantes de Carrión*; it is seen also in the culmination of the story of *Fernán González* (see above, pp. 40-42) and perhaps in the quite explicit insistence on reparation for wrongs done which marks the ends of the stories of the *Infantes de Lara*, the *Condesa traidora*, the *Infante García* and *Sancho II*—the last instance being also marked by the fictitious but highly legalistic imposition of the Oath of Santa Gadea.[5]

As to the later history of these legends, I have argued in the last chapter against the neotraditionalist view of an on-going series of poetic *refundiciones* giving rise to the more developed versions in later chronicles, and in the later part of this conclusion I shall go on to sum up some of the motives behind what I believe to be the alternative explanation of these later chronicle versions. I do not want to repeat here the arguments set out in chapter 7 concerning the most frequently discussed case of supposed *refundición*, that of the *Cid* story; it may be apposite to refer back to a previous chapter, that on the *Infantes de Lara*, to underline points made there. That is the only case, in my opinion, where there is a strong argument for the existence of a later poetic version of the story alongside the original *cantar*. There, it will be recalled, the *Cr1344* and the *Versión Interpolada* of the *Vulgata* tell, in different ways, a story containing substantially new narrative elements, differing from the version prosified in other chronicles, and do so in prose which contains strong traces of assonance. The presence of both these criteria, narrative innovation and assonantal prose, seems to make the postulation of a *refundición*, a more developed version of the original poem, altogether more realistic. This is, however, an isolated instance; and, as I have argued elsewhere, the undoubted literary qualities of the revised version may lead one to suspect a less artless—and perhaps a later—author that is sometimes assumed.[6]

How, then, are the differences between successive chronicle versions to be explained, if not by their dependence on successive poetic *refundiciones*? We may distinguish between two basic types of difference, the structural and the stylistic.

[5] There is a possibly significant overlap between some of the features noted in these paragraphs and those discussed by C. C. Smith in his essay 'On the Ethos of the *Romancero Viejo*', in *Studies of the Spanish and Portuguese Ballad*, edited by N. D. Shergold (London, 1972), pp. 5-24.

[6] See Pattison, 'Legendary material', especially pp. 179-80.

The first category includes cases where the harmonisation of sources has brought problems to the compilers of chronicles, who have dealt with such problems in a number of ways, some of which have more or less drastic structural consequences for the legendary stories in question. Two examples of this are: the way in which the compilers of the *PCG*, 'versión regia', interpolated the more sensational details of the end of the *Condesa traidora* story into their narrative (see above, p. 63), the earlier version being visible in the *Crónica najerense* and in the *CVR* as well as in the *PCG*, 'versión vulgar' and in the *Vulgata*; and the story of Fernando I's division of his kingdoms, handled in one way in the *PCG*, the *CrC* and the *Ocampiana* (which show signs of knowing the epic tradition but of not using it) and in another by the *CVR*, which gives full details of the popular version while explicitly taking leave to doubt its veracity (see above, pp. 93-97).[7]

Still on the level of structure, one may also note a general tendency of later chronicles to leave out much of the cross-referencing and the compilatorial remarks about sources—historiographical scaffolding, as it were. So, the account of *Bernardo del Carpio* in the *PCG*, with all its chronological difficulties, attempts to link together logically the elements of what may well be disparate stories: the corresponding passages in the 'Crónica fragmentaria' and in the *Vulgata* are the most developed versions of this tendency. The *Cr1344*, however, and still more so the *RefTol* which derives from it, produce a much more coherent and simplified narrative in which only rudimentary efforts are made to show the historiographic process at work (see above, pp. 17-22). A similar example is the story of *Fernán González* in the *Cr1344* again, which abandons the careful interlacing of material drawn from the Latin chronicles and the subject-matter of the legendary life of the hero in favour of a simple process of juxtaposition (see above, p. 35).[8]

Of what I have called stylistic innovation the preceding chapters also give many examples. Here I will try only to pull

---

[7] Similar conclusions may be drawn from the treatment of the legendary material by the *CVR* and the *Vulgata* in the case of the *Infante García* story (see above, pp. 74-76).

[8] The most complex instance of this kind of compilatorial uncertainty may be seen in the treatment of the *Mocedades* material in various different manuscripts of the *CrC* and in the *Cr1344* (see above, pp. 83-91).

together some of the most consistent threads. On the whole the chroniclers explain in detail both characters' motives and whole sequences of events which in the original poetic narratives are left less explicit. Consider, for example, the complex account of a minor incident involving Fernán González and the King of Navarre's men (see above, pp. 27-28), where the ruse is spelt out in painful detail in the *PCG*, 'versión regia', as opposed to the more laconic account of the 'versión vulgar'; or the similar instance in the *Infantes de Lara* story, where the revision makes much more of Mudarra's departure from Almanzor's court (see above, p. 45-46). There are many instances of the same criterion giving rise to innovations in the *Cid* story, both in the *PCG* and even more so in the more complex narratives of the *CrC* and the *Cr1344*: the circumstances surrounding the *Afrenta de Corpes* provide perhaps the best instance of this and are discussed in my 1977 article;[9] other examples are the story of the escape of the Cid's lion[10] and, perhaps, the complex ruse by which the mounting of the dead hero's body helps in the last battle of Valencia (see above, pp. 131 and 139).

On a less fundamental level, one may note the tendency of the chroniclers to include extra characters. This is again especially notable in the *Cid* story (see above, pp. 123-24, and 130-31),[11] but is also to be seen in the later version of the *Fernán González* story, particularly in the version found in the *Cr1344* (see above, p. 37). A general tendency to expansion of a purely rhetorical nature is to be seen, for instance, in various aspects of the *Sancho II* story in the *CrC* (see above, pp. 105-06) or in that of the *Cid*, especially in the *cortes* scene in the *Cr1344* (see above, pp. 135-36). This last feature leads into a general liking for sensational action and dialogue found increasingly in fourteenth-century and later chronicles: many elements of the siege of Zamora and its aftermath are given fuller treatment in the *CrC* (see above, pp. 105-06), the bloody vengeance of the end of the *Infante García* story is given in its fullest extension in the *Cr1344* (see above, pp. 77-78) and the *cortes* scene corresponding to the climax of the *Poema de mio Cid* is, in

---

[9] See Pattison, 'The *Afrenta de Corpes*', especially the summary at pp. 138-40.
[10] See Catalán, 'Poesía y novela', pp. 432-33.
[11] See Pattison, 'The *Afrenta de Corpes*', especially pp. 132-33 and 139, and Smith, 'The Personages of the *PMC*', especially p. 588.

the *PCG*, the *CrC* and the *Cr1344*, described in increasingly violent detail (see above, pp. 135-36).[12]

Finally, a moralising note undoubtedly becomes prominent. The clearest case of this is the idiosyncratic *Versión Interpolada* in its treatment of aspects of the *Infantes de Lara* story and that of the *Condesa traidora*,[13] but other chronicles are not exempt from it. The *CrC* and the *Cr1344* add pious touches to the *Cid* story (see above, pp. 123, 127, and 134-35), and indeed the whole Cardeña legend—though it presumably existed before the chroniclers adopted it—bears witness to such an attitude and to its ready acceptance into historiography. Linked with this, and of greater underlying importance, is an increase in what might be called historical exemplarity. *Fernán González*'s story must end not on the low note of defeat by the Moors but, in the *PCG*, 'versión regia', on the high one of his invented revenge (see above, pp. 29-30); the matricide of Count Sancho must be the subject of repentance—again, only in the *PCG* among early versions—and the occasion for the pious foundation of the monastery of Oña (see above, pp. 62-63);[14] and, most notably, the Cid, already an examplary heroic figure of great stature in the *Poema de mio Cid*, becomes almost a lay saint both in small things—the repayment of the Jews in the *PCG* and, with even more pious detail, in the *CrC* (see above, p. 131)[15]—and in the strong odour of sanctity surrounding his last days, his death and the miraculous happenings which followed it (see above, pp. 138-41).

These, then, are some of the ways in which the chroniclers rewrote history. I hope that the examples given in these pages, together with the far larger number of instances examined throughout this book have gone some way towards substantiating the claims made at the end of the Introduction: that if respect for historical accuracy was largely lost in the evolution of chronicle texts in the fourteenth and fifteenth centuries, there is some compensation for us in the process. This comes

---

[12] The most extreme examples of this tendency to sensationalism are to be found in the fifteenth-century *Refundición Toledana*: see also pp. 54-55, 67-69, and 78-80; and see Pattison, 'The Legend of the Sons of Sancho el Mayor', especially pp. 38-39.

[13] See Pattison, 'Legendary material', especially pp. 173-76.

[14] The *Versión Interpolada* shows the extreme case of this type of amplification in the instance under discussion (see above, pp. 34, 49-50, and 64).

[15] See Smith, 'Did the Cid repay the Jews?', especially pp. 52-53.

from the insight that contemplation of these texts gives us into the imposition of new artistic values which show the way forward to something approaching prose fiction. Perhaps one ought not to adopt too rigorous a set of historical criteria when judging the work of those whose subject matter was, after all, largely fictional in the first place.

Appendix
THE CHRONICLE TEXTS

This is not a fully descriptive catalogue of manuscripts, rather a reference list which includes bibliographical details to enable the interested reader to consult fuller descriptions of the manuscripts. To attempt to arrange the different versions chronologically poses certain problems. It seems preferable to adopt a simplified system dividing the chronicle versions into two basic groups: those which reflect a relatively primitive state of the historiographical compilation, possibly corresponding at least in part to Alfonso's own life time; and those which amplify the original narrative. The first group comprises the 'versión vulgar' of the *PCG*, the *Crónica General Vulgata*, the *CVR*, and, for the 'tercera parte', the *Crónica Abreviada*; the second, the 'versión regia' of the *PCG*, the *CrC*, the *Cr1344*, the *Ocampiana* (that is, the 'cuarta parte' published by Ocampo), likewise the 'cuarta parte' of the *Crónica Abreviada*, and, finally, the two interpolated versions, the *RefTol* of the *Cr1344* and the *Versión Interpolada* of the *Vulgata* which, alone of this second group, goes back independently to a 'primitive' version rather than depending on the original expansion of one such version by the *PCG*, 'versión regia'.

Preliminary notes

(1) The following list does not include all the manuscripts of the Alphonsine chronicles and of those which derive from them. Specifically, it excludes those partial manuscripts which do not include the material discussed in this work: for example, there are many manuscripts of the *PCG* which include only the history of Spain up to the Arab invasion, and others which include only the reigns of particular monarchs (notably that of Fernando III, *el santo*). Such manuscripts are listed briefly at the end of the appropriate section.

(2) Those manuscripts which have been used directly in the preparation of the present work figure in bold type.

(3) The following abbreviations are used for libraries; other abbreviations used for published catalogues and reference works will be found in the list of bibliographical abbreviations (pp. vii-xi):

Escorial	Biblioteca del Monasterio, San Lorenzo de el Escorial
Madrid, BN	Biblioteca Nacional, Madrid
Madrid, Pal	Biblioteca del Palacio, Madrid
Paris, BN	Bibliothèque Nationale, Paris
Salamanca	Biblioteca de la Universidad, Salamanca
Santander	Biblioteca Menéndez y Pelayo, Santander

A. PRIMITIVE VERSIONS

(i) The *Primera Crónica General*, 'versión vulgar'

This exists in five manuscripts of the 'tercera parte' and one of the 'cuarta parte'. All these manuscripts are characterised by relative concision: see above, pp. 16-17, 27-30, 45-46, 62-63, 74, 81-82, 103, etc.

Tercera parte:

G: Escorial X-I-11
    See: *PCG*, p. lix; Catalán, *De Alfonso X*, p. 99 n. 2; Zarco, *Catálogo*, II, 457-58.
    In the 'cuarta parte' this MS becomes the *CrC*; see below, p. 157.
T: Santander M.550
    See: *PCG*, p. lx; Catalán, *De Alfonso X*, p. 98 n. 2; Gómez Pérez, 'Elaboración', p. 267 (no. 8); Artigas, *Catálago*, p. 375 (no. 316).
Y: Escorial Y-II-11
    See: *PCG*, p. lx; Catalán, *De Alfonso X*, p. 98 n. 2; Gómez Pérez, 'Elaboración', p. 266 (no. 7); Zarco, *Catálogo*, III, 30-31.
Z: Escorial X-I-7
    See: *PCG*, p. lx; Catalán, *De Alfonso X*, p. 99 n. 2; Gómez Pérez, 'Elaboración', p. 269 (no. 9); Zarco, *Catálogo*, II, 454-55
Minneapolis, Minnesota University Library, Z946.O2fC881
    See: Gómez Pérez, 'La *EE* alfonsí', p. 519 (no. 10); L. L. Collins, 'An Unknown Manuscript of the *CVR*', *Scriptorium*, 28 (1974), 51-60. This MS appears to be a mixture of the *PCG* 'versión vulgar' and the *CVR*; see also below, p. 154.

Cuarta parte:

F: Salamanca 2628 (formerly Madrid, Pal II 429 / 2-E-4)
    See: *PCG*, p. lix; Gómez Pérez, 'Elaboración', p. 267 (no. 10); Menéndez Pidal, *Crónicas generales*, pp. 19-22 (no. 8).

(ii) The *Crónica General Vulgata*

This is the chronicle, sometimes called the *Tercera Crónica General*, a version of which forms the 'tercera parte' published by Ocampo. It sometimes has structural peculiarities (see above, pp. 18-19, and 30-31) and is apt to add notes of an editorial kind (as in the case of the story of Bernardo del Carpio, see pp. 19-20) and also some additional details (as in the case of the legend of the Infantes de Lara, see pp. 47-48). Towards the end of the 'tercera parte', in the story of the Infante García, the *Vulgata* takes an idiosyncratic line towards its sources: see pp. 75-76. On the whole, though, it is clearly linked with the *PCG*, 'versión vulgar', and with the *CVR*.

Ocampo : *Las quatro partes enteras de la Cronica de España que mando componer el Serenissimo rey don Alonso llamado el sabio* . . . Vista y emendada mucha parte de su impresión por el maestro Florian Docǎpo . . . (Zamora, 1541).
C : Escorial Y-I-9
    See: Catalán, *De Alfonso X*, p. 190 n. 53; Zarco, *Catálogo*, III, 12-15.

APPENDIX   153

F: Madrid, BN 828
    See: Catalán, *De Alfonso X*, p. 190 n. 55
    In the 'cuarta parte' this MS becomes a version of the *'Traducción interpolada del Toledano'*.
H: Madrid, BN 10216
    See: Catalán, *De Alfonso X*, p. 190 n. 56
L: Madrid, BN 1298
    See: *PCG*, p. lix; Catalán, *De Alfonso X*, p. 190 n. 57.
    This MS was erroneously classified by Menéndez Pidal as being the *PCG*.
R: Madrid, Pal II 2038 (formerly 2-N-4)
    See: Catalán, *De Alfonso X*, p. 190 n. 54; Menéndez Pidal, *Crónicas generales*, pp. 130-32 (no. 22).

(iii) The *Crónica de Veinte Reyes*

In the 'tercera parte', the *CVR* forms a family with the *PCG*, 'versión vulgar' and the *Vulgata*, and within that family, a sub-group with the *Vulgata*. Both are marked by a structure which sometimes differs from that of the 'versión vulgar', although there are numerous differences of detail. On the whole, the *CVR* does not share the innovations of the *Vulgata* in matters of detail, and it tends to be more concise: for examples, see above, pp. 30-34, and 46-47. Towards the end of the 'tercera parte', the *CVR* begins to depart from the family mentioned; its account of the story of the Infante García shows a marked increase in editorial confidence (see pp. 74-76), and this is yet more marked in the 'cuarta parte'. Here the *CVR* is the first chronicle to make significant use of legendary material in the episode of the Partition of the Kingdoms (see pp. 95-97), although its compilers had rejected such material in the earlier part of the reign of Fernando I (see p. 82); the *CVR* then offers a substantially revised and reorganised version of the reign of Sancho II (see pp. 107-11); finally, it is the only chronicle to continue to follow the *Poema de mio Cid* for the whole of the hero's life and to reject the *Estoria de Cardeña* material (see pp. 137-38).

B: Santander M.549
    See: Babbitt, p. 165; Powell, p. 199; Gómez Pérez, 'La *EE* alfonsí', pp. 519-20 (no. 12); Artigas, *Catálogo*, p. 378 (no. 320). [This manuscript appears now to be missing; the library staff have been unable to locate it on a number of occasions, most recently in April 1983.]
J: Escorial X-I-6
    See: Babbitt, p. 164; Powell, p. 196; Gómez Pérez, 'La *EE* alfonsí', pp. 515-16 (no. 1); Zarco, *Catálogo*, II, 453-54.
K: Salamanca 2211 (formerly Madrid, Pal II 1782 / 2-M-1)
    See: Babbitt, p. 165; Powell, p. 198; Gómez Pérez, 'La *EE* alfonsí', p. 518 (no. 8); Menéndez Pidal, *Crónicas generales*, pp. 120-23 (no. 20).
L: Escorial X-II-24
    See: Babbitt, p. 164; Powell, pp. 198-99; Gómez Pérez, 'La *EE* alfonsí', p. 516 (no. 2); Zarco, *Catálogo*, II, 492-93.

Ll: **Madrid, BN 1501**
    See: Babbitt, p. 164, Powell, p. 197; Gómez Pérez, 'La *EE* alfonsí', p. 516 (no. 4)

M: **Minneapolis, Minnesota University Library, Z946.02fC881**
    See: Powell, p. 199; Gómez Pérez, 'La *EE* alfonsí', p. 519 (no. 10); L. L. Collins, 'An Unknown Manuscript of the *CVR*', *Scriptorium*, 28 (1974), 51-60.
    This MS appears to be a mixture of the *PCG* 'versión vulgar' and the *CVR*; see also above, p. 152.

N: **Escorial Y-I-12**
    See: Babbitt, pp. 164-65; Powell, pp. 195-96; Gómez Pérez, 'La *EE* alfonsí', p. 516 (no. 3); Zarco, *Catálogo*, III, 18-20.

N': **Madrid, Pal II 2437 (formerly 2-K-8)**
    See: Babbitt, pp. 165-66; Powell, p. 197; Gómez Pérez, 'La *EE* alfonsí', pp. 518-19 (no. 9); Menéndez Pidal, *Crónicas generales*, pp. 123-24 (no. 21) and 227-28.

Ñ: **Santander M.159**
    See: Babbitt, p. 165; Powell, p. 199; Gómez Pérez, 'La *EE* alfonsí', p. 519 (no. 11); Artigas, *Catálogo*, p. 377-78 (no. 319).

P: **Madrid, BN 18416**
    See: Powell, pp. 197-98; Gómez Pérez, 'La *EE* alfonsí', pp. 517-18 (no. 6).

Q: **Madrid, BN 1507**
    See: Powell, p. 198; Gómez Pérez, 'La *EE* alfonsí', p. 517 (no. 5).

X: **Salamanca 1824 (formerly Madrid, Pal II 180 / 2-C-2)**
    See: Babbitt, p. 165; Powell, pp. 196-97; Gómez Pérez, 'La *EE* alfonsí', p. 518 (no. 7); Menéndez Pidal, *Crónicas generales*, pp. 111-20 (no. 19).

(iv) the *Crónica Abreviada*

In the 'tercera parte' the lost *Crónica Manuelina* on which the *Abreviada* was based seems to have been a representative of the 'primitive' family; see above, pp. 18 n. 13 and 30, although in at least one case (the legend of the Infantes de Lara) it seems to follow clearly the *PCG* 'versión vulgar' rather than the *Vulgata/CVR* version (see above, p. 46 n. 7). For the *Abreviada* in the 'cuarta parte', see below, p. 159.

Madrid, BN 1356
    See: Catalán, *De Alfonso X*, pp. 172-74; id., 'Don Juan Manuel ante el modelo alfonsí'; and the edition of the MS by R. L. and M. B. Grismer entitled Juan Manuel, *Crónica Abreviada* (Minneapolis, 1958).

B. EXPANDED VERSIONS

(i) The *Primera Crónica General*, 'versión regia'

    (*a*) MS *E* and its derivatives

The most straightforward representative of the 'versión regia', and the one which was responsible for its name, is MS *E*, which was the base manuscript for Menéndez Pidal's edition of the *PCG*. From this descends a group of other manuscripts; all of them, like their exemplar, are marked by a tendency to rhetorical expansion (see above, pp. 16-17, 27-30, 45-46, 62-63, 74, 81-82, 103 etc.), by attempts in some cases to justify the actions of characters (see above, pp. 29-30 for the case of Fernán González) and to make them more exemplary, and, on occasion, by a tendency to introduce new legendary material; this last tendency is seen most clearly in the case of the legend of the Condesa traidora (see above, p. 63).

E: Escorial Y-I-2 and X-I-4
  See: *PCG*, pp. lviii-lix; Catalán, *De Alfonso X*, pp. 19-93; Gómez Pérez, 'Elaboración', pp. 268-69 (no. 12); Zarco, *Catálogo*, III, 2 and II, 450-51.
I: Madrid, BN 10134 bis
  See: *PCG*, p. lix; Catalán, *De Alfonso X*, p. 42 n. 15; Gómez Pérez, 'Elaboración', p. 270 (no. 15).
J: Madrid, BN 1347
  See: *PCG*, p. lxi; Catalán, *De Alfonso X*, p. 43 n. 17.
  In the 'cuarta parte' this MS becomes the *CrC*; see below, p. 157.
Madrid, BN 643
  See: Gómez Pérez, 'Elaboración', p. 271 (no. 17).
Madrid, BN 1487
  See: Gómez Pérez, 'Elaboración', pp. 270-71 (no. 16).
Madrid, Academia de la Historia, II-1313
  See: Gómez Pérez, 'Elaboración', p. 272 (no. 19).

(b) The *Crónica Fragmentaria*

A sub-group of the 'versión regia' is formed by the following manuscripts which are marked, in the case of the legend of Bernardo del Carpio, by a critical spirit towards structure and sources (see above, pp. 17-18). Of these manuscripts, three end after this episode and before that of Fernán González (MS *B, U, X*); MS *V* is continued with the *Versión Interpolada* of the Vulgata, and MS *Xx* continues up to the end of the 'tercera parte' with the 'versión regia' according to the principal group (i.e., like MS *E*).

B: Salamanca 2022 (formerly Madrid, Pal II 18 / 2-B-2)
  See: *PCG*, p. lvii; Catalán, *De Alfonso X*, p. 38 n. 9; Gómez Pérez, 'Elaboración', p. 276 (no. 28); Menéndez Pidal, *Crónicas generales*, pp. 22-31 (no. 9).
U: Madrid, Biblioteca de la Universidad 158
  See: *PCG*, p. lx; Catalán, *De Alfonso X*, pp. 38-39 and n. 9; Gómez Pérez, 'Elaboración', pp. 274-75 (no. 25).
V: Madrid, BN 1277
  See: Catalán, *De Alfonso X*, pp. 38-39 and n. 9.
  This MS is continued as the *Versión Interpolada* of the *Vulgata*: see below, p. 159.
X: Madrid, BN 10213 and 10214
  See Catalán, *De Alfonso X*, pp. 38-39 and n. 9; Gómez Pérez, 'Elaboración', p. 274 (no. 24: N.B., Gómez Pérez calls this manuscript *H* and not *X*).

Xx: Madrid, BN 7583
   See: Catalán, 'Don Juan Manuel ante el modelo alfonsí', pp. 21 and 37 n. 67.
   This MS is continued with the 'versión regia' according to MS *E*.

(c) The *Versión Gallego-portuguesa*

Finally, mention must be made of two manuscripts which, in the 'tercera parte', consist of a translation into Galician-Portuguese of MS *E*:

A: Madrid, BN 8817
   See: *PCG*, p. lxi; Catalán, *De Alfonso X*, p. 53 n. 5; Lorenzo, *La traducción gallega*, pp. xxxvii–xlvi.
A': Salamanca 2497 (formerly Madrid, Pal II 910 / 2-H-3)
   See: *PCG*, p. lvii (N.B., Menéndez Pidal calls this MS *A* and not *A*'); Catalán, *De Alfonso X*, p. 53 n. 5; Lorenzo, *La traducción gallega*, pp. xlvii–lvii.

These two manuscripts are both continued in the 'cuarta parte' with a translation of the *CrC*; see below, p. 157.

The following manuscripts of the *PCG* are not described (see above, preliminary note 1, p. 151):

C: Madrid, BN 12837
D: Madrid, BN 10273
K: Madrid, BN 2075
M: Madrid, BN 642
N: Madrid, Pal II 2063 (formerly 2-N-1)
Q: Madrid, BN 5795
R: Madrid, BN 13002
S: Madrid, BN 9233
Escorial Z-III-3
Madrid, BN 1195

Madrid, BN 17769
Madrid, BN 1865
Madrid, BN 645
Madrid, BN 1343
Madrid, BN 1526
Madrid, Pal II 1264 (formerly 2-J-3
Salamanca, 2684 (formerly Madrid, Pal II 1793 / 2-M-1
Stockholm, Kunglinga Phil. 69
Toledo, Biblioteca Pública 104

(ii) The *Crónica de Castilla*

The *Crónica de Castilla* (or *Crónica de los Reyes de Castilla*) may be regarded as an expanded and amplified version of the 'cuarta parte' of the *PCG*, 'versión regia'. Its manuscripts fall into two main groups, one of which is marked relatively by a high degree of concision or abbreviation. Its characteristics have been described in detail by Armistead (*La gesta*) and by Catalán (*De Alfonso X*, pp. 323-49); for the freedom with which this chronicle adopts legendary material (and subsequently expands it), see above, pp. 94-95, 104-07, 122-25, 133-34, and 139-41. The point at which the manuscript tradition becomes most complex—that is, the *Mocedades* material—is also discussed above, at pp. 83-86 and 88-91; here I limit myself to listing the manuscripts, with the additional note that a version of the *CrC* is also to be found in the so-called *Crónica Particular del Cid*, details of which will be found at the end of the list of manuscripts.

B: Paris, BN 326
   See: Armistead, pp. 234-36; Catalán, *De Alfonso X*, p. 326 n. 19

D: Paris, BN 220
   See: Armistead, pp. 237-42; Catalán, *De Alfonso X*, p. 337 n. 35
G: Escorial X-I-11
   See Armistead, pp. 242-45; Catalán, *De Alfonso X*, p. 326 n. 17; Zarco, *Catálogo*, II, 457-58.
   The 'tercera parte' of this manuscript is the *PCG*, 'versión vulgar': see above, p. 152.
J: Madrid, BN 1347
   See: Armistead, p. 236-37; Catalán, *De Alfonso X*, p. 340 n. 42.
   The 'tercera parte' of this manuscript is the *PCG*, 'versión regia': see above, p. 155.
L: Madrid, Academia de la Historia, 12.26.4
   See: Catalán, *De Alfonso X*, p. 342 n. 45
M: Santander M.7
   See: Catalán, *De Alfonso X*, p. 332 n. 28; Artigas, *Catálogo*, pp. 378-79 (no. 321). This manuscript is wrongly described by Artigas as the *CVR*.
N: Madrid, BN 10210
   See: Armistead, pp. 246-48; Catalán, *De Alfonso X*, p. 339 n. 40.
P: Paris, BN 12
   See: Armistead, pp. 249-51; Catalán, *De Alfonso X*, p. 326 n. 18
R: Salamanca 2303 (formerly Madrid, Pal II 1075 / 2-J-2)
   See: *PCG*, p. lxi; Armistead, pp. 251-52; Catalán, *De Alfonso X*, p. 337 n. 34; Menéndez Pidal, *Crónicas generales*, pp. 138-40 (no. 25).
S: Madrid, BN 1810
   See: Armistead, pp. 252-56; Catalán, *De Alfonso X*, p. 338-39, n. 38.
T: Madrid, BN 7403
   See: Armistead, pp. 256-59; Catalán, *De Alfonso X*, pp. 330-32, n. 26.
U: London, British Library, Egerton 288
   See: Armistead, pp. 259-65; Catalán, *De Alfonso X*, p. 340 n. 41.
V: Madrid, BN 8539
   See: Armistead, p. 266; Catalán, *De Alfonso X*, pp. 328-29, n. 23.
Y: Rome, Biblioteca Apostolica Vaticana, Lat. 4798
   See: Armistead, 'An Unnoticed Epic Reference' p. 144 n. 9; Catalán, *De Alfonso X*, p. 328 n. 22
Z: Madrid, Biblioteca Zabálburu
   See: Catalán, *De Alfonso X*, p. 332 n. 27.
Crónica del famoso cauallero Cid Ruy Diez, campeador (Burgos, 1512)
   See: Armistead, pp. 234-36 (N.B., Armistead uses the letter *H* to designate this version); Catalán, *De Alfonso X*, pp. 326-28 and nn. 20-21.

Finally, it should be mentioned that the 'cuarta parte' of the Galician-Portuguese manuscripts A and A' (see above, p. 156) is a translation of the *CrC*.

(iii) The *Crónica de 1344*

The Galician-Portuguese manuscripts just referred to—those in which the 'tercera parte' is the 'versión regia' of the *PCG* and the 'cuarta parte' the *CrC*—are the ancestors of the *Cr1344*. This was originally composed in

Portuguese, translated into Castilian, revised in an expanded version of c. 1400 in Portuguese and again translated into Castilian. Of the first version, only the Castilian MS *M* (and the fragmentary *E*) survive; the second exists in three Portuguese manuscripts (not listed here) and the Castilian MSS *Q, S, U,* and *V*. For further details, see Lindley Cintra, *Crónica,* I; Catalán and Andrés, *Cr1344;* and Catalán, *De Alfonso X,* pp. 289-441. The characteristics of the *Cr1344* which emerge from the present work are essentially that it represents a critical rewriting of its source, whether this be the *PCG* in the 'tercera parte' or the *CrC* in the 'cuarta parte', and that this rewriting is particularly noticeable when the compilers can bring new sources to bear, be these legendary (as in the case of the legend of the Infantes de Lara: see pp. 51-54) or historiographical, (as when the stories of the *Particiones* and of Sancho II are revised on the basis of the *CVR*: see pp. 97-99 and 112-13). It is always clear that a new and critical spirit is at work, as well as one with a strong tendency to rearrange structural elements and expand the narrative rhetorically (see also pp. 20-21, 34-41, 65-67, 77-78, 86-88, etc.).

M: Salamanca 2656 (formerly Madrid, Pal II 1069 / 2-I-2)
    See: Lindley Cintra, *Crónica* I, cdxc-cdxci; Catalán and Andrés, *Cr1344,* lxxiii-lxxiv; Catalán, *De Alfonso X,* p. 291 n. 1; Menéndez Pidal, *Crónicas generales,* pp. 46-78 (no. 14).

Q: Madrid, BN 10814 and 10815
    See: Lindley Cintra, *Crónica,* I, dxxiii; Catalán and Andrés, *Cr1344,* pp. lxxvii-lxxviii; Catalán, *De Alfonso X,* p. 291 n. 1.

S: Santander M.109
    See: Catalán and Andrés, *Cr1344,* pp. lxxviii-lxxix; Artigas, *Catálogo,* pp. 376-77 (no. 318).

U: Madrid, Biblioteca Zabálburu
    See: Lindley Cintra, *Crónica,* I, dxxii-dxxiii; Catalán and Andrés, *Cr1344,* pp. lxxvi-lxxvii; Catalán, *De Alfonso X,* p. 291 n. 1

V: Madrid, Pal II 875 (formerly 2-G-3)
    See: Lindley Cintra, *Crónica,* I, dxxiv; Catalán and Andrés, *Cr1344,* p. lxxiv; Catalán, *De Alfonso X,* p. 291 n. 1; Menéndez Pidal, *Crónicas generales,* pp. 78-85 (no. 15)

Not described is the fragmentary MS *E* (Escorial &-II-1); see preliminary note 1, p. 151).

(iv) The *Crónica Ocampiana*

This is the name given to the 'cuarta parte' published by Ocampo (see above, p. 152) which, unlike the 'tercera parte', is an expanded version analogous to the *CrC*. Indeed, the MSS which have some relationship with Ocampo's edition are often described as 'mixed' versions of the *Ocampiana* and the *CrC*. There is, perhaps, a methodological difficulty in taking Ocampo's published version as one of two poles between which various 'mixed' versions may be said to lie. I shall return to this matter in a separate study. Broadly speaking, the *Ocampiana* represents a blend between the *PCG* and the *CrC*, following now one and now the other version: see above, pp. 85, 94-95, 103, 125-26, and 134-35.

Ocampo: see above, p. 152 under A (ii), the *Crónica General Vulgata*, for details of the published version.

Ch: **Madrid, BN 830**
  See: *PCG*, p. lxi; Catalán, *De Alfonso X*, pp. 329-30 n. 25 and 333-34 n. 29.

Ph: **Madrid, BN 1396**
  See: Catalán, *De Alfonso X*, pp. 328-29 n. 24 and 333-34 n. 29.

Q: **Madrid, Pal II 1877** (formerly 2-M-5)
  See: *PCG*, p. lxi; Catalán, *De Alfonso X*, pp. 192 n. 60 and 33 n. 29; id., 'Don Juan Manuel ante el modelo alfonsí', pp. 43-46; Menéndez Pidal, *Crónicas generales*, pp. 132-33 (no. 23).

Th: **Madrid, BN 1522**
  See: Catalán, *De Alfonso X*, pp. 333-34 n. 29.

W: **Madrid, BN 1335**
  See: Catalán, *De Alfonso X*, pp. 333-34 n. 29.

(v) The *Crónica Abreviada*

The now-lost *Crónica Manuelina* on which the *Abreviada* is based seems, in the 'cuarta parte', to have been a version more analogous to the *CrC/Ocampiana* branch than to the *Vulgata/CVR* as in the 'tercera parte', although in some places the most obvious relationship is to the *PCG* 'versión regia' (cf. pp. 82, 94, 103-04, 122, and 133, above, see also Pattison, 'The *Afrenta de Corpes*', pp. 136-38 and Catalán, 'Don Juan Manuel ante el modelo alfonsí'). See above, p. 154, for details of the sole manuscript.

(vi) The *Refundición Toledana* of the *Cr1344*

This is a rhetorically expanded version of the *Cr1344*. For its characteristics see above, pp. 21-22, 41-42, 54-55, 67-69, and 78-80; see also Lathrop, *The Legend*, and Pattison, 'The Legend of the Sons of Sancho el Mayor', especially pp. 38-39.

M: **Madrid, BN 7594**
  See; *PCG*, p. lxi; Lathrop, p. 77

S: **Salamanca 2585** (formerly Madrid, Pal II 1853 / 2-N-5)
  See: Lathrop, pp. 77-78; Menéndez Pidal, *Crónicas generales*, pp. 157-61 (no. 30)

(vii) The *Versión Interpolada* of the *Vulgata*

This version, in the 'tercera parte', interpolates material which is frequently of a sententious nature and, on occasion, may reflect the use of new, later versions of epic legends. For details, involving the legends of Fernán González, the Infantes de Lara, the Condesa Traidora and the Infante García, see above, pp. 34, 49-51, 64 and 76, and compare also Pattison, 'Legendary material'.

V: **Madrid, BN 1277**
  See: Catalán, *De Alfonso X*, p. 191 n. 58.

This manuscript is a continuation of the '*Crónica Fragmentaria*' version of the *PCG*: see above, p. 155.

INDEX

Alfonso II 11, 13-16, 18, 20, 21, 47
Alfonso III 12, 15, 16, 18
Alfonso VI 99, 102, 103, 105, 106, 109-11, 116, 119, 122, 125-27, 129, 130, 134-37, 144
Alfonso X 1-3, 5, 7, 13, 58
Almanzor 23, 26, 45-50, 53, 55, 59, 60, 147
Almenar 45, 49, 52
Almodafar 118, 128
Alvar Fáñez Minaya 105, 123, 124, 126, 127, 130, 131, 135, 137
Alvar Sánchez 44, 47, 52
Andrés, M. S. de 30, 89, 113, 158
Argentina 57, 60-62, 65, 67
Arias Gonzalo 97, 98, 100
Arlanza 24, 27, 141
Armistead, S. G. 4, 8, 82, 84, 86-88, 91, 157
Asur González 117, 130, 132, 135, 136
Avalle-Arce, J. B. 23, 39

Babbitt, T. 4, 5, 8, 33, 46, 48, 63, 75, 81, 82, 93, 94, 97, 99, 100, 108-11
Barbadillo 47, 48, 51
Ben Alcama 115
Bermudo III 72, 81, 82, 87, 88
Bernardo del Carpio 10, 11-22, 23, 35, 41, 44, 45, 54, 144, 146, 152, 155
Bivar 87, 122, 123, 126, 127
borrador see *Estoria de España*
Bueso 16-18, 21
Burgos 123, 125-27

Cabezón 96-100
Calahorra 83, 86
cantares de gesta 11, 14, 16, 22, 23, 27, 35, 40, 81, 82, 96-97 113, 144; *Cantar del rey don Fernando* 89, 90, 97, 99, 100; *Cantar del rey don Sancho* 101, 102, 107, 114; *Cantar de la mora Zaida* 10, 129; *Cantar de Mainete* 10
Cardeña 116, 122, 125, 126, 137, 139, 140, 141, 148
Carrión, Infantes de 116, 119, 128-36, 145
Catalán, D. 4, 5, 7-9, 13, 16, 18, 20, 28, 30, 33, 35, 44, 45, 48-50, 63, 82, 83, 85, 86, 88, 89, 100, 103, 106, 107, 112, 113, 120, 122, 124, 125, 131, 133, 134, 137, 138, 142, 147, 156, 158, 159
Chalon, L. 8, 9, 26, 37, 39, 44, 46, 48, 54, 58, 59, 63, 67, 72, 74, 94, 98, 101, 102, 107, 111, 119, 120, 125, 137, 143
Chaplin, M. 11, 24, 39, 44, 59, 101, 144
Charlemagne 12-14, 16, 19, 139
Cid 10, 44, 81-91, 94, 95, 97, 98, 103, 106, 108, 112, 115-42, 144, 148
Condesa traidora 10, 43, 57-69, 103, 143-46, 148, 154, 159
Corpes, Afrenta de 116, 129, 139, 147
Cotrait, R. 23, 39
Crónica Abreviada 7, 18, 30, 46, 63, 82, 93, 94, 99, 103, 104, 122, 133, 138, 151, 154, 159
Crónica de Castilla 6, 9, 81-91, 93-95, 97-100, 103-08, 111-14, 117, 122-28, 133-36, 139-40, 146-48, 151, 156-58
Crónica Fragmentaria 17-19, 34, 146, 155-56, 159
Crónica General Vulgata 7, 8, 18, 19, 30-35, 46-49, 62-64, 75-76, 85, 146, 151-54
Crónica Manuelina 104, 114, 121-22, 133, 138, 154, 159
Crónica de 1344 6, 7, 20, 21, 34, 36-39, 41, 42, 49-55, 58, 65-69, 77-79, 82, 83, 86-91, 93, 97-99, 101, 104, 108, 112-14, 122, 126-28, 135, 136, 139-40, 145-48, 151, 157-59
Crónica Najerense 1, 3, 25, 43, 59-63, 67, 70-73, 77, 94, 109, 114, 146
Crónica Ocampiana 5, 8, 18, 85, 93-95, 100, 103, 104, 111, 114, 121, 122, 125, 128, 133, 134, 136, 138, 146, 151, 158-59
Crónica Particular del Cid 9, 83, 157-58
Crónica de Veinte Reyes 5, 6, 20, 30-33, 35, 46-49, 61-63, 74-76, 82, 85, 90, 91, 93, 95-101, 104, 107-14, 117-20, 126, 129, 136-38, 146, 151-54, 158
Cuarta Crónica General 49

'cuarta parte' see *Estoria de España*
Cummins, J. 50-51, 53

Defourneaux, M. 12, 15
Deyermond, A. D. 8, 11, 23, 24, 39, 44, 59, 83, 84, 86, 89, 91, 101, 143, 144

Elvira 95, 96, 98, 113
Entwistle, W. J. 15, 24, 44, 137, 142
Epic sources 2, 82, 91, 143; *refundiciones* of 6, 35, 50, 51, 53-55, 120, 129, 141, 142, 145
Era Degollada 23, 26
Estoria de Cardeña 116, 136-42, 153
Estoria de España 3, 5, 100, 121, 138, 142; *borrador* 33, 49, 100, 101, 108, 117; 'cuarta parte' 5, 7, 81, 82, 85, 97-98, 115, 121, 125, 126, 151-59; 'tercera parte' 5, 7, 34, 57, 70, 82, 99, 121, 151-59; 'versión crítica' 48
Exemplarity 29-30, 114, 127, 148

Fariz 123, 125, 126
Fernán González 10, 23-42, 43, 45, 57, 70, 74, 103, 141, 143, 144-48, 155, 159
Fernán Gutiérrez 72, 78
Ferrant Lláynez 72-74, 77-79
Fernando I 6, 10, 43, 77, 78, 81-84, 86-90, 93-101, 108, 115, 125, 126, 141, 153; see also *cantares de gesta*
Fernando, Cardinal 95, 97, 98
Fraker, C. F. 101, 114
Franklin, A. B. 12, 15
Fruela II 5, 20, 88, 108

Garci-Fernández 43, 44, 52, 53, 57, 59-66, 68, 69
García of Navarre 78, 81, 82, 86, 87, 102, 103, 105, 109, 110-13
García Ordóñez 116, 117, 132
General Estoria 3
Gómez Pérez, J. 4, 10, 13, 82, 95, 97, 122
Gonzalo González 44, 47, 49, 53-55
Gonzalo Gustioz 44, 45, 46, 48, 50, 51, 53-55

Hacinas 23, 34, 41
Heinermann, M. 14, 15
Historia Arabum 120
Historia Roderici 102, 108, 109, 111, 115-17, 129, 137, 138

Hook, D. 116, 117, 133, 143
Horrent, J. 15, 101, 106

Infante García 10, 54, 57, 70-80, 143, 145-47, 152, 153, 159
Infantes de Lara 7, 10, 35, 43-55, 67, 144, 145, 148, 152, 158, 159
Isidore of Seville 2, 81, 93, 96

Jerónimo 141, 143
Jimena (sister of Alfonso II) 11, 13-15
Jimena (wife of Cid) 83, 84, 86, 88, 133-35, 137, 140, 141, 143
Juan Manuel 7, 18, 30, 63, 122, 138
juglares 11, 16, 21, 144

Keller, J. E. 23, 39

Lain Calvo, 87, 108
Lambra 44-47, 50, 52-54
Lathrop, T. A. 53-55, 67, 159
Legalism 40, 42, 134, 135, 143, 145
León 37, 70, 71-74, 77, 93, 96
Liber Regum 109
Libro de Alexandre 3
Lindley Cintra, L. F. 8, 20, 35, 37, 48, 49, 74, 85, 89, 97, 98, 100, 103, 112, 113, 125, 134, 137, 158

Mainete see *cantares de gesta*
Martín Antolínez 118, 122, 123, 130
Martín Peláez 133, 134, 135
Menéndez Pidal, R. 4, 7, 8, 11, 13, 16, 17, 23, 25, 28, 30, 35, 40, 42-44, 46-50, 52, 53, 55, 58, 61, 70-72, 79, 94, 95, 98, 101, 108, 110, 113, 115-17, 121, 124, 129, 155
Michael, I. D. L. 116, 124, 137
Mocedades de Rodrigo 8, 40, 82, 83, 86, 89, 90, 108, 143, 146, 156
Monteros de Espinosa 58, 60-63, 66, 67
Monzón 72, 78
Moralising 122-23, 127, 148
Mora Zaida see *cantares de gesta*
Mudarra 45, 47, 48, 50, 53, 54, 147
Muño Gustioz 132, 135
Muño Salido 45-47, 49, 52

neotradicionalismo 61, 145
Nuño Fernández 97-99

Ocampo 5, 7, 9, 18, 32, 47, 75, 85, 94, 98, 99, 104, 112, 125, 126, 151, 152, 158-59

INDEX

Oña 58, 60-65, 73, 148
Ordoño 130, 132
Ordoño III 25, 29

Pattison, D. G. 49, 54, 64, 69, 107, 129, 133, 136, 139, 145, 147, 148, 159
Pedro de Barcelos 6
Pedro Marcos 96, 110
Per Abbat 119, 121
Pero Vermúdez 121, 130-36
Plumpton, J. E. 58, 59, 61
Poema de Fernán González 23-42
Poema de mio Cid 35, 43, 115-42, 143, 148, 153
Powell, B. J. 119, 129, 142
Primera Crónica General passim; 'versión regia' 4, 5, 28-29, 30, 33, 35, 44, 45, 47, 49, 58, 62, 63, 74, 76, 85, 100, 103, 142, 146-48, 151, 154-56; 'versión vulgar' 4, 5, 6, 28, 30, 33, 44, 45, 49, 62-64, 74, 82, 85, 100, 103, 104, 121, 133, 146, 147, 151-52
Procter, E. S. 1-3

Ramiro II 25, 32,
Ramiro III 25, 35, 46
Ramón Berenguer 117, 118, 123, 126, 128
Refundición Toledana 7, 21, 22, 41-42, 49, 65, 67-69, 78, 91, 93, 99, 113, 146, 148, 151, 159
refundiciones see *cantares de gesta*
Reig, C. 8, 101, 108, 109, 113
Religiosity 34, 49-50, 123, 133, 143, 144
Rey Rodrigo 10
Romanz (del Infant García) 74-79
Roncesvalles 12, 14, 15, 20
Ruiz Asencio, J. M. 44, 58
Russell, P. E. 137-39, 142, 143
Ruy Blásquez 44-47, 49-54

Sancha (sister of Bermudo III and wife of Fernando I) 70-75, 77-79, 87, 89
Sancha (wife of Garci-Fernández) 57, 58, 60-52, 64-49
Sánchez Alonso, B. 1, 115, 120
Sancho I 24, 35, 40
Sancho II 79, 93-95, 97, 99, 101-14, 115, 125, 126, 145, 147, 153, 158; see also *cantares de gesta*

Sancho *el Mayor* 69, 71-73, 75, 76, 78, 79, 81
Sancho, Count of Castile 57-60, 64, 70
San Diaz, Count 11-13, 17-19, 22
Santa Gadea 101-03, 105, 107, 111, 116, 124, 145
Santarén 105
Santiago 14, 83, 84, 86
Smalley, B. 2
Smith, C. C. 118, 123, 124, 131, 137, 139, 143, 145, 147, 148
Sneyders de Vogel, K. 26, 33
Southern, R. W. 2
Sponsler, L. 54, 87
Stylistic elaboration 34, 104-06, 135-36

'tercera parte' see *Estoria de España*
Timbor 13, 17, 19, 21
Toledano 1, 2, 3, 13, 14, 16, 23, 24, 25, 29, 33, 35, 43, 70, 72-75, 76-77, 81, 82, 84, 93, 94, 96, 97, 99, 101, 102, 111, 115, 120, 128, 129, 142
Tudense 1, 3, 13-16, 23-25, 33, 43, 70, 71, 73-75, 77, 81, 82, 84, 93, 94, 96, 97, 99, 101, 102, 110, 111, 115, 128, 129

Ubieto Arteta, A. 25, 115
Urraca 87, 90, 95-98, 103, 105-08, 111, 113

Vado de Cascajares 58, 60, 61, 65, 68, 69, 144
Valencia 115, 116, 128, 129, 133, 137
Vega de Carrión 39, 40, 42
Vela family 70, 71, 73, 75-79
Vellido Adolfo 105, 106
'versión crítica' see *Estoria de España*
Versión Gallego-portuguesa 6, 65, 67, 78, 112, 126, 156, 157
Versión Interpolada 7, 8, 32, 34, 38, 49-53, 64, 69, 76, 145, 148, 151, 155, 159
'versión regia' see *Primera Crónica General*
'versión vulgar' see *Primera Crónica General*
von Richthofen, E. 15, 24, 50, 59, 101

Zamora 79, 96, 97, 101, 102, 105, 107-09, 112, 113, 147
Zaragoza 102, 117, 118, 128

www.ingramcontent.com/pod-product-compliance
Lightning Source LLC
Chambersburg PA
CBHW020332170426
43200CB00006B/358